Vanishing Voices

Vanishing Voices

The Extinction of the World's Languages

Daniel Nettle and Suzanne Romaine

OXFORD
UNIVERSITY PRESS

Oxford University Press

Oxford   New York
Auckland   Bangkok   Buenos Aires
Cape Town   Chennai   Dar es Salaam   Delhi
Hong Kong   Istanbul   Karachi   Kolkata
Kuala Lumpur   Madrid   Melbourne   Mexico City
Mumbai   Nairobi   São Paulo   Shanghai
Singapore   Taipei   Tokyo   Toronto

and an associated company in
Berlin

First published by Oxford University Press, Inc., 2000
198 Madison Avenue, New York, New York 10016
First issued as an Oxford University Press paperback, 2002

Oxford is a registered trademark of Oxford University Press

Library of Congress Cataloging-in-Publication Data
Nettle, Daniel.
Vanishing voices : the extinction of the world's languages /
Daniel Nettle and Suzanne Romaine.
p.   cm.
Includes bibliographical references and index.
ISBN 0-19-513624-1 (cloth)
ISBN: 0-19-515246-8 (pbk)
1. Language obsolescence.   2. Language maintenance.
I. Romaine, Suzanne.   II. Title.
P40.5.L33N48   2000
417'.7—dc21   99-16979

1 3 5 7 9 8 6 4 2
Printed in the United States of America

Contents

List of Illustrations

F ew people seem to know or care that most of Australia's 250 aboriginal languages have already vanished and few are likely to survive over the long term. No young children are learning any of the nearly 100 native languages spoken in what is now the state of California. The last Manx speaker died in 1974. The same gloomy story can be told for many other languages all over the world: At least half the world's languages could be extinct in the next century. What has happened to extinguish these diverse voices?

The extinction of languages is part of the larger picture of worldwide near total ecosystem collapse. Our research shows quite striking correlations between areas of biodiversity and areas of highest linguistic diversity, allowing us to talk about a common repository of what we will call "biolinguistic diversity": the rich spectrum of life encompassing all the earth's species of plants and animals along with human cultures and their languages. The greatest biolinguistic diversity is found in areas inhabited by indigenous peoples, who represent around 4 percent of the world's population, but speak at least 60 percent of the world's languages.

Despite the increasing attention given to endangered species and the environment, there has been little awareness that peoples can also be endangered. More has been said about the plight of pandas and spotted owls than about the disappearance of human language diversity. The main purpose of this book is to inform the wider scientific community and the public of the threat facing the world's languages and, by extent, its cultures.

Although our story is a largely depressing one of cultural and linguistic meltdown in progress, we think this new millennium also offers hope. In May 1992 about 500 native delegates gathered in Kari-Oca on the outskirts of Rio de Janeiro, to attend the First World Conference of Indigenous Peoples and declare their desire for self-determination, to educate their children and preserve their cultural identity. The last decades of the twentieth century have seen a resurgence of indigenous activism from the grassroots level all the way to international pressure groups. Ironically, the same forces of globalization fostering cultural and linguistic homogenization, and the spread of English in particular, are being marshalled as tools of resistance. Many native peoples and their organizations have websites in English on the internet capable of reaching millions of people all over the world. Delegates to the 1999 World Indigenous Peoples Conference on Education in Hilo, Hawai'i, were encouraged to address the meeting in their native languages. We would like to dedicate the book to the many people whose diverse voices have already vanished and to speakers of endangered languages everywhere still engaged in the struggle to preserve and strengthen theirs.

This book began as a series of lectures on "Endangered Languages: Causes and Consequences" that we presented at the University of Oxford in Hilary Term, 1998. Our collaboration revealed we were both planning books on the topic with somewhat different emphases reflecting our interests and training: Daniel Nettle, with an academic background in anthropology and fieldwork experience in Africa, and Suzanne Romaine with a background in linguistics and fieldwork experience in the UK and Pacific islands. The resulting book is naturally somewhat different than the separate ones we had each originally envisioned, but we hope the resulting whole is greater than the sum of the respective parts.

In order to make the book easily accessible to the widest possible audience, we have avoided in-text references and footnotes. At the end of the book we have included a bibliography and further reading for each chapter indicating the sources we have drawn on.

We would like to thank Leanne Hinton for helpful comments on an earlier draft of this manuscript, and Deborah Clarke and Rachel Rendall for discussions of the topic. We are also grateful to a number of people who helped with illustrative material and bibliographical matters: Colin Baker, Lily Cregeen, Nancy C. Dorian, Ed Greevy, George Hewitt, Stuart Kirsch, Charles Langlas, Ellen Okuma, Leialoha Apo Perkins, Kevin Roddy, and Craig Severance.

Oxford   Daniel Nettle
January 1999   Suzanne Romaine

Vanishing Voices

One

Where Have All the Languages Gone?

Most of us feel that we could never become extinct.
The Dodo felt that way too.

—William Cuppy

A few years ago, linguists raced to the Turkish farm village of Haci Osman to record Tevfic Esenç, a frail old man believed to be the last known speaker of the Ubykh language once spoken in the northwestern Caucasus. At that time only four or five elder tribesmen remembered some phrases of the language, but only Esenç knew it fluently. Even his own three sons were unable to converse with their father in his native language because they had become Turkish speakers. In 1984 Esenç had already written the inscription he wanted on his gravestone: "This is the grave of Tevfic Esenç. He was the last person able to speak the language they called Ubykh." With Esenç's death in 1992, Ubykh too joined the ever increasing number of extinct languages.

Four years later in South Carolina a native American named Red Thundercloud died, the last voice of a dying tongue. No longer able to converse in his native language with the remaining members of his community, he took the language of his tribe to the grave with him. Red Thundercloud was alone among his people, but not alone among native Americans. Roscinda Nolasquez of Pala, California, the last speaker of Cupeño, died in 1987 at the age of 94, and Laura Somersal, one of the last speakers of Wappo, died in 1990.

In another part of the world on the Isle of Man, Ned Maddrell passed away in 1974. With his death, the ancient Manx language left the community of the world's living tongues. Just a hundred years earlier, not long before his birth, 12,000 people (nearly a third of the island's population) still spoke Manx, but when Maddrell died, he was the only fluent speaker left. Two years before his death, Arthur Bennett died in north Queensland, Australia, the last person to know more than a few words of Mbabaram, a language he had not used himself since his mother died twenty some years before.

Tevfic Esenç, Red Thundercloud, Roscinda Nolasquez, Laura Somersal, Ned Maddrell, and Arthur Bennett lived and died thousands of miles apart, in radically different cultural and economic circumstances. Although the precise factors that destroyed their communities and left them as the last representatives of dying languages were quite different, their stories are remarkably similar in other ways. Unfortunately, their fates reveal a common pattern, which is but the tip of the iceberg: the world's languages are dying at an alarming rate. This book tells the story of how and why languages are disappearing.

About half the known languages of the world have vanished in the last five hundred years. Some languages of ancient empires, such as Etruscan, Sumerian, and Egyptian, disappeared centuries ago. Their inscriptions are but faint reminders of mostly forgotten peoples, whose cultures and languages are long since dead. Meroitic, a language which between the eighth century BC and the fourth century AD was the official language of an empire with the same name in the Sudan, survives only in inscriptions which have not been deciphered to this day. Only three words survive of Cumbria, an ancient language of Britain. Of the many more people who left no written records we know nothing.

A brief look around the world today reveals that the trickle of extinctions of the last few centuries is now turning into a flood. Our opening

Figure 1.1   Tevfic Esenç, last speaker of Ubykh.

[*Courtesy of Okan Iscan/ George Hewitt*]

Figure 1.2   Red Thundercloud, last speaker of Catawba Sioux and Laura Somersal, one of the last fluent speakers of Wappo.

[*Thundercloud reprinted from Bernard Comrie, Stephen Matthews and Maria Polinsky eds. 1996. The Atlas of Languages, Quarto Publishing plc; Somersal photograph by Scott M. Patterson; courtesy of Vicki Patterson*]

*Figure 1.3   Ned Mad-
drell, last speaker of Manx*

*[Courtesy of Lily Cregeen,
and Manx Museum,
Douglas, Isle of Man]*

examples show that language death is not an isolated phenomenon confined to ancient empires and remote backwaters. It is going on before our
very eyes in all parts of the world. Manx, for instance, is not alone
among the languages in western Europe in being near extinction. Two
hundred years before Manx died, Dolly Pentreath, the last known native
speaker of Cornish, passed away at the age of 102 in 1777. The few
remaining modern Celtic languages such as Irish, Scottish Gaelic, Welsh
and Breton are in great danger.

Though few speakers of English know it, until around AD 1000 Irish
was a militantly expanding language; it has the oldest literature in
Europe after Latin and Greek. Yet, despite the fact that virtually every
child studies Irish extensively in school, it is little used at home. Thus,
Irish has continued to die as the language of a rural peasantry in a few
remaining pockets along the west coast of the country. Scholars believe
the long-term future of the language is not any more secure now than it
was sixty years ago. According to one estimate, in 1990 there were just
under 9,000 speakers with sufficient attachment to Irish to transmit it to
their children. Languages not passed on to the younger generation will
eventually die out.

A brief look at other parts of the world confirms the same dismal picture. Australian Aboriginal languages are dying at the rate of one or
more per year. Although there may have been more than 250 languages

before European contact, some linguists predict that if nothing is done, almost all Aboriginal languages will be dead by the time this book is published. The United States alone is a graveyard for hundreds of languages. Of an estimated 300 languages spoken in the area of the present-day US when Columbus arrived in 1492, only 175 are spoken today. Most, however, are barely hanging on, possibly only a generation away from extinction.

A survey of the North American continent done some time ago in 1962 revealed that there were 79 American Indian languages, most of whose speakers were over 50 (for example, the Pomo and Yuki languages of California). There were 51 languages with fewer than 10 speakers, such as the Penobscot language of Maine; 35 languages had between 10 and 100 speakers. Only six languages—among them Navajo, Cherokee, and Mohawk—had more than 10,000 speakers. It is almost certain that at least 51 of these languages have all but disappeared. Languages with under 100 speakers are so close to extinction that revival for everyday use seems unlikely. The remaining native American languages in California are not being taught to children. Among the many native American languages already lost are some which gave the Pilgrims their first words for the new things they found in America, such as *moose* and *raccoon*. Our only reminders of them now are these words and state names such as *Massachusetts*.

Why and how are languages dying?

We have used terms such as "death" and "extinction" in relation to languages just as a biologist would in talking about species. This may sound strange or inappropriate. What justification is there for this? After all, languages are not living things which can be born and die, like butterflies and dinosaurs. They are not victims of old age and disease. They have no tangible existence like trees or people. In so far as language can be said to exist at all, its locus must be in the minds of the people who use it. In another sense, however, language might be regarded as an activity, a system of communication between human beings. A language is not a self-sustaining entity. It can only exist where there is a community to speak and transmit it. A community of people can exist only where there is a viable environment for them to live in, and a means of making a living. Where communities cannot thrive, their languages are in danger. When languages lose their speakers, they die.

Some have also used the terms "language murder" and "language suicide," suggesting that languages do not die natural deaths. They are instead murdered. English, as Glanville Price put it, is a "killer language." Thus, it has been said that Irish, for instance, was murdered by

English. Others, however, have in effect put the blame on Irish by saying that the language committed suicide. The Irish writer Flann O'Brien, although pro-Irish, resented and rejected the attempt to revive the Irish language, because he was of the opinion that the difficulties faced by Irish were "due mainly to the fact that the Gaels deliberately flung that instrument of beauty and precision from them."

Terms such as "death," "extinction," "murder," and "suicide" applied to language are metaphors, but are such metaphors useful? We will argue that the death and extinction (and even murder) perspective is useful because languages are intimately connected with humans, our cultures, and our environment. The notion of language suicide of course puts the blame squarely on the victim. This view is not constructive and in any case, is ill-founded. People do not kill themselves on a whim. Suicide is indicative of mental and often physical illness brought about by undue stress. Likewise, people do not fling away their languages for no good reason. We will show throughout this book how many instances of language shift and death occur under duress and stressful social circumstances, where there is no realistic choice but to give in. Many people stop speaking their languages out of self-defense as a survival strategy.

As a telling example, we can take what happened in El Salvador in 1932, when after a peasant uprising anyone identified as Indian either by dress or physical appearance was rounded up and killed by Salvadoran soldiers. Some 25,000 people were killed in this way. Even three years later radio broadcasts and newspapers were calling for the total extermination of the Indians of El Salvador to prevent another revolt. Many people stopped speaking their languages to avoid being identified as Indian, in order to escape what they feared was certain death in a country which officially had no Indians. Ironically, in the 1970s there was a reversal of attitudes, particularly among non-Indian Salvadorans, who lamented their lost cultural heritage. Unfortunately, we have other cases of human rights abuses to relate in this book, instances where people face punishment and imprisonment for using their own languages. Kenyan writer Ngũgĩ Wa Thiong'o's decision to write in his native language, Gikuyu, resulted in his imprisonment and eventual exile.

Likewise, the extinction of Ubhyk is the final result of a genocide of the Ubykh people, who until 1864 lived along the eastern shore of the Black Sea in the area of Sochi (northwest of Abkhazia). The entire Ubykh population left its homeland when Russia conquered the Muslim northern Caucasus in the 1860s. Tens of thousands of people were expelled and had to flee to Turkey, no doubt with heavy loss of life, and the survivors were scattered over Turkey. Russian conquest of the Caucasus continues to this day, threatening the lives, lifestyles and languages of people such as the Chechens. Meanwhile, Turkey itself is a country with a long history of human rights abuses directed against the Kurds and their language, which is banned from public use.

Linguistic diversity, then, is a benchmark of cultural diversity. Language death is symptomatic of cultural death: a way of life disappears with the death of a language. The fortunes of languages are bound up with those of its speakers. Language shift and death occur as a response to pressures of various types—social, cultural, economic, and even military—on a community. Every time a language stops performing a particular function, it will lose some ground to another that takes its place. Death occurs when one language replaces another over its entire functional range, and parents no longer transmit the language to their children.

In this book we will show how the various factors responsible in the past for language death pose an even greater threat to many languages today. Indeed, there are good reasons to believe that the processes leading to the disappearance of languages have greatly accelerated over the past two hundred years. Linguists estimate that there are around 5,000–6,700 languages in the world today. At least half, if not more, will become extinct in the next century. In the next chapter we will demonstrate that this puts the problem of linguistic extinction on a par with biologists' most pessimistic estimates for species extinction. Knowledge of the various historical events which shape the evolution of languages and lead to the expansion of some and the contraction of others is necessary if we are to do anything about the loss of linguistic diversity. Why is it, for instance, that the Greeks still speak Greek today after thousands of years, but that people in Ireland, Scotland, and Wales are losing their languages?

Where and when are languages at risk?

The Summer Institute of Linguistics (SIL), a fundamentalist mission group based in the United States and the largest Protestant missionary society sent abroad, probably has a better idea of the scope of the problem of language endangerment than most academic linguists. Although SIL's primary interest is not language maintenance, but the provision of Bible translations for the peoples of the world, their workers have more first-hand experience in documenting languages on a large scale. Their current capacity is 850 languages, cumulatively 1,200. From their work we learn that Bible translation has either begun or is needed for about 50 percent of the languages of the world. We know very little about this 50 percent, many of them perhaps in danger. The Summer Institute's publication, *Ethnologue*, suggests that as many as 20 percent of the world's languages are moribund, but this is likely to be a very conservative estimate.

The pulse of a language clearly lies in the youngest generation. Languages are at risk when they are no longer transmitted naturally to children in the home by parents or other caretakers. Even languages which older, but not younger, children in a community have acquired are at risk. The key question then is: how many languages still spoken today are no longer being learned by young children?

Using SIL's *Ethnologue* data, we can calculate that 90 percent of the world's population speaks the 100 most-used languages. This means that there are at least 6,000 languages spoken by about 10 percent of the people on earth. Linguist Michael Krauss of the Alaska Native Language Center suggests that by including all the languages which have more than 100,000 speakers, there may be only as few as 600 "safe" languages. He believes that few of the other 6,000 can be regarded as having a secure future. In other words, the overwhelming majority of the world's languages may be in danger of extinction.

More specifically, Krauss estimates that in the United States and Canada, 80 percent (149 out of 187) of the native Indian languages are no longer being learned by children. At least 60 native languages were spoken in what is now Canada, but Kinkade estimates that only 4 of these (Cree with 60,000, Ojibwa with 30,000 in Canada and 20,000 in the US, Dakota with 5,000 in Canada and 15,000 in the US, and Inuktitut with 16–18,000 in Canada, 6,000 in Alaska, and 41,000 in Greenland) are truly viable since only these few have a large enough base of speakers and younger children acquiring the languages to ensure survival. Only five of the native languages spoken in what is now the US have as many as 10,000 to 20,000 speakers, and only two have as many as 40,000 to 50,000. The Navajo language is the only native language with more than 100,000 speakers.

For Central America, Krauss suggests that 17 percent (50 out of 300) are no longer viable, and for South America, 27 percent (110 out of 400). While this region has a much smaller number of languages than, say, Africa, it has a considerable number of unique languages not related to any others. Brazil, for example, is a country still in great need of linguistic documentation: almost half its languages are located in the remotest and least accessible regions of the country and have not been studied. The only known speakers of Koaia, for example, are the women in one household in the state of Rondonia. The comparatively few languages in South America are probably the result of the near total elimination of the native population. The number of speakers of Indian languages has never returned to pre-Conquest levels. Uruguay, for instance, no longer has an Indian population and no indigenous Indian language is preserved there. No modern South American nation expresses its national culture and identity through the use of an indigenous language with the possible exception of Paraguay, where practically everyone, Indian and non-Indian alike, knows and uses Guaraní on some occasions even though Spanish is the official language.

The worst case, however, is Australia, with 90 percent of its estimated 250 Aboriginal languages near extinction. Only some 50 languages are widely spoken today and of these only 18 have at least 500 speakers. These 18 account for roughly 25,000 of the remaining 30,000 speakers of Aboriginal languages. There is no Aboriginal language that is used in all arenas of everyday life by members of a sizeable community. It is possible that only two or three of the languages will survive into the next century.

Africa and Asia are the continents with the highest number of living indigenous languages, although European languages have spread over both regions during the last 200 years. A recent attempt to assess the problem of language death in Africa revealed, not surprisingly, that virtually all African nations were affected to some degree. The conclusion determined that 54 languages were already extinct, and another 116 were in the process of extinction. These figures are not based on an actual field survey but rather on the existing literature on African languages and questionnaires sent to researchers, so they are likely to be underestimates. Kenya is the only country for which reliable estimates exist on this topic and it has already lost eight languages. Again, not surprisingly, Nigeria, which has the largest number of languages, also has the largest number of extinct and endangered languages (10 already extinct and a further 17 in the process of extinction, according to one very conservative estimate).

Although there is some obvious safety in large numbers, they do not tell the whole story, for reasons we explain in the next chapter when we take a more detailed look at what some of these statistics mean. We mentioned earlier Krauss's figure of 100,000 as a rough estimate of safety. However, we cannot automatically conclude that all small languages are at risk, or conversely that all large languages are safe. Icelandic, for instance, has only 100,000 speakers but is in no danger of extinction. Other languages with much larger numbers of speakers can be and are at risk. Some of the precarious languages of Central India such as Kurux, for instance, have over a million speakers—and so did Breton, as recently as 1926. Similarly, Navajo had well over 100,000 speakers a generation ago, but continues to decline. In Vanuatu none of the indigenous languages has more than 3,000 speakers, yet most of them seem to be maintained. In Micronesia the two languages most at risk today are the largest (Chamorro with 60,000 speakers on the island of Guam) and the smallest (Sonsorolese with about 300 speakers on the island of Sonsoral in Palau). Therefore, small population in and of itself does not tell us much without examining other indicators such as the status of the language. Unfortunately, relatively few linguists tend to work with these very small languages, so we know much less about them.

Very often all the information we have about the existence of a particular language spoken by small groups consists of the material collected by a missionary or a linguist on one field trip.

Even then, attempts to assess the health of many of these smaller languages are often frustrated by the fact that the linguist who worked on the language in question made no mention of how many people spoke the language and what its likely prognosis was. Apart from an isolated field visit, many linguists have no further contact with the languages they investigate. Although there are still many languages we know nothing about, new languages are always being discovered, but sometimes not soon enough to do anything. The Ugong people of western Thailand have been in decline ever since they were discovered by outsiders. In the 1920s a surveyor commented that the language was already on its last legs. An anthropologist who worked among the Ugong in the 1960s also noted the moribund nature of the language. In the 1970s a linguist began working on the language in the several locations where it is still used. By that time it had already become extinct in the two locations previously visited by the surveyor some five decades earlier.

In the late 1970s the Electricity Generating Authority of Thailand built two hydroelectric dams on the two branches of the River Kwai. These dams flooded the locations of two Ugong villages and the inhabitants were relocated elsewhere. With the unity of the villages destroyed and their speakers scattered, the older speakers who still preserve the language have few, if any, people to speak to in Ugong. Ugong has literally been swamped and the speakers immersed in Thai villages.

As in the case of species, languages urgently need documentation and monitoring. The state of health of a small language and its speakers can change very rapidly. For instance, in 1962 the speakers of Trumai, a language spoken in a single village on the lower Culuene River in Venezuela, were reduced by an influenza epidemic to a population of fewer than 10 speakers.

Why worry about languages dying?

At first glance, a linguist's interest in preserving languages seems both self-evident and self-serving. For scientific reasons alone, languages are worth preserving. Linguists need to study as many different languages as possible if they are to perfect their theories of language structure and to train future generations of students in linguistic analysis. Thanks to the efforts of linguists, at least there will be some record of Ubykh with its unusual sound system containing 81 consonants and only 3 vowels. (Compare English with only 24 consonants and approximately 20 vowels, depending on the combination of sounds in a particular variety; or

Rotokas, a language spoken on Bougainville island in Papua New Guinea, with the smallest number of sounds in any language, only 5 vowels and 6 consonants.) Yet, descriptions based on the last living speakers can usually capture only a fragment of what that language must have been like in its full-blown version in active use by a living community of younger and older speakers. One consequence of declining use of a language is a loss in its complexity and richness of expression.

New and exciting discoveries about language are still being made. There is every reason to believe that what we know now is but the tip of the iceberg. For many years linguists thought Ubykh to be the world record-holder for number of consonants. Now it seems that some African languages surpass Ubykh in this respect—if only there is time to find out. Many African languages are dying rapidly too. Only in the 1970s did linguists discover the existence of a language called Hixkaryana, which has about 350 speakers. It is one of many languages spoken by small numbers of speakers in Amazonia. Structurally speaking, Hixkaryana and its neighboring languages are interesting because they represent the only known cases of languages which construct sentences by putting the object first, as if we were to say in English, for instance, *a book read Mary* instead of *Mary read a book*. Other languages, for example Japanese and Guugu Yimidhirr (spoken around Cooktown in north Queensland, Australia), typically have the order Subject Object Verb (SOV), as in *ngayu Billy nhaadhi* (literally, *I Billy saw*). Modern English has the order SVO, although that has not always been the case. Around 10 percent of the world's languages put the verb first, like Irish: *is cailin og Maire*, meaning *Mary is a young girl*, translates literally as *is girl young Mary*. Hixkaryana and other object-initial languages may not survive into the next century. Except by chance, we might not have known that it was possible for human languages to have OSV word order.

Satisfying answers to many current puzzles about languages and their origins will not emerge until linguists have studied many languages. To exclude exotic languages from our study is like expecting botanists to study only florist shop roses and greenhouse tomatoes and then tell us what the plant world is like. Linguistic diversity gives us unique perspectives into the mind because it reveals the many creative ways in which humans organize and categorize their experience.

In fact, from the evidence we have to date, it would appear that the most grammatically complicated and unusual languages of the world are often isolates—unrelated to any other language—and often spoken by small tribes whose traditional way of life is under threat. The majority of "world" languages such as Chinese, English, Spanish, and Arabic, spoken by 50 million or more people, are, by contrast, not isolates and they are also not as grammatically complex as many of the world's smaller languages. There is a strong tendency for languages to simplify upon expansion and contact with other languages. After the Norman Conquest, for example, English absorbed much vocabulary from French and over the centuries has lost much of the grammatical complexity still found in more conservative Germanic languages such as German and Icelandic. The differences are obvious when we consider that a modern Icelander can still read the Icelandic sagas, while the language of Old English epics such as *Beowulf* is a completely different language to modern day English speakers. Majority languages have been grammatically streamlined. Moreover, the world's major languages are becoming more like one another through the process of intertranslation and culture contact. Most languages have borrowed English terms for words in the field of science and technology.

Speakers of isolated languages only rarely use their own languages to communicate with outsiders. Such languages are generally learned only by children growing up in the local community and almost never as second languages. Languages that are used only for in-group communication in small groups can afford complexity. We can observe the same tendency towards complexity among close friends or members of the same family who communicate regularly with one another. They often have conversations that are hard for outsiders to understand because they contain many references to things shared only by that group. In-group jokes, teenage slang, and professional jargon are some examples. When weather forecasters talk to one another at meteorological conventions they use terms such as *positive vorticity advective*—which, in lay terms, means that conditions are favorable to rain.

In small language groups innovations and new usages can quickly spread throughout a whole village. Sociologist Eliezer Ben-Rafael relates how on one Israeli kibbutz the local doctor was named Zigmund. Years after the doctor left a doctor is still a "zigmund" for the children as well as adults. It has even been known that twins have developed their own language unintelligible to other family members. The very processes that make a language more complex, more localized and specific to a small group also make it ideally suited to marking a distinctive identity. The more different it is, the better it serves this function. In Chapter 4 we will show how this has happened in Papua New Guinea, which provides a good model of linguistic equilibrium of the type that characterized human societies before the industrial revolution.

The complexity found in some of these small languages spoken in out of the way places may come as a surprise to some people, because non-linguists often think of some of these languages and communities as primitive. Consider the hundred or so people who live in the remote village of Gapun, which lies roughly midway between the Sepik and Ramu rivers in Papua New Guinea. In this isolated village most people support themselves through hunting and agriculture. They speak a language called Taiap. Up until the 1970s no linguist had worked on the language of Gapun. In fact, in 1938 a German missionary, who was the first European to discover the language, predicted that no linguist would ever want to bother with it because the village where it was spoken was so small and located in a relatively inaccessible mosquito-infested swamp. We now know that Taiap is an amazingly rich language in terms of its structural diversity and particularly distinctive vocabulary, unlike any other in the Sepik. It is not clearly related to any other language in the area or indeed to any other language in Papua New Guinea as far as we can tell. While further research might provide clues about the precise genetic relationship between Taiap and other languages, this is unlikely to happen.

Taiap is dying. The younger generation of villagers grow up speaking Tok Pisin (*talk pidgin*, or pidgin English) and are no longer fluent in Taiap. What has happened? We will see in Chapter 6 how contact with the outside world has brought many changes to the village. Roads, schools, Christianity, and the new ideas brought with these things have changed the way people think in Gapun. They see Tok Pisin as a language that will give them access to the modern world and so they shift their allegiance to it, and no longer speak exclusively in Taiap to their children. When Taiap dies, it will leave a black hole. Closer study of it may reveal a vital clue to the huge puzzle of human origins in New Guinea, an island rich in biodiversity.

In the next chapter we examine in more detail the geographic distribution of linguistic diversity and what it tells us about human evolution. We will show how cultural diversity and biological diversity are not only related, but often inseparable, perhaps causally connected through coevolution in specific habitats. Research has shown quite striking correlations between areas of biodiversity and areas of highest linguistic diversity, allowing us to talk about a common repository of what we will call *biolinguistic diversity*: the rich spectrum of life encompassing all the earth's species of plants and animals along with human cultures and their languages.

The greatest biolinguistic diversity is found in areas inhabited by indigenous peoples, who represent around 4 percent of the world's population, but speak at least 60 percent of its languages and control or manage some of the ecosystems richest in biodiversity. Although the fate of indigenous peoples is decisive for the maintenance of biolinguistic diversity, they too are endangered. In 1993, the United Nations Year of Indigenous Peoples, most of the world's fourteen million refugees were indigenous people. According to one estimate, as many as 200,000 indigenous people are killed every year.

If Taiap were a rare species of bird or Ubykh a dying coral reef, maybe more people would know of their plight and be concerned. Yet in Papua New Guinea and all over the world, many unique local languages are dying at an unparalleled rate. Few people know or care. Should we be any less concerned about Taiap than we are about the passing of the California condor? Although the greatest threat is posed to the languages spoken by peoples whose cultures and traditional lifestyles are also at risk, language death is a problem found within modern nations as well, as our earlier examples of the Celtic languages show. In the Hawaiian islands, for instance, the majority of native plants and animals are, like the Hawaiian language, found nowhere else on earth and face impending extinction. Although the island state represents less than 1 percent of the US total land mass, it has 363 (over 30 percent) of 1,104 species federally listed as threatened or endangered, including the yellow hibiscus, the state flower, and the Hawaiian goose (*nēnē*), the state bird. It is not coincidental that language endangerment has gone hand in hand with species endangerment. Languages are like the miner's canary: where languages are in danger, it is a sign of environmental distress.

We think there are many reasons why all of us—not just linguists, or those whose languages are under threat—should be alarmed at what is happening and try to do something to stop it. As a uniquely human invention, language is what has made everything possible for us as a species: our cultures, our technology, our art, music, and much more. In our languages lies a rich source of the accumulated wisdom of all humans. While one technology may be substituted for another, this is not true of languages. Each language has its own window on the world. Every language is a living museum, a monument to every culture it has been vehicle to. It is a loss to every one of us if a fraction of that diversity disappears when there is something that can have been done to prevent it. Moreover, every people has a right to their own language, to preserve it as a cultural resource and to transmit it to their children.

It is hard for most English speakers to imagine what it might mean if the English language were to die and they would no longer be able to speak it as they went about their daily activities. How would it feel to be the last speaker of English on earth? Marie Smith, the last Eyak Indian of Cordova, Alaska explained how she felt at being the only full-blooded Eyak and the only speaker of her language: "I don't know why it's me, why I'm the one. I tell you, it hurts. It really hurts. . . . My father was the last Eyak chief, and I've taken his place. I'm the chief now, and I have to go down to Cordova to try to stop the clear cutting on our land."

English has always seemed such a secure possession, despite the fact that after the Norman Conquest, its future was actually in some doubt. Yet it was likewise difficult for English speakers at that time to imagine that their language would one day spread all over the globe. Most English speakers take the present position and status of English for granted, and do not realize that English was very much once a minority language initially in all of the places where it has since become the mother tongue of millions. It has gained its present position by replacing the languages of indigenous groups such as Native Americans, the Celts, and the Australian Aborigines, and now many more.

Most of us also take the diversity found in the world's languages for granted, just as the cow takes her tail for granted in this Jamaican proverb: *Kau neva no di yus of im tel til di butcha kot it of* ("the cow didn't know what use her tail was until the butcher cut it off"). While campaigns are mounted to protect and conserve whales, spotted owls, and other natural resources, languages are overlooked. There has been little support from international organizations like the United Nations for preserving languages. As we will show in this book, there are many reasons why the plight of languages has been neglected. This is, however, a strategic error that will be regretted as time goes on.

In Chapter 3 we will illustrate how some of the detailed knowledge of the natural environment encoded in human languages spoken by small groups who have lived for centuries in close contact with their surroundings may provide useful insights into management of resources on which we all depend. At the moment, as many as one-quarter of the prescription medicines used in the United States are derived from plants which grow in the world's rain forests. We know that many more plants and trees growing in tropical rain forests may contain remedies and even cures for human diseases, but we may never learn about some of them because the rain forests are being destroyed.

Figure 1.4   Marie Smith, last speaker of Eyak

[*Courtesy of Art Wolfe*]

Moreover, traditional knowledge tends not to be valued as a human resource unless it makes an economic contribution to the West. Even though the United States government recognized the Pacific yew as the most valuable tree in American forests because its bark can be processed to yield taxol, a drug useful in the treatment of ovarian cancer, the bark is still being burned as scrap or left to rot on the forest floor in the aftermath of wasteful logging operations. The next great steps in scientific development may lie locked up in some obscure language in a distant rain forest.

The Inuit people who inhabit northern Arctic regions developed ways for surviving in an extremely cold and adverse climate. Knowledge of which kinds of ice and snow could support the weight of a man, a dog, or a kayak was critical for the continued survival of the Inuit, so they were named individually. In the Native American language, Micmac, trees are named for the sound the wind makes when it blows through them during the autumn, about an hour after sunset when the wind always comes from a certain direction. Moreover, these names are not fixed but change as the sound changes. If an elder remembers, for example, that a certain stand of trees used to be called by a particular name 75 years ago but is now called by another, these terms can be seen as scientific markers for the effects of acid rain over that time period. One Palauan traditional fisherman born in 1894 and interviewed by marine biologist R.E. Johannes had names for more than 300 different species of fish, and knew the lunar spawning cycles of several times as many species of fish as have been described in the scientific literature for the entire world.

Today scientists have much to learn from the Inuit people about the Arctic climate, and from Pacific Islanders about the management of marine resources. Much of this indigenous knowledge has been passed down orally for thousands of years in their languages. Now it is being forgotten as their languages disappear. Unfortunately, much of what is culturally distinctive in language—for example vocabulary for flora, fauna—is lost when language shift takes place. The typical youngster today in Koror, Palau's capital, cannot identify most of Palau's native fish; nor can his father. The forgetting of this knowledge has gone hand in hand with over-fishing and degradation of the marine environment.

The next two chapters will reveal many striking similarities between the loss of linguistic diversity and the loss of biodiversity. We believe these are not accidental. The areas with the greatest biological diversity also have the greatest linguistic/cultural diversity. These correlations require close examination and must be accounted for. Extinctions in general, whether of languages or species, are part of a more general pattern of human activities contributing to radical alterations in our ecosystem. In the past, these extinctions took place largely without human intervention. Now they are taking place on an unprecedented scale through our intervention—in particular, through our alteration of the environment. The extinction of languages can be seen as part of the larger picture of worldwide near total ecosystem collapse. Our failure to recognize our intimate connection with the global ecosystem lies behind what we will call the biolinguistic diversity crisis facing us today. What has brought us to this brink?

Paleontologist Niles Eldredge is of the opinion that humans first began to impose a significant and different kind of impact on the environment when they made the transition from hunter-gatherers to sedentary farmer societies, a change we will examine in more detail in Chapter 5. Hunters may have been responsible for the destruction of individual species, but farmers and the alteration of the landscape required for agricultural subsistence enabled humans to destroy the ecosystems necessary for the support of species, including our own. Several other major transformations in human history require further consideration as well, in particular, the expansion of Europeans into the New World from 1492, and the Industrial Revolution of the 18th century, which was responsible for many farmers leaving the countryside to become urban factory workers. By the latter half of the nineteenth century Britain had already become a largely urban nation, and its capital, London, the largest metropolis in Europe. Later, the application of science to industry in the twentieth century would create what C.P. Snow refers to as the "scientific revolution." The agrarian revolution and the industrial-scientific revolution are in his view the two major transformations in human social history.

We are accustomed nowadays to hearing people say that everything is interconnected. We live in what Marshall McLuhan called the "global village," where international languages, and English in particular, are key links. The world is now tightly linked by electronic media. With the launching of Intelsat III in 1967, for the first time in history no part of the globe was completely out of touch with any other part. Now there are hundreds of such satellites orbiting the earth. Increasingly sophisticated and rapid telecommunications brought about through computers in the late twentieth century have created a network of computers, popularly called the "information superhighway." Following this revolution in mass communications, some few languages have spread all over the world. Because the technology facilitating these developments originated largely in the English-speaking world, not surprisingly, English has become its lingua franca. Until 1995 it was difficult to communicate via the internet in any language that could not be expressed in the standard English alphabet as defined by the American Standard Code for Information Interchange (ASCII), set down in 1982.

Similarly, the corporations and financial institutions of the English-speaking countries have dominated world trade and made English the international language of business. Books in the English language have dominated the publishing business; there are few countries in the world where English books cannot find a market of some kind. Even other major languages, such as French and German, have continued to lose ground against English over the course of this century as mediums of scholarly publication. By 1966, 70 percent of the world's mail and 60 percent of its radio and television broadcasts were already in English. Compare this to the state of the language in the year 1600, however, when the idea that English might become a world language was not seriously entertained since it was thought to have many flaws. At that time knowledge of English was virtually useless in traveling abroad. Nowadays, it is regarded as essential.

Language shift is thus symptomatic of much larger-scale social processes that have brought about the global village phenomenon, affecting people everywhere, even in the remotest regions of the Amazon. Many smaller languages are dying out due to the spread of a few world languages such as English, French, Chinese, and so on. In today's global village, a mere handful of about 100 languages are spoken by around 90 percent of the world's population. We will argue that this radical restructuring of human societies, which has led to the dominance of English and a few other world languages, is not a case of "survival of the fittest," nor the outcome of competition or free choice among equals in an idealized market place. It is instead the result of unequal rates of social change resulting in striking disparities in resources between developed and developing countries.

Another reason why language death has been ignored reflects a common but mistaken belief that the existence of many languages poses a barrier to communication, to economic development, and to modernization more generally. Shouldn't we instead be glad that so many languages are dying out? Isn't multilingualism the curse of Babel? Wouldn't the sharing of a common language lead to better understanding? Monolingual English speakers are usually unaware of the fact that their circumstances are NOT the norm in a world that has long been and is still predominantly multilingual.

Danish linguist Louis Hjelmslev related how a Finnish colleague told him of an American visitor to Finland who had heard about the complexity of Finnish, a language with over twenty cases and a pronunciation of considerable difficulty to the average English speaker, and unrelated to most other western European languages. The American seemed amazed that a small population of only four million should maintain such a seemingly impractical language, which in effect cut them off from their neighbors and their neighbors from them. He proposed an exceedingly drastic measure to get rid of it by ceasing to teach Finnish and engaging instead a sufficient number of teachers of English to teach all Finnish children English. In one generation this little practical problem would be overcome once and for all.

We can either laugh at the American's naive utilitarianism or decry his solution as draconian and imperialistic. Such misinformed views blinded by monolingualism, are, however, all too common, and part of the legacy of the Tower of Babel. Genesis relates how all people once spoke the same language, but God decided to punish them for their presumptuousness by erecting the tower and making them speak different languages. The association of multilingualism with pernicious outcomes is still with us, as was evident, for instance, in media mogul Rupert Murdoch's speech on Australian radio in 1994. His gist was that multilingualism was divisive, and monolingualism, cohesive. Multilingualism was in his view the cause of Indian disunity, and monolingualism the reason for the unity of the English-speaking world. He rejoiced in the fact, however, that Hindi was finally spreading as a major lingua franca, due to the availability of Hindi TV programming being spread by his Asian television company, Star.

It takes but little reflection to find the many obvious flaws in Murdoch's reasoning, and to come up with cases in which the sharing of a common language has not gone hand in hand with political or indeed any other kind of unity. Northern Ireland is one such example from the English-speaking world that comes readily to mind. But there are many others from other parts of the globe. A very high degree of linguistic and religious uniformity in Somalia, for example, did not prevent a brutal civil war from breaking out there. Certainly, the attempt at Russification of the former republics of the Soviet Union did not ensure unity in that part of the world either. Indeed, one of the first political acts undertaken by the newly independent Baltic states was to reassert their linguistic and cultural autonomy by reinstating their own national languages in place of Russian. After the demotion in status of Russian, Russia was not slow to accuse these countries of depriving Russian speakers of their linguistic human rights.

Because languages and dialects are often potent symbols of class, gender, ethnicity, religion, and other differences, it is easy to think that language underlies conflict. Yet disputes involving language are not really about language, but instead about fundamental inequalities between groups who happen to speak different languages. It is easy to lose sight of this point when language is often such a prominent symbol in the much larger struggle for minority rights. In 1951, for example, Frisian language activists were involved in a street riot in the Dutch town of Ljouwert, protesting the inadmissibility of the Frisian language spoken by many of the members of the major indigenous minority group in Dutch courts.

As we demonstrate in Chapter 8, language has played a key role in past struggles for cultural and political distinctiveness all over the world, and it continues to do so today. In Quebec the controversial law requiring all signs to be in French only represented the symbolic ability of the Quebec government to control and maintain the Frenchness of Quebec in the midst of a predominantly anglophone Canada. Above all, however, it is an attempt on the part of Francophones to gain control over their own affairs, to exist as a people with their own identity and culture, and their own language. In introducing legislation designed to protect French, Quebec Francophones seek no more than to guarantee for themselves similar rights that anglophone Canadians have felt unnecessary to state as policy because they were implicit in practice already. There has also been violence in Wales over the presence of English signs, and the purchase of vacation homes by people from England.

Not surprisingly, signs carry a lot of symbolic freight. They do more than identify places and things. They reveal social hierarchies. Jerusalem's political history is encapsulated in the city's multilingual signs. Trilingual signs with English on top and Arabic and Hebrew underneath, such as the Jaffa Gate sign in Figure 1.6, date from the period when Palestine was ruled under British mandate from 1919 to 1948. When the Jordanians conquered the Old City, their use of Arabic-English signs with Arabic on top signaled the political pre-eminence of Jordan. The absence of Hebrew in effect

Figure 1.5   Welsh Language Society protest against sale of houses

[Courtesy of Marian Delyth]

Figure 1.6   Trilingual signs in Jerusalem

[Adapted from Spolsky and R.L. Cooper, The Languages of Jerusalem. Oxford: Oxford University Press, 1991, p. 7, Fig. 5.1 and p. 94, Fig. 6.8]

declared Jewish claims as illegitimate. When the Israelis captured the Old City in 1967, they put up trilingual signs, this time with Hebrew on top, and English and Arabic underneath. The Arabic on a number of street signs in the Jewish quarter was painted over around 1984, or defaced.

Languages and language varieties are always in competition, and at times in conflict, as the cases of Quebec and Jerusalem illustrate. There may be approximately 6,000 languages in the world, but there are only about 200 countries—which means that multilingualism is present in practically every country in the world. As the following chapters will show, however, the boundaries of modern nation-states have been arbitrarily drawn, with many of them created by the political and economic interests of Western colonial powers. Many indigenous people today, such as the Welsh, Hawaiians, and Basques, find themselves living in nations they had no say in creating and are controlled by groups who do not represent their interests—and, in some cases, actively seek to exterminate them, as is the case with the Kurds in Iraq and Turkey. More than

80 percent of the conflicts in the world today are between nation-states and minority peoples.

All nation-states, whatever their political ideology, have persecuted minorities in the past and many continue to do so today. While not all states are actively seeking the eradication of minorities within their borders, they pursue policies designed to assimilate indigenous people into the mainstream or dominant culture. Many immigrants to the United States, for instance, were brainwashed into thinking that their languages and cultures were inferior and therefore had to be abandoned for the sake of being American. As recently as 1971 it was illegal to speak Spanish in a public school building in Texas. The widespread assimilation of minorities in this way in democratic countries such as the US is generally ignored, since it is assumed that assimilation is voluntary and not coerced. Consideration of the larger picture, however, reveals a fuzzy boundary between forced and voluntary assimilation.

Most older Saami (Laplanders) in Finland, for instance, were indoctrinated by the school system into believing that the speaking of Saami even at home weakened the child's knowledge of Finnish. Many parents from various south Asian minorities now living in Britain have been told by teachers and social workers that speaking languages other than English at home would put their children's learning of English at risk. The research evidence indicates otherwise, as we show in Chapter 8, but most of the so-called experts who offer such advice are monolinguals and think of bilingualism as a problem in need of remediation. Children all over the world have been punished and ridiculed at school for speaking their parents' languages.

Political scientists once thought that the spread of both global capitalism as well as communism would eventually eliminate long-standing narrow allegiances to local ethnicities in favor of a broader loyalty to modern nation-states. Yet ethnic nationalism has repeatedly resisted the melting pot. Ethnicity also grows stronger when actively denied or suppressed. Throughout its 74 years of existence the territory once called Yugoslavia has been a powder keg of ethnic rivalries going back centuries. The country that has been dissolving these past few years was an artificial creation of conflicting cultures held in check by a centralized Communist government until 1980; once the old regime crumbled, old tensions surfaced, leading to the unraveling of the country. We will see in more detail in Chapter 8 how the virtual collapse of the economies of the former Soviet bloc countries has revealed the difficulties of centralized planning that rides roughshod over regional and ethnic affiliations and their related languages.

We see in these examples that languages perform a fundamental act of identity for their speakers: you are what you speak. Sir James Henare, a Maori leader who died in 1989, expressed such sentiments about the

Maori language: "The language is the life force of our Maori culture and *mana* ['power']. If the language dies, as some predict, what do we have left to us? Then, I ask our own people who are we?" Likewise, a Romani saying, *Varesave foki nai-len pengi nogi chib, si kokoro posh foki*, translates as *a people without their own language is only half a people*, and the Welsh proverb *Heb iaith, heb genedl* means *no language, no nation*.

Although the existence of distinct cultures within one nation has often been seen by the powers that be as a threat to the cohesiveness of the state, our examples (and many more like them that we consider in coming chapters) show that denying people the right to their own language and culture does not provide a workable solution either. When large portions of the population are denied forms of self-expression, the nation's political and social foundations are weakened. This is not to deny the existence of considerable problems, particularly where the traditional patterns of behavior of a minority group conflict with those of the dominant culture in a society. We argue in Chapter 8 that a nation that incorporates cultural and linguistic diversity is also richer than one that denies their existence. Difference itself is not the problem, but rather lack of respect for difference, its meanings, and its values.

To preserve our languages is also to preserve ourselves and our diverse heritage—admittedly an ultimately selfish goal. Sociolinguist Joshua Fishman says that we should not be embarrassed about the fact that support of language maintenance is basically a value position, because the position of its opponents is also a value position. They assume it would be better if small cultures and languages were simply to die out. Just because people can evidently survive without their languages and traditional cultures does not necessarily mean that enforced uniformity is a good thing, or that nothing of consequence is lost when a people loses a language.

What can be done?

The first step in the solution to any problem is to acknowledge its existence and understand its origins. Only by understanding the historical and social circumstances which have created this threat can we hope to reverse it. Hence, the main purpose of this book is to inform the wider scientific community and the public of the threat facing the world's languages and cultures.

The language endangerment crisis is only just beginning to be taken seriously among linguists and their professional organizations. It very much needs to be brought to the public's attention in the way that the environmental crisis has been popularized through activities such as Earth Day, held annually since 1970. Before the popular environmental movement, for instance, the US had no Environmental Protection Agency, no

Clean Air Acts, no Endangered Species Act, and there were few environmental laws at either the federal or state level. Consumer knowledge today, however, is such that many people now refuse to buy furs or sprays which damage the ozone layer, or other products known to have a negative impact on the environment. Recycling is today a household word.

We are encouraged by the fact that even though it is only relatively recently that serious thought has been given to the possibility that human interference with nature was having disastrous consequences for the environment, many people now recognize that resources must be managed if we are to survive. Although there is still a long way to go, this increased awareness has contributed to a slowing of environmental damage. Yet few people think of languages in the same way they do of other natural resources such as air, water, and oil, which need careful planning. Of the many similarities between threatened languages and endangered species, the most obvious one is their irreplaceability. There is no substitute for either type of resource.

By directing our efforts to saving the components of our global village—our peoples, languages, and cultures—we aim to preserve ourselves as a species with all its rich variation. As Joshua Fishman points out, in this sense the task of preserving languages is a "good problem" because its solution will contribute to solving related problems rather than to making things worse. The solution to the environmental crisis involves preserving local ecosystems through the empowerment of indigenous peoples who live there. Preserving and creating small-scale community habitats in turn support languages and cultures.

Environmental damage, like language death, has global effects, but the burden at the moment falls most heavily on the developing countries, which have some of the highest rates of biolinguistic diversity. This is yet another reason why the extinction of biolinguistic diversity has been ignored: it is seen as largely a Third World problem. The destruction of the rain forest, for instance, affects directly and immediately developing countries in the tropics for the most part, but the aftermath affects us all. When the forests are burned or otherwise cleared, biodiversity is lost and there is atmospheric buildup of greenhouse gases, which contributes to global warming.

To explain what is happening to languages, and what it means, we have to understand the broader and more fundamental social pressures that are active in the world today, such as the huge differences in numbers and economic power between the peoples of the world. These contemporary disparities have not come out of nowhere in the last few decades. To explain their existence, we have to consider the broad sweep of human history over the very long term, perhaps as much as ten thousand years. The task of this book is thus a very large one indeed. We will not try to duck any aspect of it, as we are determined to pursue the inequalities of the contemporary world all the way back to first causes as far as we can.

However, this does mean that our treatment of the issues in a book of this length will have to be painted for the most part with a rather broad brush. Although we will use concrete examples wherever we can, these are at times necessarily shorter on detail and nuance than we would like. It is not that we think that detail and nuance are unimportant; they can make the difference between a culture surviving and its dying out. However, both the patterns seen through a telescope and those seen through a microscope are true patterns, and telescopes are good for finding forests, in which microscopes can then tell us a great deal about individual trees.

In the next chapter we will take a telescopic look at the distribution of languages and linguistic diversity in order to assess the extent of language endangerment around the world. Chapters 3 and 4 zero in on some specific examples of diversity. Chapters 5 and 6 provide a broad overview of the agrarian and industrial revolutions in terms of their consequences for the spread of languages and their speakers. Having identified the major forces that now threaten the common repository of biolinguistic diversity, the final two chapters focus on planning strategies for survival of the world's biolinguistic diversity, with Chapter 8 containing some specific examples of language maintenance efforts underway around the world.

Two

A World of Diversity

Languages die like rivers
Words wrapped around your tongue today
and broken to the shape of thought
between your teeth and lips speaking
now and today
shall be faded hieroglyphics
ten thousand years from now.
—*Carl Sandburg*

I f asked to name as many languages as possible, the average person could probably easily name a dozen, but would certainly not come up with this list: Abenaki, Bella Coola, Rama, Guguu Yimidhirr, Kabana, Adzera, Boiken, Toba Batak, Fyem, Tzotzil, Cebuano, Mokilese. You have probably never heard of these languages, or thousands more like them. One of us asked some graduate students in linguistics at the University of Oxford to write down the names of as many languages as they could think of. The number ranged from 50 to 75.

Even professional linguists perhaps would not be able to name more than a hundred. A recent advertisement for "Teach yourself language courses" appearing in a popular magazine claimed to "offer introductory and advanced courses in most of the world's languages." To be precise, they boasted a total of 215 courses in 76 languages! However, this number represents but 1 percent of the total number of languages. Most ordinary readers are surprised to find that linguists estimate the number of languages in the world to be between 5,000 and 6,700.

This chapter assesses the extent of the world's linguistic diversity, and its endangerment. We will show that the geographic distribution of languages and speakers is very uneven. Certain parts of the world such as the Asia/Pacific region are hotbeds of linguistic diversity, while others, such as Europe, are more uniform. Unfortunately, the linguistic hotbeds are also very much at risk. We will show that by one estimate, 60 percent of all languages are at risk. This puts the problem of linguistic extinction on a par with the worst case scenarios for species extinction. More than half the world's languages and species could be gone by the turn of the next century.

There are remarkable overlaps between the areas of greatest biological and greatest linguistic/cultural diversity around the world, allowing us to speak of a common repository of biolinguistic diversity. These striking correlations require close examination and must be accounted for. As we emphasized in Chapter 1, the loss of linguistic and cultural diversity should be seen as an integral part of larger processes threatening biodiversity on earth. Because language plays a crucial role in the acquisition, accumulation, maintenance, and transmission of human knowledge concerning the natural environment and ways of interacting with it, the problem of language endangerment raises critical issues about the survival of knowledge that may be of use in the conservation of the world's ecosystems.

How many languages are there and where are they spoken?

There are a number of reasons why it is difficult to say precisely how many languages there are in the world. In addition to languages, there are also varieties or dialects of languages, many of which are also at risk. We confine ourselves here, however, to the topic of language endangerment. Another problem in deciding precisely how many languages there are in the world arises from the fact that many have no special names. The Sare people of the Sepik region of Papua New Guinea, for example, call their language Sare, but this means simply "to speak or talk." The Gitksan people of British Columbia have no conventional native name for their language which sets it apart from other varieties such as Nisgha and Tsimshian. The Gitksan generally refer to their own language as *Sim'algax*, "the real or true language," but the Nigsha and Tsimshian people do the same.

Some languages have many different names. *The Ethnologue*, for example, one of the best sources of information on the languages in the world, lists over 39,000 language names, dialect names, and alternate names. Sometimes linguists use names which are different from those that speakers themselves use. The language some linguists now call Kabana, spoken in Northwest New Britain, Papua New Guinea, was earlier called Barriai by one observer, which is a name the Kabana and Amara people give to their land. The name *Nez Perce*, given to the native American tribes in what is now Washington, Oregon, and Idaho, comes from French for "pierced nose"; the tribes call themselves *Numi-pu*, which means simply "our people."

In some cases an identical name is used for two completely different languages, and different sources often do not agree either about the name of a language or its status. *The Ethnologue*, for example, says that Alagwa, a Southern Cushitic language spoken in central Tanzania, had 13,000 speakers in 1984, but another source says it is extinct. Recent fieldwork in 1989 indicates there are about 10,000 Alagwa people, nearly all of whom are bilingual in Rangi, and that Alagwa children now tend to speak Rangi among themselves.

However, the most important reason the majority of the world's languages are known only to specialists and the speakers themselves is that many linguists work on only one language or sometimes a handful of related languages, and linguists have tended to work on the familiar and easily accessible languages of Western Europe spoken by large numbers of people. One linguist estimates that some 4,000 of the world's languages have never been described adequately. In Papua New Guinea, for instance, which we discuss in the next chapter, perhaps a dozen of its 800 some languages have been described in any detail. So while thousands of linguists have probably worked on French or English over the last 100 years or so, there are thousands of other languages that have received little attention, and many hundreds that have received none at all.

The distribution of languages across the space of the world is strikingly uneven. Table 2.1 lists the top fifteen languages, in terms of number of speakers. Almost half (47.5%) of the world's population of around 5.9 billion speaks one of these languages, while much of the rest of the world speaks languages with fewer than 10,000 speakers.

You will probably recognize most of these names. Most of these languages are spoken in more than one country, such as English, for instance,

Table 2.1   *Top fifteen languages in terms of number of speakers*

Rank	Language	Population	% of World's Pop.
1	CHINESE, Mandarin	885,000,000	15
2	ENGLISH	322,000,000	5.4
3	SPANISH	266,000,000	4.5
4	BENGALI	189,000,000	3.2
5	HINDI	182,000,000	3.0
6	PORTUGUESE	170,000,000	2.8
7	RUSSIAN	170,000,000	2.8
8	JAPANESE	125,000,000	2.1
9	GERMAN	98,000,000	1.6
10	CHINESE, Wu	77,175,000	1.3
11	JAVANESE	75,500,800	1.2
12	KOREAN	75,000,000	1.2
13	FRENCH	72,000,000	1.2
14	VIETNAMESE	66,897,000	1.1
15	TELEGU	66,350,000	1.1

Source: *Ethnologue,* 1996

with large groups of speakers in the UK, USA, New Zealand, Canada, Australia, and South Africa. For similar historical reasons, Spanish and Portuguese are widely spoken in Latin America; French in parts of Africa, the Pacific, and North America; and languages such as Bengali and Hindi in the UK. Similarly, Mandarin (in addition to other Chinese languages such as Wu) is spoken not only in mainland China, but also in Singapore, Taiwan, and Hong Kong. This is one reason the populations speaking these top fifteen languages are so large.

Most of the world's languages, however, do not show the same geographic spread as these top fifteen. Although as many as 250 languages are spoken by a million or more people, 83 percent of the world's languages are spoken only in one country. Moreover, most languages do not even claim a territory as large as a country. In fact, there are approximately 25 to 30 times as many languages as there are countries, which means some degree of bi- or multilingualism is present to some degree in practically every country in the world.

Accurate information on many languages is difficult to come by, however, because governments often ignore and even ban certain languages—

in some cases because they do not recognize them as languages, in other cases because they deny the right of a group who speaks that language to exist. *The Ethnologue* counts 27 Quechuan languages in Peru, for instance, while the Peruvian government accords only six of these the status of language. The government's decision is political rather than linguistic.

Another way to look at the uneven distribution of the world's languages is to look at the functions they are used for. Most languages at present exist in what sociolinguists call a *diglossic relationship*, a term used to refer to functional specialization between languages so that the language used within the home and in other personal domains of interaction between community members is different from the one used in higher functions such as government, media, education. In Paraguay, for instance, Spanish is the official language of government and education, while Guaraní, spoken by 90 percent of the population, is the language of most homes and everyday informal interaction.

Languages compete continually with one another for speakers and functions, for reasons we will discuss in more detail in the next few chapters. When diglossia is stable, each language has its own set of functions and space without threatening the other. When one language encroaches on a domain typically controlled by another, this indicates a shift in the relative balance of power between groups speaking these languages. Latin, for instance, at one time fulfilled all the functions a language could. It was the language of home, government, empire, science, art, literature, and church. One by one these functions were taken over by other languages until only the religious function remained.

Most speakers of today's European languages do not realize that their languages were once in a diglossic relationship with Latin. It took some centuries before English, for example, replaced Latin and French as the language of court proceedings, official correspondence, educational and scientific treatises. Isaac Newton and many other scientists wrote their works in Latin. Richard Mulcaster was among the first to question, in 1582, why everything could not be written in English; it was not until 1700, however, that the tradition of writing academic texts in Latin finally died out. By comparison with classical Latin, English was still in many respects stylistically limited because it was not used across the broad range of contexts that Latin served. Furthermore, its use was confined to England and therefore its utility as the lingua franca of science and technology it was to claim in later centuries was at that stage doubtful.

We saw in the previous chapter how the spread of English around the world was linked to the dominance of English speakers in the areas of science and technology, which in turn led to significant control of the world's economy. Those who control particular linguistic resources are in a position of power over others. Linguistic capital, like all other forms of capital, is unequally distributed in society. The higher the profit to be achieved through knowledge of a particular language, the more it will be viewed as worthy of acquisition. The language of the global village (or McWorld, as some have called it) is English: not to use it is to risk ostracization from the benefits of the global economy. It is at least partly for this reason that many newly independent countries have opted to use the language of their former colonizers rather than try to develop their own languages. Moreover, the elite in these countries generally acquire languages through schooling, and use this knowledge to retain their positions of power over the majority of citizens who do not know them.

This means that world languages such as English are widely used by people as second languages. Indeed, there are now more speakers of English as a second language—350 million, according to one estimate— than there are native English speakers. Two thousand years ago there were about 250 million people in the whole world; now more than that number speak English.

Globalization has increasingly led to layers of diglossia on an international scale. Within Sweden, for instance, Swedish is in a diglossic relationship with a number of other languages such as Finnish, Saami, and the newer migrant communities such as the Greeks. While it is usually sufficient for a Swede to know Swedish and English, the Saami cannot afford the luxury of monolingualism, or even bilingualism in Saami and an international language. The Saami need to know the dominant language of the state in which they live—either Swedish, Norwegian or Finnish—as well as some language that allows them to communicate beyond national borders. Within Scandinavia, Swedish has a diglossic relationship with other Scandinavian languages, with Swedish more often learned by others than Swedes learn other Scandinavian languages. Within the larger context of Europe and beyond, however, Swedish is on a par with other Scandinavian languages and continental European languages such as Dutch in relation to other European languages of wider currency such as English, French, and German.

The more specialized the function a language fulfills, the fewer language options there are. The United Nations, for instance, has a small set of six "official languages" and a slightly larger set of "working languages," but the majority of languages of its nearly 200 member countries have no status at all. In many cases English or another language such as French or Arabic is the declared "official" language of a country, most of whose inhabitants speak another language at home. The total number of official languages in the world is quite small—probably no more than 100 languages have this status. English is now the dominant or official language in more than 60 of the world's 185 nation-states recognized by the United Nations. Most of the scientific journals of the world are written in English and a few other international languages such as French, German, and Russian, which over the centuries have been expanding their functional and geographical territories at the same time as the space filled by other languages has contracted.

Most languages of the world are unwritten, not recognized officially, and restricted to local community and home functions. They are spoken by very small groups of people. The median number of speakers for the languages of the world is only 5,000 to 6,000, and nearly 85 percent of languages have fewer than 100,000. These small languages are unevenly shared between the continents and countries of the world.

The map in Figure 2.1 shows an estimate of the relative language densities of the world's major countries. Though the statistics involved are complex, this is effectively a measure of languages per square mile. As the map shows, there are zones of high density amidst areas of relative paucity. In particular, the map reveals a dark band running through the tropics, with density falling away as one moves towards the poles.

Most of the world's languages are spoken in the tropical countries of the dark band on the map. There are two great belts of high density: one running from the West African coast through the Congo basin and to East Africa, and another running from South India and peninsula Southeast Asia into the islands of Indonesia, New Guinea, and the Pacific. The seventeen major countries of these two belts contain most of the world's language giants: Nigeria, with 427 languages, Cameroon (270), Zaire (210), Ivory Coast (73), Togo (43), Ghana (72), Benin (51), Tanzania (131), India (380, including 3 of the top 15), Vietnam (86), Laos (92), the Philippines (160), Malaysia (137), Indonesia (670, including 1 of the top 15), Papua New Guinea (860), Vanuatu (105), and the Solomon Islands (66). These seventeen countries between them hold 60 percent of all languages (around 4,000 in all), but only 27 percent of the world's population and 9 percent of the world's land area. If we add the three other giants, Australia (with 250 languages), Mexico (240), and Brazil (210), we have over 70 percent of all languages in just twenty nation-states, among them some of the poorest countries in the world.

These great belts of high language density shown in Figure 2.1—the heart of Africa, Southeast Asia to the Pacific, plus Brazil, central America, and parts of Australia—are also the locations of the tropical forests which harbor so many of the world's species. These forests provide a home for 50 to 90 percent of all the earth's species, as well as a majority of the world's languages. We believe this correlation is no accident, and later in the chapter we will return to the idea that linguistic and biological diversity have common locations, common causes, and face common threats.

In contrast to the profusion of languages in the tropics, the temperate latitudes are rather impoverished. Europe has only 3 percent of all languages, and China, despite having 21.5 percent of the earth's population and 8.6 percent of its land area, has just 2.6 percent of the world's lan-

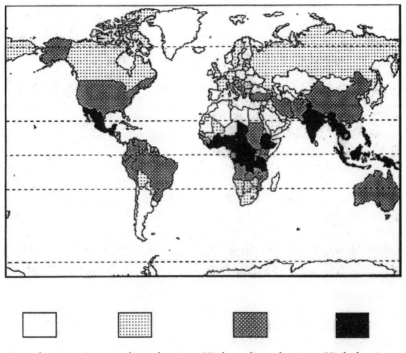

Low density   Low medium density   High medium density   High density

Figure 2.1   Map of the World showing the relative language diversity of the major countries

[*From Daniel Nettle,* Journal of Anthropological Archaeology *17 (1998):354–74; Adapted courtesy of Academic Press*]

guages (a total of 96). In Chapters 4, 5, and 6 we will consider the processes which have so inhibited diversity in these locations.

The patterns we have shown in Figure 2.1 are striking. However, just counting languages is not itself the way to assess either linguistic diversity or linguistic endangerment, as we shall now see.

Hotbeds of linguistic diversity

If some horrific catastrophe wiped out all the languages of western Europe tomorrow, we would lose relatively little of the world's linguistic diversity. As we have just seen, Europe has only about three percent of the world's languages, and most of the largest European languages are also widely spoken outside Europe. More importantly, however, most of the languages of Europe are structurally quite similar, because they are related historically. If we were to lose the same number of languages in Papua New Guinea or South America, the loss would be far more significant, because the divergence between languages there runs much deeper. Unfortunately, such catastrophes have happened in the past and have probably already resulted in the loss of a great amount of diversity, as we shall see in Chapters 5 and 6.

Clearly, we need a way of quantifying the divergence between languages, and to do this we must have a way of classifying them. Linguists have several such techniques. Here we mention only two of the most important ones: *genetic* and *typological classification*. Genetic classification takes account of the common historical origins of languages. Typological classification, on the other hand, disregards this factor in order to group languages together on the basis of contemporary structural similarities, such as a common word order, or the same number and type of vowel sounds.

Japanese and Panjabi, for instance, do not stem from a common parent and are therefore completely unrelated, but they share the grammatical property of being verb-final. This means they put the verb at the end of the sentence instead of between the subject and object as SVO (Subject-Verb-Object) languages like English do. This is significant because the basic word order of sentences is very often a good predictor of the word order of other constituents. For example, the Celtic languages such as Breton and Welsh, as well as Polynesian languages such as Maori and Hawaiian, are verb-initial (VSO) languages. Not only do verbs come before subjects (for example in Hawaiian, where *'ike ka wahine ia'u*, meaning "the woman sees me," translates literally as *sees the woman me*: nouns also come before the adjectives that modify them (*hale ke'oke'o li'ili'i* in Hawaiian, for "small white house," is literally *house white small*). The fact that the Polynesian and Celtic languages have VSO word order in common is not due to a common historical origin, but simply an important and far-reaching structural property that happens to have evolved in both cases.

Genetic classification, on the other hand, is concerned with historical relationships, and groups languages together into so-called families that share a common origin. This common history is the explanation for the structural and other similarities found in a family. Looking at the words in Table 2.2, for instance, you can see that there are regular similarities between Hawaiian and Maori, between Welsh and Breton, and between German and Swedish—but not between German and Maori, or Hawaiian and Swedish, and so on. The German and Swedish words also resem-

Table 2.2   *An example of genetic relationship*

	Hawaiian	Maori	Welsh	Breton	German	Swedish
house	hale	whare	ty	ti	haus	hus
fish	iʻa	ika	pysgodyn	pesk	fisch	fisk
name	inoa	ingoa	enw	anw	name	namn
water	wai	wai	dwr	dour	wasser	vatten
man	kanaka	tangata	dyn	den	mann	mann

ble English quite closely because all three are part of the Germanic family of languages, which in turn is part of Indo-European. Hawaiian and Maori, on the other hand, are Polynesian languages belonging to the Austronesian family.

Linguists have used genetic classification to assign most of the world's languages to a smaller number of families. Some of these are well known. We give but two examples here, Indo-European and Sino-Tibetan.

The Indo-European family, containing 200 some languages, is one of the most widespread and certainly the best documented. It covers most of Europe and extends through Asia Minor into India. Of the top fifteen languages in Table 2.1, only Japanese, Korean, Javanese, Vietnamese, Telegu, and Chinese do not belong to this family. Since 1492 Indo-European languages have been carried to other continents: English in the United States and Australia, Hindi in Trinidad, French in Haiti, Portuguese in Macao, Dutch in South Africa, and Spanish in Latin America. Today an Indo-European language—either English, Spanish, or Portuguese—is the dominant language and culture in every country in North, Central, and South America. Despite the successful spread of Indo-European languages, however, there are also branches of the family at risk. Four Celtic languages (Scottish Gaelic, Irish Gaelic, Welsh, and Breton) are all that remain of a family that once extended through Europe into Asia Minor. It is one of the most threatened groups of the indigenous languages of Europe, with Manx and Cornish already extinct, as we shall see in Chapter 6.

After the Indo-European family, Sino-Tibetan is the most populous family in the world, containing close to a billion speakers. The languages are found mainly in Nepal, China, India, and Myanmar but also in the north of Laos, Thailand, and Vietnam. Most of these languages, however, have fairly small numbers of speakers, except for Chinese. The eight languages grouped together under the label "Chinese" account for the vast majority of Sino-Tibetan speakers.

Just as there are many more languages than is commonly realized, there are many more language families than most people are familiar with. Linguist Johanna Nichols, in a recent comprehensive survey, estimates that there are 249 families of about the same internal divergence as Indo-European in the world.

She calls these families *stocks*. Some of the stocks may be linked to others into higher-level, more distant units, though more distant relationships than the stock level are difficult to prove and often controversial. On the other hand, some linguists would not accept the reduction even to 250 stocks. For example, some authorities recognize at least that many families for South America alone.

The distribution of stocks is also very uneven. A couple of huge stocks, Austronesian in the Pacific basin and Niger-Congo in Africa, have nearly 1,000 languages each. In Chapter 5, we will consider the forces which gave these peoples, and hence their languages, such a large geographic range. On the other hand, there are a number of stocks consisting of just one language. These are known as *isolates*, languages which have no demonstrable relationship with any other. Japanese and Korean are probably the best-known and largest isolates. New Guinea has more than its fair share, such as Taiap, whose case we encountered in Chapter 1 and will consider further in Chapter 6. Basque, spoken in parts of France and Spain, is another. There are many more, especially in parts of the world where little research has been done, and many are in danger of dying before they can be discovered and documented. Isolates are particularly intriguing because they may represent what is left of an area containing much diversity in the past. As last vestiges of an earlier population, they give us invaluable hints about the prehistory of regions.

The geographic distribution of the 249 stocks identified by Nichols is shown in Figure 2.2. As we can see, the Old World is rather poor in stocks. Africa, for all its 2,000 languages, has just 20 stocks, and despite the huge expanse of Eurasia, it musters just 28 stocks (6 in Europe, 12 in Northern Asia, 10 in South and Southeast Asia). In sharp contrast are New Guinea—with almost as many stocks as all of Eurasia—Australia, and above all, the Americas, with over 150 of the world's 249 stocks.

The distribution of typological diversity, as Nichols shows, is also extremely uneven. Certain areas, generally those with many stocks, also show a wide diversity of structural language types. The Americas and the Pacific basin emerge from Nichols's study as centers of great structural diversification, while Eurasia is, once again, rather impoverished. This is true despite the fact that the study probably underestimates the extent of diversity outside Eurasia to a considerable degree. This is because Nichols needed to rely on a sample of well-described languages in order to have the information needed for mapping, and non-Eurasian languages are mostly underdocumented and in some cases near to extinction. Although

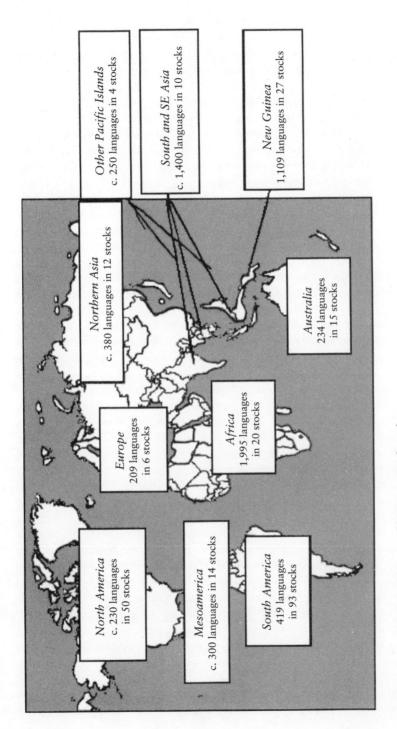

Other Pacific Islands
c. 250 languages in 4 stocks

South and SE Asia
c. 1,400 languages in 10 stocks

New Guinea
1,109 languages in 27 stocks

Northern Asia
c. 380 languages in 12 stocks

Australia
234 languages in 15 stocks

Europe
209 languages in 6 stocks

Africa
1,995 languages in 20 stocks

North America
c. 230 languages in 50 stocks

Mesoamerica
c. 300 languages in 14 stocks

South America
419 languages in 93 stocks

Figure 2.2   Global distribution of languages and stocks

information was included from 174 languages, there are few Niger-Congo, Sino-Tibetan, or Austro-Thai languages, and no Eskimo-Aleut languages. There are also some imbalances with the Americas, represented by 59 languages and South America by only 15.

Nichols captures the distribution of diversity by identifying what she calls *residual* and *spread* zones. Residual zones have high diversity; they are inhabited by small groups, from many different stocks, with many different language types, among whom bilingualism or multilingualism is the norm. Papua New Guinea is the classic case, as we shall see in Chapter 4. A residual zone will contain a good deal of the world's possible linguistic diversity in microcosm.

In the spread zones, on the other hand, some historical processes (involving differentials of power, as we shall see in Chapters 5 and 6) have allowed one language or set of closely related languages to push out over a wide geographical area. This spread obliterates, displaces, or absorbs other languages.

It is important to stress that the reasons particular languages spread and others contract has nothing to do with the languages themselves. It is people who spread languages. In early human history these spreads were motivated by considerations of local ecology: people tended to move from a poor resource base to a richer one. Where another group already occupied a desirable area, there was potential conflict. More recent spreads have occurred due to the rise of agriculture and conquest. For example, the spread of Latin led to the extinction of Etruscan and various other languages. Before the Roman conquest there were probably more non-Indo-European languages, such as the survivor Basque, in western Europe. The spread of a new language in an area causes some structural features to spread at the expense of others. Spreads, then, deplete the linguistic diversity of an area.

The current low diversity of Eurasia and Africa is the result of several millennia of sustained spreading of a few groups, as we shall discover in Chapter 5. However, even here there are pockets of residual diversity which have escaped the forces of homogenization, such as the Caucasus mountains, whose fiercely independent residents have been shielded from the march of peoples on the plains below; Ethiopia and Kenya, off the main route of the Bantu expansion (which we will discuss in Chapter 5); the Kalahari desert, home to the San hunter-gatherers with their unparalleled "click" languages; and Tanzania, the only African country with all four of the higher-level language family groupings.

Most of the rest of the world—the Americas, Australia, the Pacific basin—is effectively a residual zone, which accounts for its greater stock richness. Within each area, of course, there are local spreads and local residua, but the background level of diversity is high. However, the spreads which began by depleting the diversity of Eurasia and Africa are now continuing their business overseas. If Johanna Nichols had arrived on the scene one hundred years later, she would very likely have found a New World completely covered by Indo-European, a residual zone turned into a spread zone. The causes of this threat are the subject of much of the rest of our book.

Nichols concludes, surely correctly, that the pattern of high diversity found in the Pacific and the Americas can be regarded as primordial: that is, close to what we would expect of language in its natural or default state. Indeed, in Chapters 4 and 5, we will argue that for around 90 percent of human history the whole world was probably a vast residual zone. Thus, our closest perspective on what human language is like should come from these relatively undisturbed areas. Unfortunately, these are the very places we know least about—and time is running out, as we shall now see.

Endangerment: the extent of the threat

How much of the world's linguistic diversity is endangered? The honest answer at this stage is that we don't know precisely, but when forced to guess, the proportion different linguists come up with is alarmingly high. In Chapter 1, we cited Krauss's statistics on the number of languages that are moribund in different parts of the world. These are useful, but extremely partial; many languages are endangered that are not yet moribund. These are the languages which might yet be saved.

Another way to look at it is to examine the functions that different languages fill. As we have said, by 1966, English was the language of 70 percent of the world's mail and 60 percent of radio and television broadcasts, and it is increasingly the sole language of international trade, finance, higher education, and science. Fewer than 4 percent of languages have any kind of official status in the countries where they are spoken, although over recent decades this situation has been improving, with Welsh, Maori, and Aymara, for example, obtaining recognition in their respective countries.

However, even official support is no guarantee of vitality. After having been banned in 1896, for instance, the Hawaiian language has been co-official with English in the state of Hawai'i since 1978, but it is still in a precarious condition with fewer than 1,000 native speakers. Irish, which has the strongest public support, is ironically probably the demographically weakest of the modern Celtic languages. As the national language of Ireland, it has the dubious distinction of being one of the few endangered languages with a state ostensibly dedicated to its preservation, and yet it is still dying because it is not being passed on to the next generation. We will examine both of these cases in more detail in Chapter 8. Conferring status

on the language of a group relatively lacking in power doesn't necessarily
ensure the reproduction of a language, unless other measures are in place
to ensure intergenerational transmission at home. As we will see over the
coming chapters, conferring power on the people would be much more
likely to do the trick. It is political, geographical, and economic factors
which support the maintenance of linguistic and cultural diversity. These
need to be considered holistically, as part of an ecology of language, an
approach that sees language as part of the larger natural environment.

Perhaps the only way to get some idea of the extent of endangerment
is to look at the sizes of living languages. Table 2.3 shows the percentage
of the languages in different continents which have fewer than some
number of speakers. The differences between the continents are readily
apparent. The languages in Australia and the Pacific and the Americas
are mostly very small, over 20 percent having fewer than 150 speakers,
and almost all with fewer than 100,000. Africa, Asia, and Europe, by
contrast, as well as some giant languages, have a fair number of medium-
sized languages (100,000–1 million speakers). Such languages are probably safe from extinction in the short term at least.

Recall from Chapter 1 Krauss's belief that a language with fewer than
10,000 speakers is probably at risk. This is a crude generalization, but it
may nonetheless be useful as a first approximation. It would mean that
60 percent of all languages are already endangered. The situation is
slightly better in Africa (33%), Asia (53%), and Europe (30%), but
much worse in North and South America (78% and 77%) and Australia
and the Pacific (93%). These latter areas are the hotbeds of genetic and
typological diversity we have just identified.

Table 2.3   *Percentages of languages according to continent of origin
having fewer than indicated number of speakers*

Continent	<150	<1000	<10,000	<100,000	<1,000,000
Africa	1.7	7.5	32.6	72.5	94.2
Asia	5.5	21.4	52.8	81	93.8
Europe	1.9	9.9	30.2	46.9	71.6
North America	22.6	41.6	77.8	96.3	100
Central Am.	6.1	12.1	36.4	89.4	100
South Am.	27.8	51.8	76.5	89.1	94.1
Aus/Pacific	22.9	60.4	92.8	99.5	100
World	11.5	30.1	59.4	83.8	95.2

[Source: Nettle, *Linguistic Diversity*. Oxford University Press, 1999: 114]

These figures are based simply on size, and size may not be the best guide to endangerment, as we indicated in Chapter 1. At present, however, it is probably the best measure until more research is done. A large language could be endangered if the external pressures on it were great, while a very small language could be perfectly safe as long as the community was functional and the environment stable. For example, small size has been a stable characteristic of languages in Australia for millennia, and this does not mean they have always been dying out. However, small languages can disappear much faster than large ones, and current technological and socioeconomic forces are difficult for small communities to resist, although larger groups may have the resources to do so. Thus, in present circumstances size may be quite critical in determining survival.

These figures, then, may give a reasonable projection of endangerment. If they do, the situation for languages is just as bad as biologists' worst projections for species diversity. Indeed, there are many commonalities and concerns in the biological and the linguistic extinction crises. It is to these linkages we now turn.

Biolinguistic diversity: some correlations between the linguistic and biological worlds

We mentioned at the outset of this chapter that according to biologists' more pessimistic predictions, half of the world's species will be extinct or on the verge of extinction by the end of the next century. Most estimates of extinction rates show them to be significantly higher than the processes creating biodiversity could compensate for because it takes much more time for evolution than extinction. Niles Eldredge, for example, estimates rather conservatively that we are currently losing species at the rate of about one a day—which adds up to 365 over the course of a year. E.O. Wilson, on the other hand, suggests an annual extinction rate of about 27,000 species, or about three species every hour! This amounts to more than 50,000 times the so-called background rate before human intervention. Nowadays, the rate of extinction may be as high as 60,000 to 90,000 species annually. Even Eldredge's much smaller figure is dramatic on its own, but to put these estimates in proper perspective, we need to know first how many species there are, and where they are found. Only then can we assess the size of the problem of extinction of the world's biodiversity.

Ecologists have unfortunately faced similar difficulties to those of linguists in trying to answer the question of how many species there are, and how many are at risk. Despite more than 250 years of research, no one really knows how many species of organisms inhabit the earth today. Estimates vary widely from 3 million to 80 million or more overall, with similar variation in estimates for groups such as insects, plants, and animals. Only some 1.4 million species have been described and given names.

As we found was the case with languages, much of the world's biodiversity has not yet been catalogued, particularly in the tropics, which are among the richest areas. According to Robert May, scientific adviser to the UK government, only 4 percent of the researchers engaged in classifying plants and animals work in those parts of the world where the greatest diversity exists. The distribution of these scientists is also ill-matched to the species richness of the various taxa. We saw that the same was true of linguists, who have tended to concentrate on more familiar languages spoken by large numbers of people, most of which belong to the Indo-European family.

The attention of biologists, like that of linguists, has also been highly selective. We know much more about particular kinds of species — namely animals with feathers and fur — than we do about insects or plants. Plants, for example, have commanded little public attention in conservation campaigns, although they are more fundamental than animals in supporting life on earth. People around the world utilize over 40,000 species a day, and most of them are plants. They provide the raw material for many medicines and the genetic stock from which agricultural strains of plants are developed. Insects, which account for 85 percent of all animal life, have attracted less scientific investigation and aroused little public concern despite their significance. In Africa termites and ants alone outweigh all the mammals put together. E.O. Wilson, for instance, says that if insects were to disappear, humanity probably could not last more than a few months. Most of the amphibians, reptiles, birds, and mammals would crash to extinction about the same time. Next would go the bulk of flowering plants and other terrestrial habitats of the world, and the land surface would literally rot.

Although most of the 4,000 some mammal species of the world have been classified, quite a different picture emerges for creatures other than mammals or birds. There may, for instance, be somewhere between 20,000 and 40,000 species of fish. No one knows for sure. One biologist was amazed when he first went to Lake Malawi to study its rich fish life. Half the fish pulled up in every trawl were unnamed species. It is the most species-rich lake in the world, with as many as 1,000 different types of fish — more than in all of the Atlantic Ocean. Virtually all of them are endemic: that is, they exist nowhere else in the world. The significance of Lake Malawi can be better appreciated when we consider that a total of only 75 to 100 new species of fish are described annually. Although every place is unique with respect to its combination of flora, fauna, language, and customs, some places are more unique than others. We examine one such place in Chapter 4 when we take a close look at Papua New Guinea, a country with about 5 percent of the world's biodiversity in its 400,000 some species, but only 1 percent of its land area.

As we saw was the case for languages, we need some way of assessing which parts of the world are most diverse and which are most at risk. To do this, we must have a measure more revealing of diversity than simply counting numbers of species. No single measure will capture completely the enormous complexity of life on earth. How do we factor in dimensions such as rarity and endemism (the equivalent of language isolates), in relation to the genetic variety and species richness in a particular area, in order to arrive at a measure of overall ecosystem richness? Our earlier example of Lake Malawi would score high on measures based on sheer numbers of species of fish as well as on endemism. Presumably we would also want to recognize greater diversity in an area containing both redwoods and dandelions (the equivalent of typological diversity in linguistic systems) than one containing a pair of more similar species such as dandelions and daisies.

Figure 2.3 represents one attempt at an overall assessment. It depicts global biodiversity values on the basis of the distribution of some of the most highly valued mammals, reptiles, amphibians, and seed plants. Although this measure gives greater weight to the higher plants and vertebrates, it does allow us to identify hotbeds of biodiversity.

Comparing this map to the one in Figure 2.1, we see that those areas which are rich in languages also tend to be rich in biodiversity value. Biodiversity is concentrated through the tropics and tails off towards the poles, just as linguistic diversity does. There are similar hotbeds of great diversity, such as in New Guinea. Thus, we can really speak of a common area of biolinguistic diversity. How has this come about?

Residents of temperate climates need little convincing of the greater biological diversity of the tropics compared to more northerly latitudes if they have ever traveled to a place like New Guinea. They are immediately struck by the profusion of trees, flowers, birds, and insects. The more heterogeneous the physical environment is, the more species are found there. This is incidentally true for both land and sea. Heterogeneity in the physical environment enables a greater of number of microenvironments to exist which can support a greater number of species. This is another way of saying that complexity begets more complexity. The more richly complex a system is, the more stable it tends to be—a point to which we return in Chapter 8. Local ecosystems contain populations of different species, each playing a different role in the recycling of nutrients and the flow of energy through the system.

Linguistic diversity is an important part of this pattern of richness and stability. Languages, like species, are highly adapted to their environments. The koala requires the leaves of the eucalyptus tree for its survival. If a habitat is drastically altered or destroyed, the organisms that

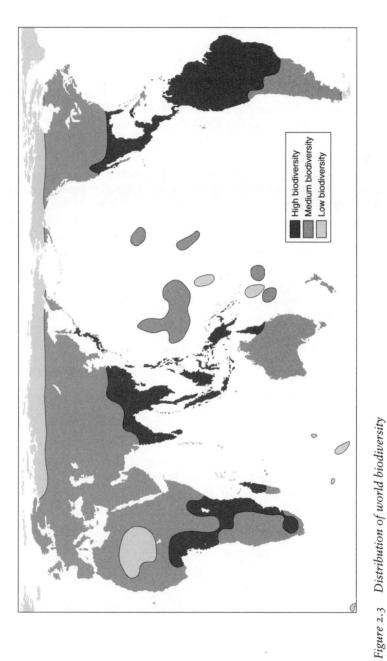

Figure 2.3   Distribution of world biodiversity

[*Adapted from P.H. Williams, K.J. Gaston, & C.J. Humphries, Proceedings of the Royal Society, Biological Sciences (1997), 264:141–148.*]

once inhabited it will be wiped out. Just as languages claim territories of various sizes, every species has a niche. Niches, in turn, have various widths or limits to their distribution. Horseshoe crabs are always the last of the larger organisms to disappear from polluted estuaries along the eastern coast of North America, for example, because they can tolerate a wider range of temperature variation and degree of salinity than other species. They are, in other words, relatively broad-niched. Narrow-niched species are, by contrast, more specialized to a particular environment. The higher the latitude, the greater the average area and latitudinal extent of a species range. This is known as *Rapoport's Rule*. Thus, the relatively fewer species in the northern latitudes have much more extensive ranges than do the more numerous species inhabiting the tropics. Temperatures vary widely in the more temperate climes, and high latitude organisms must be able to withstand these extremes. This makes them better able to cope with change.

Like species, languages too can be thought of as occupying ecological niches. The majority of the world's languages are, however, narrow-niched, like Taiap in Papua New Guinea. Relatively few languages — such as English, Arabic, or Chinese — are broad-niched. At the same time tropical ecosystems are typically rich in number of species, they are poor in the number of organisms — the opposite of northern latitudes. Thus, the population of any one species may be relatively small; it is variety which is great — another characteristic of a stable ecosystem. If we apply this biological analogy to languages, then we would expect to find great numbers of languages spoken by relatively small numbers of speakers in the tropics. And that's precisely what we tend to find, as we show in more detail in Chapter 4 when we consider Papua New Guinea: an enormous number of languages spoken by relatively small numbers of people.

Consider the niche occupied by coral reefs, for instance, restricted to a belt which runs no higher than 40 degrees north and south of the equator. Reef communities are severely affected in major mass extinctions. They are intolerant of climate fluctuation because for millions of years conditions have remained stable. One reason the tropics have more species of organisms is the availability of relatively constant amounts of energy, in particular from the sun.

Niche widths can change, however, and disrupt a relatively stable ecosystem. Any global cooling would reduce the width of the tropical regions. Even more serious than climate change, however, is human intervention, in the form of agriculture, and more recently, resource extraction activities such as mining and logging. The availability of food, water, and other resources in local ecosystems puts natural limits on expansion of any species, including our own — until relatively recently. It was cultural invention that enabled the human species to spread around the globe. As we argue in Chapter 5, however, the invention that really changed our position in the natural world was the invention of agriculture some 10,000 years ago. After humans took control over the production of our food supply, we became the first species in the 3.5 billion year history of life to live outside the confines of our local ecosystem. Now all but a handful of hunter-gatherer societies live outside their local ecosystems. Agriculture was thus an ecological revolution that triggered a population explosion that has not abated as more and more people require land on which to grow food. The whole earth has become our local ecosystem and our entire species functions as a single massive population within that ecosystem. Yet, because the vast majority of us no longer are functional parts of local ecosystems, we don't see the importance of preserving them.

However, as we will show in Chapter 8, we did not really leave our ecosystem as much as redefine our position in it, and our future is not independent of this global ecosystem. The modern world of human activities and production appears at first glance to take place largely outside nature. Take a look at what's in your refrigerator. Most of our food comes not from crops grown in our back yards, but from a wide range of substances processed in factories all over the industrialized world. Living in buildings we have constructed from artificial materials, making weekend forays in our cars to visit "nature" for hikes and camping trips, it is easy for us to imagine that we could live by technological innovations alone and that we can exist apart from nature. Our approach to "living with nature" has been to distance ourselves from it to use our technologies to increase our abilities to exploit natural resources, preferably someone else's. According to a 1998 estimate of the World Wide Fund for Nature, we consumed a third of the world's natural resources between 1975 and 1995, with North America and Europe the areas of highest consumption.

Now that supertankers have the power to disgorge millions of gallons of oil into the ocean, farmers can introduce genetic mutations into the life cycle through the use of pesticides and herbicides, and scientists have the capability to unleash bioengineered organisms into the world, we can also destroy the resources on which we depend at a much faster rate than natural processes can replenish them. The evidence we have presented in this chapter also allows us to understand why the same amount of habitat destruction in the tropics would lead to many more biolinguistic extinctions than would occur in the higher latitudes.

The developed nations of the world are now rapidly destroying the habitats which sustain much of the world's biolinguistic diversity. Much attention has focused on the world's remaining tropical rain forests as a major repository of this biodiversity. A survey of ten hectares of the Borneo rainforest, the oldest in the world and possibly the most diverse, revealed nearly 800 species of trees, and the earth's last substantial

Figure 2.4   Penan tribesmen in the Sarawak rain forest

[Courtesy of Art Wolfe]

stands of the enormous dipterocarp hardwood trees that grow to 150 feet in height and many yards in circumference. The rate of destruction of the tropical forest almost doubled in the 1980s. Although the area is less than one-tenth the size of the Amazonian rain forest, it provides most of Malaysia's exports of tropical logs, amounting to two-thirds of the world's trade in tropical roundwood. Parts of the forest were logged out by 1995. A small group of politicians in the two states of Borneo control the timber trade, with Sarawak's Chief Minister awarding lucrative contracts to political allies and family friends.

The Penan people of northeast Sarawak who live in longhouses in the forest are nowadays lucky to find a monkey to eat because the loggers have scared them away. Their trucks and bulldozers have muddied the waters and poisons in the bark of fallen trees have killed the fish. Chief Loli Mirai of Long Leng longhouse was prosecuted for burning four bridges built by logging companies, and most members of his family were arrested and detained by the police. He and many others felt it was a waste of time joining protests. Like the once thriving forests in which they lived, the Penan too are disappearing. In 1970 the population was 13,000; two decades later, fewer than 500. Soon there may be none.

The world's indigenous peoples and their languages are dying out or being assimilated into modern civilization because their habitats are

being destroyed. Since 1900, 90 of Brazil's 270 Indian tribes have completely disappeared. More than two-thirds of the remaining tribes have
fewer than 1,000 members. The story is the same for other parts of the
world such as Papua New Guinea, as we will see in Chapter 4. Shifting
from traditional ways of life has often involved loss of languages, as in
the case of the Saami of the Arctic region, who formerly earned their
livelihood almost exclusively from reindeer herding. In some cases the
move from traditional lifestyles has been precipitated by environmental
damage and away from a local habitat which was self-sustaining in terms
of its natural resources through pressures of an expanding or an invading
population. The Saami, for instance, have suffered from all these things.
The disaster at Chernobyl meant the extermination of many herds of
reindeer on which their livelihood depended, and there is increasing pressure from the Swedish state to build hydroelectric generating stations on
lands where reindeer once roamed.

Of course, it may happen that a local extinction of an organism in a
particular environment does not spell extinction for the species as a
whole, since a species may have many habitats. The species may be well
in one location but under threat in another. So it is with languages. Panjabi is in no danger of dying on the Indian subcontinent, where it has a
secure position as one of the major regional languages of India. Yet its
use is on the decline in Britain, where many speakers of the language
have emigrated. The same is true for Spanish, which is secure in Spain
and many parts of Latin America, but threatened in the United States.

If Panjabi dies in Britain, it will still exist as a language. Its plight is
not so severe as other languages, for which local death spells total extinction. When the last speaker of Manx died some years ago, that was the
end of the Manx language. But still there are degrees. Manx has close living linguistic relatives that are structurally similar. If Taiap or Basque
dies, it will leave a linguistic black hole.

Overall, the commonalities between biological and linguistic diversity
are striking. The richness is concentrated in similar places, and in both
cases, the destabilizing activities of a few powerful groups have potentially catastrophic consequences. Much of the world is now being covered by a few species of Eurasian origin—wheat, barley, cattle, rice.
These monocultures are replacing a profusion of endemic diversity
whose functions we are only now beginning to understand and appreciate. The linguistic situation is uncannily similar, but the spreading varieties are English, Spanish, and Chinese. Moreover, the underlying causes,
and even the rates of spread, are extremely similar in both cases, as we
shall see in coming chapters.

In the next chapter we take a more detailed look at some kinds of
diversity contained in the world's languages and how it is being lost.
Although all languages change over time, what distinguishes the changes

affecting a dying language is the rate at which they take place, and more-over, how they conspire to eliminate what is culturally unique and distinctive about that language. Our examples will serve to emphasize again the complexity of human-environment relationships on earth, and suggest fundamental links between human languages and cultures, non-human species, and the earth's ecosystems. Moreover, the disappearance of hundreds of species of fish, birds, and other forms of life along with their names and related knowledge of their habitat and behavior represents a huge loss to science at precisely the time when we need most urgently to manage local ecosystems more effectively.

Three

Lost Words/Lost Worlds

On Disko Island [Greenland] in 1981 I helped test the corrosion effects of sea fog on the carabiners used for safety lines on glacier crossings. . . . [T]hree months later . . . it turned out that we could pull them apart with a fingernail. Exposed to a hostile environment, they had disintegrated.

You lose your language through a similar process of deterioration. When we moved from the village school to Qaanaaq [Thule], we had teachers who didn't know one word of Greenlandic, nor did they have any plans to learn it. They told us that, for those who excelled, there would be an admission ticket to Denmark and a degree and a way out of the Arctic misery. This golden ascent would take place in Danish. This was when the foundation was being laid for the politics of the sixties. Which led to Greenland officially becoming "Denmark's northernmost county" and the Inuit were officially supposed to be called "Northern Danes" and "be educated to the same rights as all other Danes," as the Prime Minister put it.

That's how the foundation is laid. Then you arrive in Denmark and six months pass and it feels as if you will never forget your mother tongue. It's the language you think in, the way you remember your past. Then you meet a Greenlander on the street. You exchange a few words. And suddenly you have to search for a completely ordinary word. Another six months pass. A girl friend takes you along to the Greenlanders' House on Lov Lane. That's where you discover that your own Greenlandic can be picked apart with a fingernail.

—Smilia's Sense of Snow, *Peter Hoeg, 1993*

We saw in the last chapter how languages, like species, are highly adapted to their environments and that all extinctions have as their cause environmental change. Although our opening quotation to this chapter is taken from a work of fiction, it provides a useful metaphor of a process of unraveling or disintegrating, a language being picked apart in pieces after exposure to a hostile environment—in this case, to the gradual encroachment of another culture and language.

In this chapter we examine this process of change and its consequences in more detail with some case studies. In particular, we illustrate how many of the changes affecting endangered languages tend to eliminate linguistic complexity, along with much of what is culturally distinctive—for example, vocabulary for local flora, fauna, native traditions and knowledge. The knowledge contained in indigenous languages has much to contribute to scientific theories through the uncovering of potentially invaluable perspectives on a variety of problems such as land management, marine technology, plant cultivation, and animal husbandry.

Sudden versus gradual death

We can make an initial distinction between sudden and gradual death of a language. In sudden death, a language dies more or less intact as its speakers are exterminated. As an example of sudden death caused by environmental change in the form of a natural disaster, we can take the case of the volcanic eruption in 1815 on the island of Sumbawa in the Indonesian archipelago, which caused the death of all the speakers of the Tamboran language. All that remains of Tamboran is a short word list collected by Sir Thomas Raffles.

As examples of sudden or near sudden death caused by genocide, we can take the case of Yahi, last spoken by Ishi, believed to be the last survivor of the Yahi Indians, murdered and driven into exile by white settlers in California.

Other such extinctions have affected the Aboriginal peoples and their languages since first contact with Europeans in the latter part of the eighteenth century. These have been particularly acute in the areas of early settlement, now Australia's major urban centers. Most of the full-blooded Aboriginal population was wiped out around Sydney, Brisbane, Adelaide, Perth, Melbourne, and the whole of Tasmania. The Aboriginal population of Tasmania (around 3,000–4,000 people), for instance, was exterminated within seventy-five years of contact with Europeans. Hardly a trace of their language survives today. More people survived in remoter areas, but many languages vanished without having been recorded, or were passed down only in a few word lists written down by doctors, surveyors, clergymen, and others acting as amateur linguists.

Certainly it can be difficult to decide when the last speaker of a language has died, and some written languages survive their speakers in texts, and can in some cases be restored (such as Hebrew, which we examine in Chapter 8). We mentioned in the first chapter how Cornish

Figure 3.1   Ishi, the last Yahi Indian

[*Courtesy of Department of Library Services, American Museum of Natural History*]

apparently met its end in 1777 with the death of Dolly Pentreath, believed to be its last speaker. Yet nearly 100 years later, in 1875, six people in their sixties were discovered who knew some Cornish. In another case from California, linguist William Elmendorf found a single last speaker remaining for each of two languages, Wappo and Yuki, although neither language was in active use and there were no young people learning them. By the mid 1960s Laura Fish Somersal was the last person capable of carrying on a Wappo conversation. She used the language several times a week when her sister visited her. The language survived so long with Somersal because she did not go to school at all, where she would have been exposed to more English. She cared for her blind mother at home and used Wappo when speaking with her. The last person to remember Yuki, Arthur Anderson, hadn't spoken the language since 1908. He had been schooled in English and had long since shifted to that language for everyday use.

These examples show how it can be difficult to pinpoint precisely the absolute end of any language, and that means the distinction between sudden and gradual death can be blurred. It is not always possible to locate all the remaining speakers in a dwindling and sometimes scattered population. Moreover, a language can be effectively gone from active everyday use, but not forgotten. "Rememberers" may survive the active use of a language by several generations. In some cases such people may recall things from a language they never fully learned or used. In 1974 linguist Lyle Campbell found several old men in El Salvador, for example, who could remember a few words and phrases of a language called Cacopera. Only two men had learned more than a few words, either from a grandmother or grandfather. There are many languages which survive only in these remembered bits and pieces and are no longer regularly used.

What happens in gradual death?

When a dying language declines gradually over a period of generations, it goes through a period when it is not used for all the functions and purposes it was previously. Like a limb not used, it atrophies. Anyone who has had the experience of learning a second language will vouch for the fact that if you don't continue to use it, you will forget it. This is also true of our native language. The popular adage "use it or lose it" points to the vicious circle created by disuse. The less often that speakers use the old language, the more difficult it seems to be to use. More and more of it is forgotten and it is difficult to recall the old words for things, especially when some of the things referred to have become obsolete because they refer to traditional customs no longer practiced. One of us worked with younger speakers in rural Papua New Guinea who knew no traditional stories. The contexts for such stories do not occur as often as in the past and so children do not hear them. In parts of Australia the same thing is happening because children do not sit around the camp fires at night to listen to stories as much as they used to. Indeed, the stories children now hear are more likely to be in English, but key elements and concepts along with certain aspects of style are inevitably lost in translation.

In a study of the Dyirbal spoken by younger people in Australia, Annette Schmidt interviewed the children and grandchildren of the older speakers linguist Bob Dixon had previously worked with. She found that less fluent speakers were able to recall fewer words than more fluent ones. Some of the younger people were able to remember fewer than half of 500 items of basic and culturally distinctive vocabulary. Nowadays, no one under the age of 15 is even able to construct a Dyirbal sentence. Young people between the ages of 15 and 39 who do speak the language speak a variety quite different from its traditional form Dixon described only a few years earlier. New words were rarely coined. There is a lack of base forms to which to apply once-productive word formation rules to create new words—much as we would in English by adding suffixes such as *-ful* onto existing basic words such as *help* or *boast*, yielding *helpful, boastful,* and so on.

We all rely a great deal on certain repeated phrases in our everyday speech. As children, we are generally taught to say "hello," "thanks," and "how are you?" and have simply memorized these things as formulas. However, fluent speakers of a language can also easily create new utterances on the spot. They constantly say new things they have never said before. Speakers of a dying language, however, depend much more on routine and formulaic speech rather than on spontaneous conversation. Limited productive competence in a dying language forces terminal speakers to rely more and more on fixed phrases and less on creative new utterances.

In Schmidt's study of Dyirbal, nouns referring to objects such as "kangaroo" and "sun" seemed to be more resistant to change than verbs such as "to run" and adjectives like "small," which describe actions and qualities. Another difference between younger and older people's Dyirbal lies in the tendency for the younger people to lose more specific words and replace them with general ones. For instance, there are many words which are equivalent to the English adjective "big." To call an eel big, one would say it was *qunuii*, but to call a scrub turkey big, one would say it was *waqala*. Young people, however, use only one word to refer to all kinds of big things.

Younger Dyirbal speakers now also use the term *iaban*, which originally referred to a spotted eel, to refer to all kinds of eels. In traditional Dyirbal eels had individual names. On a bush expedition one younger speaker was able to name various species of trees such as bottlebrush and ironbark in English, but could give only the general Dyirbal word for "tree" (*yuqu*) for all of them. In earlier years, Bob Dixon had recorded names for over 600 plants from older speakers.

Younger people were also prone to lose names referring to culture-specific items relating to weather, geography, ceremonies, and kinship. When Dixon first worked with Dyirbal speakers there were 20 traditional kin categories an individual could belong to. He says it would now be impossible to work out the rules of the system on the basis of evidence obtained from the younger generation. The same applies to a lot of traditional lore and knowledge. Now most younger speakers can give names for only more basic kinship relations such as brother, wife, and husband. In traditional Dyirbal there are four words corresponding to the English term "uncle": *muqu* means "mother's elder brother," *qaya* is "mother's younger brother," *bimu* means "father's elder brother," and *nquma* is "father's younger brother." Younger speakers used only the terms *qaya* or *bimu* to refer to all persons having the relationship which in English we would call simply "uncle." Thus, some of the traditional terms have widened their meaning. Likewise, among certain Native Alaskans such as the Tlingit, Haida, and Tsimshian, clan names are being replaced by English words as their original names become increasingly difficult for younger people (all now English speakers) to pronounce and understand. The loss of these traditional kinship terms and clan names is clearly related to the disintegration of tribal structure. The disappearance of this knowledge weakens the younger generation's connection to their past because clan names evoke the people's relationship to one another—as well as to their spiritual and physical world.

Schmidt found that other words had widened their meanings too so that they now included modern objects introduced by whites into Dyirbal culture. One such example is *bulmban,* which meant originally "grass spread out for a mattress," but now refers also to a European-style bed. Dyirbal *waquy,* meaning "sand," now also means "sugar." By and large, however, it is more common for English words to be borrowed wholesale into Dyirbal. In general, the degree to which foreign words are adopted into a language's vocabulary can be taken as a measure of culture contact. In its final stages, a dying language may have taken in a lot of words from the new language, some of them for new things, but others replace native words. This too is a vicious circle because many people object to speaking a language which they no longer regard as pure.

Another thing noticed by various researchers working with a number of dying languages of linguistically different types is that complex syntactic constructions may be less frequently used or lost altogether. A particularly clear case of loss of this type going hand in hand with functional restriction comes from Jane Hill's work on Luiseño and Cupeño. In Cupeño, a Uto-Aztecan language spoken by a small number of speakers in southern California, Hill examined the use of relative clauses in the speech of one of the last speakers. She found that there were many fewer relative clauses (for example, "she liked the chair *that/which I had bought*") in use by comparison with narratives recorded in 1920. Among the terminal speakers, adjectives seem to be used instead of relative clauses and have taken over their stylistic function. The ceremonial contexts for these complex sentence types have been lost and so speakers are no longer used to using them.

More generally speaking, in a community whose language is dying, opportunities to acquire writing and the more formal styles of expression that go with it may simply not exist. Although all children are capable of learning any language as long as they have adequate input from others in the community, they begin by learning the simpler aspects of their language first and then move on to what is more complex. The more complex a structure is, the longer it takes to learn. English-speaking children don't fully master all of the details of relative clauses until they are well into their school years. One reason this is so is that relative clauses, particularly types like "the chair *on which I sat* was painted red" are much more frequently used in writing than in speech. Children are not exposed to them until they reach school and learn to write essays. Children's acquisition of an endangered language may be interrupted at the very age when this kind of grammatical complexity is being acquired, and they are forced to shift to another language at school.

Other grammatical economies result in cases where speakers have been unable to use a language regularly through childhood. This poses problems for attempts at revival, as we will see in Chapter 8, because the last generation may not remember the language well enough to allow linguists to reconstruct what the language was like in its healthier days.

In the rest of this chapter we will take some more detailed examples of the changes taking place as a result of gradual death in order to highlight some of the rich diversity that is currently being lost in many of the world's threatened languages.

What is being lost 1: a rose by any other name?

Centuries before there were marine biologists and scientific methods of classifying fish and other marine life, Pacific Islanders were passing on orally their accumulated knowledge about the behavior of each of hundreds of varieties of fish. According to some scientists, Hawaiians probably knew more about the fish of their islands when Captain Cook first arrived in 1778 than scientists know today. Indeed, many Hawaiians have now forgotten more of that local knowledge accumulated and handed down orally over the past 2,000 years than western scientists will ever learn. American author Charles Nordhoff, resident for a time in Tahiti, where he fished nearly daily for eight years with local fishermen in the early decades of this century, wrote in a similar vein that the islanders' knowledge of fish was encyclopedic and much in need of documentation.

Like many people living intimately with the sea and dependent on it for their living, island languages are rich in words, proverbs, and metaphorical expressions relating to marine life. Tahitians, for instance, called a restless person a *tunahaavaro* (a species of eel). A person who is difficult to find is termed an *ohua* (a species of fish that hides under a rock). Long forgotten fish names are still preserved in stories, myths, and proverbs. In Hawaiian, for instance, one of the largest categories of proverbs concern fish, fishermen, and fishing activities, such as *Aia a kau ka i'a i ka wa'a, mana'o ke ola*, meaning "one can think of life after the fish is in the canoe." Palauans say a person who is hard to wake up *bad el wel* ("sleeps like a turtle"). Many such expressions have little or no meaning to today's younger generation who have grown up eating canned fish bought from supermarkets.

Some of the Pacific languages also have a secret or special vocabulary or protocol used at sea that is different from that used on land. In Palauan, for instance, *tekoi l'chei* ("words of the lagoon") can be hurled by anyone, regardless of rank, at someone who does not measure up to traditional standards. On land, such a reproach by a person of lower status would not be tolerated.

Figure 3.2   Hawaiian fisherman using traditional method for catching ulua with pole made from 'ōhi'a set between rocks and eel for bait.

[Courtesy of Charles Langlas]

What does it matter if Pacific islanders are no longer able to name hundreds of fish and Dyirbal speakers, hundreds of plants or many varieties of eels? To paraphrase Shakespeare, isn't a tree or fish by any other name as good?

Such reports about the existence of hundreds of names for fish or plants often surprise speakers of English and other European languages, many of whom have stereotypes about languages spoken by small groups of people like the Dyirbal. One commonly heard myth is that such languages have only a few hundred words. The question of thinking in so-called primitive cultures was one that engaged many anthropologists in the earlier part of this century. It came as a rude shock to many that the languages spoken in small remote villages could be so intricate and complicated. In the nineteenth century some linguists thought that the Indo-European languages represented the apex of human evolution, and took their wide spread as evidence of "survival of the fittest" rather than as accidents of history. Colonial governments and missionaries commonly used their beliefs about the inferiority of indigenous languages to justify replacing them with European languages such as French or English. Thus, one French historian remarked about one of the indigenous Kanak languages of New Caledonia that it "could not be the language of a culture, and we appreciate the favour done to them by Father Gougon when he decided to teach them French back in 1860. This initiative enabled them to be connected up with the high culture of the West . . . " And the following remark, made by a European explorer in Papua New Guinea about the languages of Rossel Island, is also typical of the dismissive attitude held by many Europeans toward linguistic diversity:

> To be addressed in reasonably good English of the "pidgin" variety, by hideous savages who made murder a profession, and had never come into contact with civilization, is perplexing enough to make the observer wonder if he is awake. Yet this is what happens on Rossel Island. English is the lingua franca of the place, filling up the gaps—and there are many—in the hideous, snapping, barking dialect that passes for speech along the coast, and making communication possible among the tribes of the interior, who vary so much in language that many of them cannot understand one another. How did this come about? I fancy, through the unsatisfactory nature of the Rossel dialects. Any that we heard were scarcely like human speech in sound, and were evidently very poor and restricted in expression. Noises like sneezes, snarls and the preliminary stages of choking—impossible to reproduce on paper—represented the names of villages, people and things.

There are many false claims and erroneous assumptions in these two examples. Sociolinguistic studies of language attitudes have demonstrated how stereotypes about peoples are projected onto their languages and cultures. Europeans dismissed as primitive and barbaric the languages spoken by those whom they regarded as uncivilized, both overseas and at home, as we will see in Chapter 6. The word *barbarian* comes to us from Greek *barbarus*, meaning "one who babbles." The Greeks called others barbarians if they could not speak Greek or pronounced it improperly. Even before them, the Aztec people of ancient Mexico called those who could not speak their language savages or mutes. Their own language, however, they called Nahuatl, which means "pleasant sounding." Being linguistically different condemns the Other to being savage.

The quote about Rossel Island suggests that the reason why people there are adopting pidgin English is due to the "unsatisfactory nature" of the indigenous languages, said to be "very poor and restricted in expression." As we explained briefly in Chapter 1, it is clearly a mistake to assume that a language will have a simple structure because it is spoken in a society which is not complex technologically or politically. Yet it is widely believed that English owes its position as a world language to its efficiency, and that languages which survive and spread do so because they are more modern and better able to adapt to technology.

Even otherwise distinguished scholars such as Stephen Ullmann took the elaborate vocabularies used by small groups of people as evidence of mental inefficiency. In his view, having a separate word for all the things we may talk about would impose a crippling burden on our memory. There is absolutely no evidence for this. In any case, there is no language that has separate words for all the things its speakers might want to discuss—not even English, with its half million words, only a very small fraction of which (perhaps about 16,000) are in ordinary everyday use. Ullmann goes on to say that "we should be no worse off than the savage who has special terms for wash oneself . . . wash someone else . . . but none for the simple act of washing." He is actually responding here to earlier accounts of the existence of 14 separate words in the Cherokee languages referring to different kinds of washing.

The Cherokee example became a favorite (if not also apocryphal) example of primitive inefficiency, touted by some of the leading scholars of the early twentieth century. Otto Jespersen, for instance, who passed on a version of the story, suggested that the primitive mind did not see the wood for the trees. Yet neither he nor others who equated the alleged lack of abstract terms in Cherokee with cognitive deficiencies looked for similar patterns in supposedly more advanced languages. English, for example, does not have an abstract term to refer to a limb or extremity containing both the hand and the arm, or one containing both the leg and the foot. Many Austronesian languages, however, do have such terms: compare Hawaiian *wāwae*, meaning "leg/foot," and *lima*, "hand/arm." Clearly, it would be foolish to use such an example to argue that English speakers were incapable of thinking abstractly.

However, those who cited the Cherokee example and passed it on to others typically had no knowledge whatsoever of the language and had grossly distorted the data as well as misunderstood its implications. What we have here is simply a difference in the categories selected for encoding by different languages. One word in one language may correspond to many in another or vice versa. English, for instance, has only one word meaning "to marry," while Central Pomo, a Californian language, has two different words, one to refer to a woman's marrying and another to refer to a man's. Through being used by a particular group of people over generations for particular purposes, each of the world's languages has come to express the things important to that culture in a distinctive and efficient way by naming them individually.

Another way to look at the issue of efficiency is to consider the proposal offered by one economist who defined it in terms of the ability of one language to transmit more information than another over a period of time. He too believed that survival itself was proof of efficiency. However, it is difficult to see how to measure an amount of information except very crudely, or indeed what kind of information to take into account.

Although pidgin English was undoubtedly useful on Rossel Island and elsewhere, and therefore the most efficient way of communicating across language/group boundaries, pidgins are by definition simple languages native to no one. To achieve that simplicity, they sacrifice a great deal of the complexity that permits precision. When precision is needed, speakers of pidgin languages can always draw on their own native languages. To take one striking example, one of us asked some villagers in Papua New Guinea the names for some of the local birds. In the indigenous language of that village there are separate names for hundreds of birds that people are able to name, while in pidgin, with its limited vocabulary, they are lumped into two named categories: *pisin bilong de* and *pisin bilong nait*—birds that are seen during the day, and birds seen at night. If you want to talk about specific kinds of birds, pidgin and English are inefficient for transmitting information because neither has an extensive, exact vocabulary for naming the birds found in that region. Most of them have not even been classified scientifically yet, and scientists still use Latin terms in their classifications.

The vocabulary of a language is an inventory of the items a culture talks about and has categorized in order to make sense of the world and to survive in a local ecosystem. Thus, the economic and cultural importance of fish is reflected in the Oceanic languages of the Pacific. Because languages give individual names to concepts of cultural importance just as they mark certain distinctions in their grammars (for example, differences between male and female, or differences between one and more than one), the many languages of the world are also a rich source of data concerning the structure of conceptual categories and a window into the rich creativity of the human mind.

Consider this example from the Tuyuca language, spoken by around 465 people in Brazil and another 315 in Colombia, where there are five degrees of a grammatical distinction that linguists call *evidentiality*. All of the following sentences could be translated into English as "He played soccer," but in each case the choice of the particular verb form tells us more about the status of who is making this claim than the verb *play* does in English. The paraphrases give some idea of the additional meanings the verbs carry in Tuyuca.

1. *díiga apé-wi* (I saw him play soccer): visual
2. *díiga apé-ti* (I heard the game and him but didn't see it): nonvisual
3. *díiga apé-yi* (I have seen evidence that he played, e.g., the shoe print on the playing field, but did not see him play): apparent
4. *díiga apé-yigɨ* (I got the information from someone else): secondhand
5. *díiga apé-hɨ́yi* (it is reasonable to assume that he played soccer)

Tuyuca distinguishes between sensory information and reports derived second-hand. Of course, English can make such distinctions by saying things such as "he played soccer and I saw him with my own eyes." You may think such distinctions put too fine a point on things, but these are in fact just the kinds of fine points that are argued about in court when judges and juries have to evaluate the reliability of the testimony of witnesses. Consider this comment made by Jo Thomas, who reviewed Leo Dunmore's book about the Chappaquiddick incident involving Senator Edward Kennedy. It illustrates some of the ambiguities caused by the lack of evidential or other grammatical marking indicative of the status of report in English. She writes:

> What undermines Mr. Damore's account is that these accusations, while seeming to come from a first-hand source, are not direct quotes from Mr. Gargan [Senator Edward Kennedy's cousin], nor are they attributed directly to the 1983 interviews. . . . One cannot tell if they are true, Mr. Gargan's interpretation of the Senator's behavior or, worse, based on what Mr. Gargan told him in 1983.

Some European languages such as French or German use special tenses or moods of verb forms to convey some, but not all, of the information that Tuyuca encodes efficiently in its verb forms. Languages like Turkish, Kwakiutl, Navajo, and Hopi have different conjugations of the verb which distinguish hearsay from what is the speaker's own knowledge.

English also does not distinguish in its third person pronouns between something done to or for oneself, as opposed to some other third person. A sentence like *John washed his car* is ambiguous. Normally, unless there is evidence to the contrary, we assume that John washed his own car, but it could well be the case that he washed Bill's car. Swedish, however, distinguishes these two cases with separate pronouns. *Jan tvättade sin bil* means that John washed his own car, while *Jan tvättade hans bil* means that he washed some other male person's car. Such a system would be of obvious use in English legal language where cumbersome circumlocutions such as "the party of the first part" are required to disambiguate the reference of the third person pronouns. English does, however, unlike some other languages such as Finnish and Hawaiian, distinguish between male and female third person pronouns, at least in the singular, (*he/she*) and French does so in both the singular and plural (*il/elle* for 'he'/'she' and *ils/elles* for the plurals).

Although it is always possible to compare part of one language with another language and show that there are some things some languages can do more easily or more elegantly than others by virtue of some particular grammatical structure, there is no such thing as a primitive language (with the exception of pidgins). When we look at our own language through the eyes of another language and culture, we can see that there is no necessity to what we regard as logical. No language has a privileged window into reality.

Moreover, no linguistic structure has ever prevented adaptation to changing circumstances. Morris Swadesh pointed out that there was no such thing as an inherently weak language, a language that by its nature is unable to survive changed circumstances. Every language used today was once used at a time when its speakers lived in technologically simpler societies. Many languages still have no word for *television*, but there was no word for it in English either before its invention. Speakers of any language have no trouble coining new words for things.

Indeed, English did not establish itself as a language of science without considerable borrowing from Latin and Greek and coining of new terms based on Latin and Greek models—including *television* and thousands of others we think of today as ordinary English words. The medical profession still relies heavily on a vocabulary based on Greek and Latin largely inaccessible to ordinary people: doctors will refer to a myocardial infarction, which the rest of us know as a heart attack.

Moreover, as we will show in the concluding section, western science (now conducted primarily in English to the exclusion of virtually all other languages) has no privileged position in the solution of critical problems faced in local ecosystem management. Almost all major scientific breakthroughs have been made not so much by accumulating new facts as by radical departures from ordinary and habitual ways of thinking about things. Indeed, most real advances in science are resisted at first precisely because they do not fit in with our preconceived ways of thinking about things.

What is being lost 2: what's mine is mine?

We saw in the last chapter that Johanna Nichols found clusters of typological diversity—parts of the world where certain grammatical features are found in abundance. The languages of the world exhibit a range of types of so-called classifier systems which categorize nouns into different classes on the basis of a variety of semantic parameters, including size, shape, color, animacy, personhood, sex, and status (to name the most common dimensions). There are strong areal correlations with certain regions such as Africa, northern Australia, Oceania, North America (Algonquian), and Southeast Asia containing many languages with noun classification and classifier systems.

Such systems are of interest because they allow us to examine how human experience is meaningfully categorized and culturally structured.

Table 3.1   *Counting with numeral classifiers in Pohnpeian*

Classifier	-u	-men	-umw	-pali
used with:	*round things*	*animates*	*baked foods*	*body extremities*
one	ehu	emen	oumw	apali
two	riau	riemen	rioumw	riapali
three	siluh	silimen	siluhmw	silipali

Generally speaking, in such languages each concrete noun has to be used with a classifier. In Pohnpeian, for instance, every concrete noun belongs to one or more of 29 classes. Table 3.1 gives an example of how you would count from one to three different kinds of things belonging to different classifier groups in Pohnpeian.

To talk about "two pigs," for example, you would say *pwihk riemen*, where *pwihk* means "pig" and the second word is a compound containing a form of the number two plus the classifier *men* used with animate things. To talk about two hands, however, you would have to say *peh riapali*, where *peh* is "hand," and *riapali* is a compound containing a form of the number two plus the classifier. "Two drinking coconuts" would be *uhpw riau*, because drinking coconut takes the classifier for round things. "Two bunches of bananas" when baked in a traditional stone oven would be *uht rioumw*.

Some nouns can be used with more than one classifier. Compare, for instance, the meaning of *mahi riau*, "two bread fruit," with *mahi rioap-waot*, "two bread fruit trees." When *mahi* occurs with the classifier for round things, it means the fruit of the tree, but when it occurs with *-pwoat*, the classifier for long things such as trees, canoes, and more recently cigarettes, it refers to the bread fruit tree.

The Micronesian languages are especially rich in both numeral and possessive classifiers. Kiribati, for instance, has 66 numeral classifiers. Some further distinguish between rigid and flexible things, which may reflect a distinction between manipulation of materials in human technologies—for example in Trukese, a coconut palm versus a fishing line. Kusaiean has separate classifiers for various categories of relatives, and distinguishes decorations according to whether they are worn on the head, neck, or ears. Pohnpeian also distinguishes between honorific and common speech and has classifiers reflecting the social status of persons.

The semantics of the so-called possessive classifiers is deeply rooted in cultural practices. In Pohnpeian, for instance, a person's catch of fish and her share at a feast are classified differently from other food. Maternal relatives have specific classifiers because rank and land are inherited matrilineally. Edibles and drinkables are in turn related to rank because food share is determined hierarchically according to rank, both within the family and at community events. The noun *pwihk*, for instance, can be used with several different possessive classifiers that express subtle semantic differences concerning the relationship between the pig and its possessor. Compare, for instance, *nah-i-pwihk*, *ah pwihk*, and *kene-i-pwihk* (all of which mean "my pig"), where *nah* is a classifier used for small or precious things, and people or things over which the possessor has a dominant relationship, while *ah* refers to things harvested or butchered to be prepared as food, and *kene* is a classifier for edible things. The first of these examples would be used to refer to a person's live pig, the second to a pig after being butchered, and the third to the pig as a person's share of food, or roughly "my piece of pork."

Many Oceanic languages distinguish between what we can call *alienable* and *inalienable possession*, terms which also refer to the nature of the relationship between the possessor and the things possessed. In her survey of linguistic diversity, Johanna Nichols found that languages which classify nouns into alienable and inalienable also show strong areal distributions. Geographically speaking, the Eurasian and African areas have the lowest frequency of inalienable marking (27%); Europe, the Americas, and Australia are intermediate (51%) and the Pacific, high (84%).

In such classification systems all nouns are regarded as either being under the speaker's control (alienably possessed) or not (inalienably possessed). For example, in Hawaiian parents and grandparents, along with certain other relatives and body parts, are inalienable because a person does not choose to be born, or to have arms, and legs. Husbands, wives, and children, however, are chosen and so are alienable. Compare *ka'u keiki*, "my child" with *ko'u makuahine*, "my mother," where the word "my" has different forms depending on the nature of what is possessed, child or mother.

In the Panyjima language, still used by about 50 fluent speakers in the Pilbara region of Western Australia, the two types of possession are marked grammatically in different ways. Alienable possession is marked by means of a suffix on the thing which is the possessor (as in English, *Mary's coat*), while inalienable possession involves putting the possessor and the thing possessed side by side (as if in English it were possible to say *Mary language*). In Guugu Yimidhirr, *yugu ngarra munhi* means "the tree's bark is black" (literally, *tree skin black*) or *yarrga mangal munhi*, "the boy's hand is black" (literally, *boy hand black*): however, to say "the boy's house is black" we would use *yarrga-wi bayan munhi*, where *wi* is a suffix of possession marking the possessor "boy."

What is considered alienable and inalienable, however, may differ from language to language and therefore is influenced by cultural beliefs about ownership, property, and so on. The concept of land, for instance, is inalienable in Hawaiian and many other indigenous languages of the Pacific, reflecting the deeply felt connection of islanders with their ancestral lands. Tribal and clan names are often names of local species or places which serve to root islanders' identities firmly in the local ecosystem. The fundamental inalienability of the land is also reflected in traditional systems of land tenure in which land was not a marketable commodity.

Generally, only human beings are capable of possessing things or exerting control over them. The inalienables are also typically a small closed set in a language, while the alienable is open—though there is some fluidity, especially in Polynesian languages, where some interesting distinctions can be made. In Hawaiian, for example, *ko'u lei* means "my lei that I wear," *ka'u lei* is "my lei that I give to someone." In Yagaria, a non-Austronesian language spoken in the highlands of Papua New Guinea, bodily secretions such as tears, saliva, sweat, and mucus are inalienably possessed, but urine and blood are not. Sorcery is generally practiced on things that are inalienably possessed, such as saliva or tears, but not blood.

In many cases possessive classification has far-reaching grammatical ramifications. In Hawaiian and many other Polynesian languages there is no verb "to have" or "to be," so that meanings such as *I have a car* or *I have a child* are expressed by means of possessive pronouns requiring a choice between *o/a* class pronouns (for example, *he ka'a ko'u/he keiki ka'u*, literally "a car mine/a child mine"). Likewise, a number of constructions which in English would be expressed by subordinate clauses would be expressed in Hawaiian by means of a possessive pronoun followed by a gerund: *i ko'u hele 'ana*, meaning "when I went," is literally at/on my going."

One could argue that the distinctive system of Polynesian possessive marking is the backbone of the language. If this distinction disappears, as it indeed tends to in the speech of those who have learned Hawaiian at school rather than naturally at home, one could argue that Hawaiian ceases to be characteristically Polynesian. The language then becomes but a shadow of its former self, and so does the traditional culture and worldview it encoded.

Unfortunately, a whole range of classifier systems may be especially vulnerable on at least two counts. First, they are highly concentrated in languages spoken in parts of the world whose ecosystems and languages are under severe threat. Secondly, because such systems must have arisen through long-standing and intimate relationships between ways of speaking and cultural practices, they involve a considerable amount of complexity of the kind that is likely to be simplified or lost by attrition processes affecting many dying languages. Stephen Wurm has drawn attention to the decay and simplification of complex grammatical systems in the Pacific languages. Other reports indicate that substantial changes can take place in a short time scale. Buna, a Papuan language of the Torricelli phylum of northern New Guinea, was reported to have a highly complex noun class system in 1936, but Laycock found no trace of it in 1975, even among the oldest speakers. Ken Rehg reports that younger speakers of Pohnpeian have an imperfect command of the classifier system and limited control of the rich honorific system.

What is lost 3: women, fire, and dangerous things

As a detailed example, let us consider noun classification in Dyirbal, the dying aboriginal language studied by Annette Schmidt. The semantic basis of Dyirbal noun classes is dependent on a knowledge of traditional myths and cultural beliefs. As in other complex noun classification systems, there is a great deal of variation in noun class assignment that cannot be explained on semantic grounds. As shown in Figure 3.3, there is a four-way classification in the traditional Dyirbal used by its remaining elderly speakers, so that each noun must be preceded by a classifier telling what category it belongs to. The *bayi* class includes men, kangaroos, possums, bats, most snakes, and the moon. Man is thus *bayi yara*. The *balan* class includes women, bandicoots, dogs, anything connected with fire or water, sun, and stars. Woman is *balan jugumbil*. The *balam*

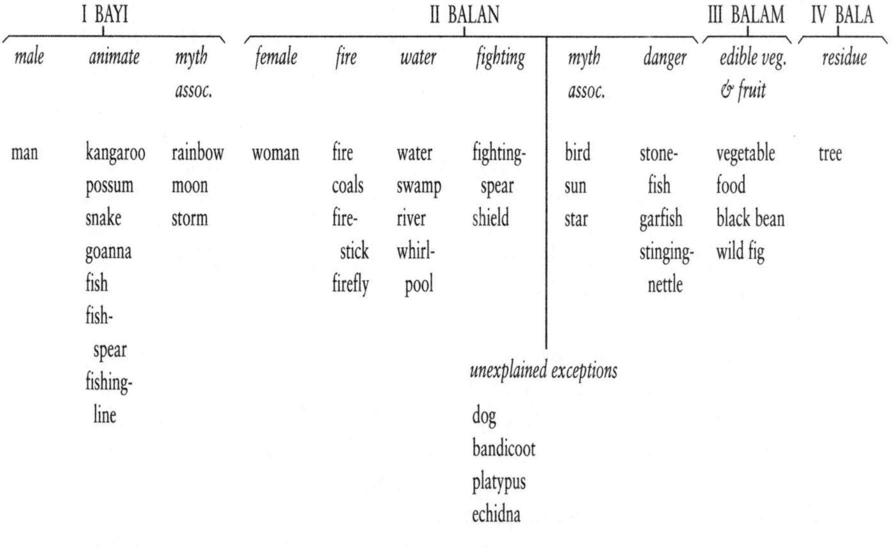

I BAYI			II BALAN						III BALAM	IV BALA
male	animate	myth assoc.	female	fire	water	fighting	myth assoc.	danger	edible veg. & fruit	residue
man	kangaroo	rainbow	woman	fire	water	fighting-	bird	stone-	vegetable	tree
	possum	moon		coals	swamp	spear	sun	fish	food	
	snake	storm		fire-	river	shield	star	garfish	black bean	
	goanna			stick	whirl-			stinging-	wild fig	
	fish			firefly	pool			nettle		
	fish-									
	spear									
	fishing-					*unexplained exceptions*				
	line									
						dog				
						bandicoot				
						platypus				
						echidna				

Figure 3.3   Noun classification in traditional Dyirbal

[*Adapted from Annette Schmidt,* Young People's Dyirbal: A Case of Language Death from Australia. *Cambridge: Cambridge University Press, 1985, fig. 6.1, p. 154]* class includes all edible fruits and the plants that bear them, ferns, honey, and cigarettes. Vegetable food is *balam wuju*. The *bala* class includes body parts, meat, bees, most trees, mud, and stones. Tree is therefore *bala yugu*. What organizing principles lie behind this system? The first class obviously includes human males and animals, while the second contains human females, birds, water, and fire. The third has nonflesh food and the last, everything not in the other classes.

In Dyirbal, however, there is also a general rule at work that puts everything associated with the entities in a category in that particular class. Fish are in the *bayi* class with men because they are seen as animals: fishing lines and spears are included because they are associated with fish. This shows that sharing similarities is not the only basis for categorization. Cultural beliefs too affect classification. In order to understand why birds are not in the first category, one has to understand that to the Dyirbal birds are the spirits of dead human females. Therefore, they belong in the second class with other female beings. The affinity between birds and female spirits is more obvious in mother-in-law language, a special version of Dyirbal men use in addressing their mothers-in-law and certain other female kin where both are referred to by the same word. Similarly, according to Dyirbal myth, the moon and sun are husband and wife, so the moon goes in the class with men and husbands, while the sun belongs with females and wives, as does fire, which is associated with the sun.

There is one further principle at work. If some members of a set differ in some important way from the others, usually in terms of their danger or harmfulness, they are put into another group. Thus, while fish belong to class I *bayi* words with other animate beings, the stone fish and gar fish, which are harmful and therefore potentially dangerous, are in the *balan* class. There is nothing in objective reality corresponding to the Dyirbal noun categories in the sense that the classes do not correspond to groups of entities that share similar properties, but the rationale for the categorization tells us something about how Dyirbal people conceive of their social world and interact with it.

Younger people are now less familiar with the kind of ancestral knowledge which motivated this system of noun classification. This has affected their Dyirbal, and the less fluent speakers operate with a simplified system shown in Figure 3.4, which classifies all nouns into just two groups, animate and inanimate. All inanimate nouns such as "tree" and "table" are grouped in class IV, with the marker *bala*. Animate nouns such as "woman" and "kangaroo" are further divided into males and females, with males as class I *bayi* words and females as class II *balan*. The distinction between class III and IV has been lost for the younger less fluent speakers, who no longer use the Class III marker *balam* for edible fruits and vegetables. In the new simplified system everything not belonging to the other classes is put into class IV *bala* words.

	I BAYI			II BALAN	
	animate male (unmarked)			*animate female*	
yara	"man"	bingu	"bandicoot"	jugumbil	"woman"
yuri	"kangaroo"	gugula	"platypus"		
midin	"possum"	gumbiyan	"echidna"		
girimu	"snake"	jangan	"stonefish"		
gugar	"goanna"				
jabu	"fish"	garram	"garfish"		
guda	"dog"	dundu	"bird"		
		bulal*	"firefly"		

*Some speakers place bulal "firefly" in class I and others put it in class IV.

IV BALA (including III)

		inanimate	
wuju	"veg. food"	buni	"fire"
mirrany	"black bean"	jilin	"coals"
banba	"wild fig"	jiman	"firestick"
yugu	"tree"	bulal*	"firefly"
yumani	"rainbow"	bana	"water"
gunyjuy	"storm"	burba	"swamp"
gagara	"moon"	malan	"river"
garri	"sun"	barin	"whirlpool"
girnyja	"star"	bangay	"fighting spear"
yarra	"fish. line"	bigin	"shield"
barrban	"fish spear"	bumbilam	"stinging nettle"

Figure 3.4   Noun classification in young people's Dyribal

[Adapted from Annette Schmidt, Young People's Dyirbal: A Case of Language Death *from Australia. Cambridge: Cambridge University Press, 1985, fig. 6.1, p. 154]*

This reorganization means too that the basis for putting items into the various classes has also been simplified. The concepts of water, fire, and fighting which were traditionally associated with class II have now been lost. Only one basic criterion, femininity, is used for counting nouns as members of that class. Less fluent speakers classify birds with other animate things in class I, while traditional speakers put them into class II because they are believed to be spirits of dead female human beings and therefore feminine. Less fluent speakers put both sun and moon into class IV with other inanimate objects, but traditional speakers put the moon in class I and the sun in class II because in Dyirbal myth the two are husband and wife. Younger speakers do not treat harmful and dangerous items like stonefish and stinging nettle as exceptions, but instead put them into class I if they are animate, and class IV if they are inanimate. In traditional Dyirbal they would have belonged to class II.

Vast changes have affected Dyirbal within the past two decades. The most complex parts of the language which take the longest to acquire seem to be the first to go. This has its roots in the transmission process. The more complex a grammatical feature is, the longer it may take to acquire it. Children's language acquisition is often interrupted or receives no support from school. The reductions in young people's Dyirbal are not compensated for by structural expansions elsewhere in the system, as they are in other languages undergoing normal change. When Dyirbal speakers lose traditional kinship terms, they do not replace them. They rely instead on English words to fill the gaps, but the English words do so only very imperfectly. In some cases there is nothing in English that can replace what is lost.

Noun classification in Dyirbal is, however, still different from English and is partially maintained, but it is less rich in its semantic associations than the traditional system. One can also argue that some aspects of Aboriginal identity live on in the local and highly distinctive (though stigmatized) variety of English spoken among young people now. The version of the dominant language acquired in such cases of language shift is usually different from that used by the mainstream population in that it preserves traces of influence from the dying language. Yet, as we will show in Chapter 8, one could still argue that it is a different kind of identity than the one associated with traditional Dyirbal.

Lost languages, lost knowledge

One obvious implication of the loss of linguistic diversity that we mentioned in Chapter 1 is a severely reduced conception of what is possible in human languages. The Amazonian languages, for example, provide rare examples of object-initial languages. Dixon stated at one point that there were no known examples of a language with two distinct systems of noun classes. Yet Palikur, a North Arawakan language in Brazil, turns out to have a system of three genders and a system of over 20 noun classes. This is a very neat example of a small and obscure language providing crucial information to test such claims, and, as it happens, disconfirm a previously held generalization. The implications of the loss of linguistic diversity, however, go far beyond the science of linguistics to affect scientific knowledge and progress more generally.

In the most general terms, science is all about naming and categorizing the things we find in the world around us and constructing theories to explain them. Because language does the same sort of thing, we can think of each language as a way of coming to grips with the external world and developing a symbolism to represent it so that it can be talked and thought about. We have seen that indigenous languages in many parts of the world are verbal botanies. That's precisely why the loss of such languages with rich detailed knowledge about the environment is such a tragedy. A cover story for *Time* magazine entitled "Lost Tribes, Lost Knowledge" in 1991 claimed that when native cultures disappear, so does a trove of scientific and medical wisdom. Despite the convincing case made for the loss of knowledge entailed by the loss of traditional cultures all over the world, the role of human languages as the main agents of cultural transmission was barely acknowledged.

Some of those who have dismissed indigenous languages and cultures as primitive and backward-looking and seen their replacement by western languages and cultures as prerequisites to modernization and progress envision a future ideal world in which everyone speaks only one language. Such views are misguided for many reasons, some of which we considered in Chapter 1 and will examine in more detail in Chapter 8. For the moment, however, we wish to stress that an elimination of linguistic diversity on such a massive scale would do the evolution of the human mind a great disservice. Thousands of languages have arrived at quite different, but equally valid, analyses of the world; there is much to learn from these languages, if we only knew about them and understood them. The most important revisions to current ways of thinking may lie in investigations of the very languages most remote in type from our own, but it is these languages which are most in danger of disappearing before our very eyes.

More critically, however, classification systems of the type we have just illustrated represent ways of organizing indigenous cultural knowledge and categorizing the natural environment. The Australian continent, for instance, has been inhabited for about 50,000 years. This is almost ten times the postulated age for the Indo-European language family, which spread from its homeland across Europe and subsequently around the globe.

Vital clues about the settlement history of the Australian continent may be contained within the remaining languages in the form of oral histories passed down for generations. Aboriginal legends say that it was once possible to walk across to the islands in the Coral Sea from the mainland. The final separation of Tasmania from the mainland is also recorded in Aboriginal oral tradition. Geographers believe that 8,000 to 10,000 years ago, at the end of the last ice age, the sea level was low enough to walk to all the islands in the Coral Sea. At the peak of the Ice Age, Tasmania too was joined to the Australian mainland. Western science did not accept Ice Age theories which would have accounted for the fluctuations in sea level until the twentieth century.

Through wandering the Australian continent for generations, Aboriginal people knew the land intimately and were able to survive in relatively harsh terrain. During World War II an American fighter plane returned from New Guinea into northern Australia, where it crashed. The four survivors had no compasses or navigational equipment, but proceeded to set out to try to find help. Three starved to death, with food all around them. Unlike the Aborigines, the Americans had no idea what was edible and inedible. Many of the trees and vines have parts which can be made edible if treated in certain ways. One plant, for instance, yields *mirang*, or "black bean." After the beans have been gathered, the nuts are removed and placed in piles inside ovens dug in the ground. They are then covered with leaves and sand and a fire is lit on top of them. They are steamed inside in a matter of hours or for whole days. When they are taken out of the oven, they are sliced up with a knife made from snail shell and put into dilly bags in a running stream for a couple of days. Then they are ready to be eaten. If the beans are not sliced fine enough, they remain bitter. None of this knowledge is written down but is passed on orally from generation to generation, much of it encoded in classification systems of the type we have just examined. Thus, it is always only one generation away from extinction. Some of the Aborigines' knowledge is now sought after by the Australian government to provide maps of the area which include a guide to the edible flora and fauna of the region and their nutritional value.

So far, however, little serious effort has been made to tap this indigenous knowledge about local ecosystems. Western scientific knowledge about effective marine management, for instance, is still scarce. Strategic planning is particularly difficult in the tropics due to the greater diversity of the marine (and other forms of) life there. In Palau, for example, the number of fish species probably approaches 1,000. Using conventional methods of scientific research, it would take decades to accumulate enough information to manage the most important marine species as effectively as salmon or other species of temperate waters. At the same time, proper management of marine and other resources is critical. Coral reef communities cover around 230,000 square miles of shallow tropical sea bottom, which represents an enormous potential of 6 to 7 million tons of fish per year. This would yield enough fish to feed the United States for about four years at its current rate of fish consumption.

Unfortunately, many reef areas in the Pacific are being heavily overfished due to the impact of western technology on traditional fishing practices in small atoll communities, while others are not being used effectively at all. At the same time, the islanders' detailed knowledge of the environment essential to their self-sufficiency is being eroded through the introduction of western education and a cash economy. Until recently, for instance, Kapingamarangi islanders (part of present-day Pohnpei in the Federated States of Micronesia) spread catch activity evenly over 200 indigenous varieties of fish, with none of them being exploited to the point of threatening their numbers. One of the most important conservation measures in the Pacific islands was the system of traditional land tenure. Traditionally, no one could fish in an area where he did not have fishing rights, which are controlled by village chiefs. There were also laws against taking more fish than could be used, and laws allowing certain species to spawn for a day before catching them. In Hawai'i both the *aku* (ocean bonito) and *'ōpelu* (mackerel) were protected during spawning, with the open season on one covering the closed season on the other.

Some fish are now being threatened by extinction due to use of the handheld spear gun, which is not actually as efficient as a traditional net. What makes this technological change so devastating on Kapingamarangi is the way in which it is used. The elders do not control access to the spear gun; anyone who can afford to buy a gun can go out to fish. Outboard engines affixed to outrigger booms make access to any part of the lagoon or deep sea quick and easy. There are no longer any constraints on fishermen's activities other than bait, the weather, and the fuel supply.

Like indigenous peoples elsewhere, many Pacific islanders have abandoned their own traditional (and in many cases superior) technologies and methods of subsistence, for reasons we examine more fully in Chapter 7. Even Captain Cook commented of the native Hawaiian fish hooks he found in use that they were a "triumph of stone age technology . . . their strength and neatness are really astonishing; and in fact, we found them, upon trial, much superior to our own." Traditional fish hooks were fashioned in many different ways, often seemingly ineffective to outsiders, but their manufacture was based on centuries of knowledge of local fishing conditions.

In Tahiti, for instance, hooks for catching tuna were traditionally fashioned from numerous varieties of pearl shell, with each shell distinctive to a particular stretch of coast of an island. A good fisherman would know the names of every kind of shell from every district of every island. In particular, the use of hooks with a strongly inward-curving (rather than straight) point, or hooks without barbs, are more efficient for catching many varieties of fish than imported metal fish hooks which have to be purchased with cash. The advantage of modern western hooks now used by many Pacific fishermen lies, like that of the spear gun, in their availability, providing one has the cash to buy them.

Figure 3.5 shows some of the so-called rotating hooks with inward facing points used on Tobi (one of the smallest, most isolated of the inhabited Micronesian islands, lying 200 to 300 miles southwest of Palau). This kind of hook is used under conditions where it is difficult to set the hook by jerking the line sharply when a fish bites: for example, when dropline fishing in deep water or in strong currents.

Traditional fishermen, particularly on small islands where the people still depend on the sea for most of their food, are still rich sources of information unknown to western scientists. Centuries before biologists existed, Palauans

Metch

- The name is derived from the Tobian name for cone shells, and refers to the spiral groove on the crown of the shell; the lower shank, bend, and point form a spiral.
- Strongly curved point facing inward (shallower water version) or downward (deeper water version).
- Used with a weight in dropline fishing for large-mouthed fish such as grouper. This is the hook of choice when fishing very deep.
- The fish must be allowed to run with the hook and then retrieved while keeping steady moderate tension on the line.

Fahum

- Bend almost circular.
- A deep water dropline hook used for fish with smaller mouths (e.g. lethrinids) than those sought with a metch.
- As many as five may be baited and attached to a single line at intervals.
- Used without a weight (a rock is tied loosely to the line to take the hook down, then shaken loose with a jerk).
- The hooking technique is intermediate between that used for a conventional rotating hook and a jabbing hook. The fish is played gently for a while until the hook sets itself lightly. Then the line is jerked hard to set the hook more firmly.

Ramatiho

- Similar in shape to fahum, but point does not approach the shank so closely and the shank has more inward curvature.
- Used for dropline fishing in fairly deep water.
- The bait is placed on the hook loosely to allow maximum penetration; when a fish bites the bait usually slides up the shank.
- Used for groupers and also for fish that suck the bait in and out of their mouths cautiously; the wide bend makes the hook hard to spit out.
- Always hooks in the jaws, not in the lips; good for fish with easily torn lips.
- A strong fish is liable to bend this hook and escape.

Figure 3.5   Some traditional fish hooks used on Tobi, Palau

[*Reprinted from R.E. Johannes,* Words of the Lagoon. Fishing and Marine Lore in the Palau District of Micronesia. *Berkeley: University of California Press, 1981, pp. 196–97]*

knew that certain types of vibrations could be used to attract sharks. Sea cucumbers, for instance, have been traditionally used in Oceania as a fish poison, but biologists established their toxicity only in the 1950s. Palauans have a remedy for the venomous sting of the rabbitfish, which could be of more general pharmacological use. They rub the raw internal organs (or sometimes just the gallbladder) of the fish on the wound and the pain subsides in a few minutes. The fact that the sting never causes pain if a person is attacked only once suggests that the reaction is of an immunological nature.

Local fishing techniques relied on the fishermen's intimate knowledge of anatomy, behavior, and habitat of many different species. The average reader of this book will hardly be conscious of the many phases of the moon and their relation to the timing of the tides, but to the Palauan fisherman, they provided information about the location of different fish and their vulnerability to capture. Throughout Oceania seasonal environmental changes are charted in a calendar based on the lunar month. The names given to certain days of the lunar month on various Pacific islands foretell the likelihood of successful fishing. On Namoluk Atoll in the Caroline Islands, the night before the new moon is called *Otolol*, which means "to swarm." In Kiribati (formerly the Gilbert Islands) the name of the day after the new moon means the same thing. The Trukese name for the night of the full moon is *bonung aro*, meaning "night of laying eggs." In Hawai'i and Tahiti there were two sets of nights with names containing *'ole/'ore*, one beginning on the seventh night in the ascending moon, and another beginning on the twenty-first in the descending moon. These times during which the *'Ole/'Ore* wind prevailed (in what we call the first and third quarters of the moon) were the periods of greatest scarcity. In Hawai'i these nights were considered unlucky for fishing as well as planting because *'ole* also means "nothing."

All these names indicate that good fishing days tend to cluster around the new moon. Only a few cases of lunar spawning cycles are recorded in the western scientific literature, but islanders were familiar with these rhythms. Furthermore, our own western calendar obscures this pattern of environmental rhythms. Although marine organisms whose spawning patterns are tied to a lunar cycle lay their eggs during the same portion of the lunar month year after year, their spawning dates vary, apparently, by up to a month or more without any reason within the western calendar. A lunar month averages 29.5 days, so 12 lunar months add up to only 354 days, or 11 days short of a solar year. The need to keep the lunar calendar in synchrony with the seasons meant that an extra month had to be inserted every so often. Palauans did this automatically and unconsciously. For them the New Year starts only when the stars and moon are "right," no matter how many lunar months have passed since the last New Year. Learning and committing to memory the timing and location of the spawnings of various species was part of the fisherman's training.

The tides are also timed in relation to lunar phases, and these too were committed to memory. Most of the languages and dialects have specific terms for the paired currents which form on either side of the islands, a region in which these currents converge downstream, and a back current flowing toward the island from this convergence point. The islanders were using their knowledge of current patterns in both fishing and navigation long before they were documented by oceanographers.

While Western scientific taxonomies attend more to formal similarities, native taxonomies may reflect functional concerns. Some species of fish in Tobi have been given a kind of generic name, based on the type of hook used to catch them. The term *bwerre*, for instance, given to certain groupers, refers to the multihooked dropline method of catching them. Other Tobian fish names often refer to behavioral characteristics, such as *hari*, "to bite," the name for brightly colored groupers. One of these groupers is called *hari merong*, which means "always bites, takes any bait." Another set of groupers is called *haugus*, which means "vacuum" and refers to the ability of these large groupers to inhale their prey by means of the sudden expansion of their oral cavities. The term *moghu* refers to a common illness on Tobi accompanied by chancre sores and fever, and is also the name given to the surgeon fish used in its treatment. The fish is ground up without removing its internal organs and then eaten. Hawaiians also gave names to fish according to some prominent characteristic or color. The *humuhumu 'ele'ele* is the "black trigger fish" while the *humuhumu nukunukuapua'a* refers to a "trigger fish with nose like a pig" and *humuhumu umaumalei* means "trigger fish with a lei (flower garland) on its chest." One group of fish called *a'u*, meaning "to prod," included all fish with long sharp beaks such as sailfish, marlin, swordfish, and garfish. To fishermen the strong beak of these fish was of most importance because a swordfish could pierce a canoe.

Important species relied heavily upon for food such as *aku* (ocean bonito), *manini* (surgeon fish), and *'ama'ama* (mullett) have more than one name, depending on the stage the fish has reached in its life cycle (see Figure 3.6). The names may refer to different habitats, behavioral patterns, characteristic colors, or to different fishing techniques used in catching them. The mullett, for instance, is usually referred to as *'ama'ama* when it is finger-length and most delicious, rather than as *'anae*, the name given to the adult fish a foot or more in length. Because fish spawn are very similar in appearance across species, a single term was sometimes used to indicate them. Thus, the term *kīna'u* was applied to the spawn of both the *kawakawa* (bonito or little tunny) and *aku*, which are found together and indistinguishable until they mature. The young stage of both was called *'āhua* or *'ōhua*. As the *manini* (surgeon fish) increases in age and size, it is called *'ōhua liko* ("young leaf bud") when in its transparent stage, *'ōhua kāni'o* ("striped") when stripes

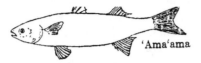

mullet: *Mugil cephalus* (Linné)

Young Stages: finger length, *pua ʻamaʻama*, or one of the following: *pua, poʻolā* (young life), *ʻoʻolā*; hand length, *kahaha*; about 8 inches, *ʻamaʻama*; 12 inches or more, *ʻanae*.

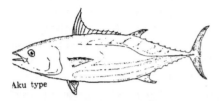

ocean bonito: *Katsuwonus pelamys* (Linné)

bonito, little tunny: *Euthynnus alletteratus* (Rafinesque)

The young called *kīnaʻu* (immature); second stage, *ʻāhua* (larger); adult stage *kawakawa*. The *aku* shares these terms, *kīnaʻu* and *ʻāhua*, until adult, for the two fish are difficult to tell apart until maturity.

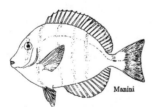

Manini, a surgeon fish: *Acanthurus triostegus* (Linné)

Stages of growth are: *ʻōhua-liko* (tender leaf bud), transparent, size of postage stamp, *ʻōhua-kāniʻo*, stripes appear when the fish is about a day old, *ʻōhua-pala-pōhaku* (stone slime), or *ʻōhua-hāʻekaʻeka* (grimy looking); at this stage they begin to nibble at fine *pala-pōhaku* seaweed and the skin begins to darken, *kākala-manini*, half-grown, and *manini*, adult stage.

Figure 3.6 *Some important Hawaiian fish with their names at different stages in their lifecycle*

[Reprinted from Margaret Titcomb, Native Use of Fish in Hawaiʻi. Honolulu: University of Hawaiʻi Press, 1977, 2d ed.]

emerge after about a day, *'ōhua pala pōhaku* or *'ōhua hā'eka'eka* ("dirty/smudged") when it begins to nibble at the *pala pōhaku* seaweed and its skin darkens, *kākala manini* ("caudal spine," the knifelike cartilage near the end of tail) when it is half-grown, and finally *manini*.

Our examples have shown that language is part of a complex ecology that must be supported if biodiversity is to be maintained. Despite the existence of a vast amount of largely undocumented scientific knowledge in the world's indigenous languages, what goes by the name of modern science is still based largely on the worldview of Europeans and their languages, especially English. As we will show in more detail in Chapter 7, most scientific research is still done by scientists from the world's industrialized countries who are interested primarily in "First World" problems. This is not because western science and languages are particularly well suited to technology. Indeed, our examples of the naming of fish and fishing practices in the Pacific islands show how native perceptions and detailed knowledge of the environment have been encoded in patterns of naming of fish, fish behaviors, fishing practices, and technology. When these words are lost, it becomes increasingly difficult even to frame problems and solve them in any but the dominant culture's terms and scientific classification schemes, which are not always adequate to the task. Moreover, as we will see in Chapters 5 and 6, it was largely due to accident rather than to any inherent superiority that dominant economic, technological, and cultural power developed in that part of the world where European languages were spoken. Before considering those processes, however, we ask a simpler question: Where has all this diversity come from?

Four

The Ecology of Language

[The] struggle between dominated and dominant groups for the right to survive includes what I have called "the ecology of language." By this I mean that the preservation of language is part of human ecology.

—*Einar Haugen*

We saw in the previous three chapters that the world contains a diversity of languages and peoples far greater than most people realize. This diversity is now under dramatic threat. In the next three chapters, we will give an account of how this situation came about. One cannot understand why languages die out, however, without also understanding the other side of the coin—namely, why so many different languages have developed and persisted throughout human history. In this chapter, then, we consider how language diversity comes about, the social forces which maintain it, and then the factors which may destroy it.

Languages do not exist in a vacuum. In fact, the term *ecology* is a particularly apt one to use in connection with languages, in several senses. The word ecology comes from the Greek *oikos*, meaning "home." A language can only thrive to the extent that there is a functioning community speaking it, and passing it on from parent to child at home. A community can only function where there is a decent environment to live in, and a sustainable economic system. To understand why languages are born, and why they die, then, entails looking not just at the languages themselves, but at all aspects of the lives of the people who speak them. This is what we mean by an ecological view of society; people are actors in a complex field whose boundaries are set by physical geography and natural resources, by their own knowledge and opportunities, and by the behavior of others around them. A language is enmeshed in a social and geographical matrix just as a rare species is enmeshed in an ecosystem. A small amount of environmental change can cause a cascade of extinction as the dependent species become stressed. Take, for example, the rare Kirtland's warbler, of which only a few hundred individuals remain. It lives in just six counties in Michigan where the habitat it needs is found: five- to six-year-old jack pine trees growing in sandy soil. If for any reason the pine trees were to be threatened or destroyed, through climate change or logging, the warbler would disappear.

A similar principle applies in language loss. A small change in the social environment, such as the loss of control of resources to outsiders, can have drastic consequences which pass right through to the domains of culture and language. In late 1987, for example, gold was found on the lands inhabited by the 8,000 forest-dwelling Yanomami Indians of North Brazil. Within eight months the region was inundated with nearly 30,000 Brazilian prospectors who came to get rich. The Brazilian government says that at least one Indian a day has died since the gold rush began, but that it was powerless to prevent this onslaught.

The first causes in language loss, then, are not themselves linguistic. As we indicated in Chapter 1, language use is more like a litmus test for what is happening in the wider society. Where language use changes, there is an underlying social upheaval that may have environmental, economic, or political causes. This litmus-test property of language is immensely significant. It means that the loss of a language—like the death of a miner's canary—is a good indicator of less visible stresses which might need investigating. This is one of the reasons we feel that the topic of language loss is such an important one. On the other hand, the embeddedness of language in society makes the task of explaining language loss a very large and complex one.

The best way to see the interconnectedness of language and society is through an example. For this, we have chosen the Pacific, because it is a major repository of the world's linguistic diversity. Its pattern of high genetic and typological diversity (with over 1,300 native languages) can be regarded as primordial, by which we mean it is close to what we would expect of language in its natural state. Within the Pacific, there is no richer example than the island of New Guinea, lying roughly 100 miles north of Australia.

New Guinea is the second largest island in the world and contains over 1,000 languages—about one-sixth of the world's total. We will focus on Papua New Guinea, the country which occupies the eastern half of the island of New Guinea, and some 600 associated islands, the largest of which are New Britain, New Ireland, and Bougainville. This country, with 13.2 percent of the world's languages, but only 0.1 percent of the world's population and 0.4 percent of the world's land area, is an outstanding hotbed within an ocean of diversity.

Babel in Paradise: Papua New Guinea

Papua New Guinea is perhaps the most biolinguistically diverse country in the world. Geographically speaking, it consists of a great crest of mountains, jutting from the sea to altitudes over 15,000 feet, surrounded by slopes and valleys. The terrain is extremely rugged with mountains and fast-flowing rivers, which have long cut the interior of the country off from outsiders. Port Moresby, located on the southern coast in what used to be the territory of Papua, is probably the most poorly located capital city in the world. It is situated in a sparsely populated area on the periphery of the country, cut off from the highlands, where most of the people live, and not connected by road to any other urban area in the country. Many villages have no road or river links with other centers and some can be reached only by walking for up to two weeks.

Over 80 percent of Papua New Guinea's land area is covered by forests. It is home to one of four significant rain forest wildernesses remaining on the planet. There is also an incredible wealth of some 22,000 plant species, 90 percent of which are found nowhere else in the world. The forests are home to over 200 kinds of mammals, 1,500 species of trees, and 780 different birds, including 90 percent of the world's spectacular Bird of Paradise, the country's national emblem. There are 252 different reptiles and amphibians, including huge saltwater crocodiles. The greatest diversity of corals in the world is found off the south coast at Port Moresby.

Figure 4.1   A typical village scene in the interior of Papua New Guinea

[Photograph by Suzanne Romaine]

Forest resources are vital in sustaining the livelihood of the country's 4 million inhabitants, who live between and astride the mountain ridges, in an area the size of France. These people speak an astonishing number of different languages—860 according to one recent estimate. The overall ratio of languages to people is thus only about 1 to 5,000. If this ratio were repeated in the United States of America, there would be 50,000 languages spoken there.

Even within this small country, however, there is an uneven distribution of languages to people. The ten largest indigenous languages belong to the large groups of the interior highlands; they have from 30,000 to 100,000 speakers, and between them they account for nearly one-third of the population. Perhaps 80 percent of the languages have fewer than 5,000 speakers, and as many as one-third have fewer than 500. This distribution does not appear to be a recent development, resulting from a depopulation of small groups. On the contrary, the evidence suggests that the extremely small scale of language groups has been a stable phenomenon for some time. Papua New Guinea is thus a perfect laboratory for understanding how linguistic diversity evolves.

Although human habitation of the island of New Guinea extends back some 40,000 years, recorded history is very recent and in some cases goes back only a few decades. It was the last major land area in the world to be colonized by European powers and almost all regions have a history of contact of less than a century.

New Guinea was originally peopled by many different waves of migrants, whose prehistory is largely unknown. Linguists generally recognize two major groupings among the languages: Austronesian and non-Austronesian (or Papuan). The Austronesian languages clearly constitute a family. The relationships among the non-Austronesian (Papuan) languages are less clear, and the label is best seen as a cover term for perhaps a couple of dozen of distinct families. Figure 4.2 shows the distribution of the Austronesian languages, and the 26 Papuan families identified by linguist William Foley. Most linguists agree that the coastal distribution of most of the Austronesian languages indicates the later arrival of their speakers compared to speakers of the non-Austronesian languages.

Typologically speaking, the languages are also diverse. As far as word order is concerned, for instance, we can find examples of SVO, SOV, VSO, VOS, and OSV. In fact, the only word order not attested is OVS, which is vanishingly rare across the world. In addition, there are examples of noun classifier systems—for example in Papuan languages such as Abu' with its 19 classes—and many other interesting and unusual linguistic features.

The peoples of New Guinea are mainly settled villagers living in a subsistence economy. Their productive activities vary according to the zone they inhabit on the island's extraordinary vertical ecology. The extreme highlands have an alpine climate, with widespread frost. There, an intensive agriculture based on the sweet potato has developed over the last few hundred years. This highly productive system has given rise to a local population boom, and the highlands support large, dense groups with large languages, as we have seen. Highland groups are constrained from spreading downward, however. The competitive advantages of the sweet potato over other plants decline with decreasing altitude, and lower down, endemic malaria, which is absent from the relatively cool highlands, is a powerful check on population growth and aggregation.

The coastal lowlands and the intermediate areas known as the highland fringe consist of pockets of rainforest, swamps, and grassland. The population is low and thinly spread, making a living from mixed farming, fishing, or from gathering forest sago palm, depending on the local conditions. It is in these areas that the really extraordinary diversity of languages is to be found. The basic unit of social organization is a local group—a village or hamlet—which occupies and works a common territory. Local groups number from 50 to a few hundred people, and there are many cases of local groups with a unique language. Elsewhere, a language may be shared between a few local groups, giving a language population of at most a few thousand.

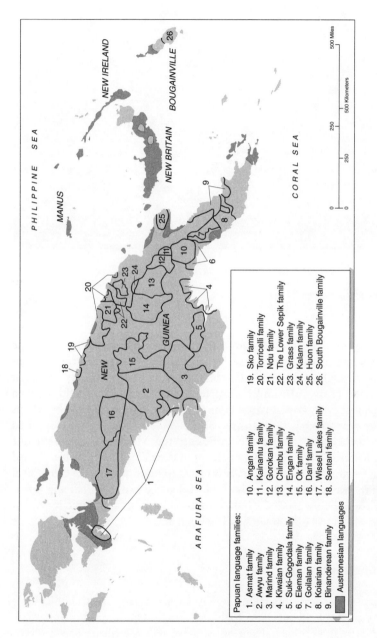

Figure 4.2   *Language families in New Guinea*

[*Adapted from W. Foley,* The Papuan Languages of New Guinea, *Cambridge University Press, 1986, pp. 230–31*]

Papuan language families:

1. Asmat family
2. Awyu family
3. Marind family
4. Kiwaian family
5. Suki-Gogodala family
6. Eleman family
7. Goilalan family
8. Koiarian family
9. Binanderean family
10. Angan family
11. Kainantu family
12. Gorokan family
13. Chimbu family
14. Engan family
15. Ok family
16. Dani family
17. Wissel Lakes family
18. Sentani family
19. Sko family
20. Torricelli family
21. Ndu family
22. The Lower Sepik family
23. Grass family
24. Kalam family
25. Huon family
26. South Bougainville family

▨ Austronesian languages

Figure 4.3   A Papua New Guinean villager harvests his yams

[*Photograph by Suzanne Romaine*]

These groupings, though small, are economically productive. As most of New Guinea is warm and wet at all seasons, food production is continuous throughout the year. Gardens growing a wide variety of crops are planted every year, and after a few months, begin to yield a small food harvest every day. A garden will produce for several years, by which time the next one has been cleared and planted and is productive. Local groups are therefore very self-sufficient; the Maring of the highland fringe, for example, produce 99 percent of their diet by horticulture, and, despite numbering only 200, have no need to import food. For a lowland group, the Kubo, a recent study showed that the system of banana farming was so reliably productive that it would have been possible for a single household to be completely self-sufficient.

Why are there so many languages?

We now turn to the question of why so many languages should have evolved in the lowlands and highland fringe. One important factor is provided by the ecological setting we have just described. The continuous productivity of the ecosystem allows very small groups of people to be self-sufficient if they choose. Furthermore, malaria and other diseases,

Figure 4.4   Villagers exchange produce at a local market

[*Photograph by Suzanne Romaine*]

and the need to fallow land, encourage disaggregation of population. These factors certainly facilitate fragmentation into small groups. However, they are not the whole picture.

One might imagine that, given the mountainous terrain and potential for self-sufficiency, New Guinean linguistic diversity came about because the peoples were physically isolated from each other. It now seems that this was not entirely so. Though self-sufficient in staples, local groups engaged in extensive and enthusiastic trade with other goods. Shells moved up from the coast, and feathers down from the interior. Stone tools, pottery, and salt moved from their centers of origin through long chains of supply and were made available throughout the country.

These types of trade were often accompanied by festivals and other ceremonial occasions, in which huge quantities of prestige goods were exchanged, often across language boundaries. These served to cement alliances between local groups, which would often combine in warfare. Warfare in Papua New Guinea seems to have been endemic, if not particularly destructive, and those who could command the greatest networks of alliances tended to fare best.

As well as goods, people crossed language boundaries in order to marry, as, like small societies everywhere, New Guinean groups had difficulty supplying spouses from among their own. The social system overall was very fluid; when local groups were defeated in war, they might disperse into allied or neighboring groups, where they assumed cultural membership. Conversely, groups would also fission as they became large and unwieldy, and either disease, politics, or depletion of resources caused stress.

There was thus a constant flow of interaction between local groups. This interlinkage is best illustrated by the fact that most people spoke several languages. As well as the vernacular of their local group, many people, especially men, would know the languages of one or two neighboring groups, or perhaps a language that had come to have wider currency around their valley or coastline. The extent of this multilingualism varied. Where language groups were large, as in the highlands, only those in the border areas tended to be multilingual. Where groups were small, everyone was effectively in a border area and knowledge of multiple languages was universal. In the lowland village of Gapun, studied by Don Kulick, the average number of languages understood by men over 40 was five: the vernacular, a lingua franca, and three or so of the other local languages. From another part of the country, the island of New Britain, linguist Bill Thurston relates how he was left in the company of a six-year-old while the village men went off to look for wood to cut for flooring. The boy brought plants collected from the vicinity and told Thurston the name of each in four different languages.

Speaking foreign languages was not only routine, but a source of prestige, and influential men would use them in rhetorical and verbal arts. Boys would be sent out for periods to neighboring groups to pick up the language, so that they might later have skills as mediators and orators. The extent of endemic multilingualism in Papua New Guinea is interesting and important, for it forces us to rethink the reasons why distinct languages persist. We might, naively, have supposed that the diversity was solely a product of sheer physical isolation, and that new roads or trade routes would therefore be bound to make it go away. But traditional multilingualism shows that people did in fact have access to languages of wider communication, had they wanted to adopt them. Diversity did not, however, disappear before European contact. The extensive interaction meant that many languages borrowed words and structures from each other. The residual differences, though, were maintained and even accentuated. Contact between groups, in the words of Gillian Sankoff, led "not to levelling but to heightened consciousness of and pride in difference." The boundaries were fuzzy, in the sense that people moved across them, and many villages had affiliations on both sides. This shows that they were the product not of nature, but of human action, and, as Terence Hays points out in a recent article on Papua New Guinea, "if it is people, as much as 'Nature,' that create, maintain, and ignore boundaries, we need to know why, and under what circumstances."

We might adopt a naively economistic perspective on human behavior and assume that people will always adopt the most widespread language of those they are exposed to, since this will be the most useful in terms of exchanging information and services with the largest number of people. If people persist with a small language, it is perhaps because alternatives are not available, or the cost of acquiring them is for some reason too high. Such a perspective is clearly wrong, because it ignores the cultural value of a language to its users.

Much of the struggle for success in human social life has been, and remains, about achieving good standing in a close-knit local community. Many forms of human behavior—from gift-giving to gossiping to joining religious or secular associations—aim at precisely this. Such activities have often been portrayed by economists as quaint or irrational leftovers from some primitive mentality, as when development theorists berate tribesmen for blowing all their hard-won surpluses on huge feasts. However, such activities only appear irrational if the economic perspective we adopt is unrealistically narrow.

For most of human history, a person's access to resources, help in times of need, and ability to attract a spouse and produce a family have all depended on the ability to command favorable social relations within a local group. This has become rather unclear in contemporary Western societies, where work and resources are allocated mainly through specialized institutions (firms, backed up with money, for example), which for most people are quite distinct from their friends and families. It was not always thus, however, and in descriptions of New Guinean societies one sees very clearly how one's position within a clan and in the eyes of other clans was all-important in forming and protecting one's household. This was not just a social nicety; it was a matter of survival.

We need to recognize, then, that human beings hold social as well as financial capital. Being a respected part of a strong community is a form of capital which under many circumstances will be more useful than goods or chattels. In Papua New Guinea, this seems to have been particularly important. The societies were basically egalitarian, though there were influential "big men" whose special status was more marked in the larger highlands societies. Such men would go out of their way not to accumulate stocks of personal economic capital. They would instead use wealth to create networks of social obligation among their allies, with gifts, loans, and hospitality. This is most dramatically illustrated in the periodic pig festivals of the highlands and highland fringe, where thousands of pigs would be slaughtered and their meat distributed to all and sundry in a single, ritually charged episode of apparent wealth destruction. In these episodes, big men were trading concrete economic capital for social capital among their group, and at some level, it was probably quite rational.

The idea of social capital brings us back to language and the benefits of local varieties. Using the form of speech of a locality is a way of tapping into the social network of that area. It shows that one belongs, that one is committed, and it engenders solidarity with others. Observational studies show that bilinguals (or those who command several varieties of the same language) will switch to the more local form whenever they are trying to invoke the solidarity of the local team. This can be seen very clearly whenever a populist politician adopts different accents when campaigning in a working-class area or speaking at a dinner for business leaders. Mainstream politicians have to try to maximize their solidarity with everyone, and one's success at obtaining the cooperation and esteem of one's peers is heavily dependent on having the right form of speech with which to address them.

Language is, to adopt the terminology of the French sociologist Pierre Bourdieu, a form of symbolic capital that may be as valuable in its way as are concrete goods. The traditional New Guinea situation makes sense from this perspective. Larger languages were available to be learned at minimal cost. Indeed, many people knew them already. However, people were concerned to maximize their social capital within their immediate surroundings. It was, after all, the local group's territory on which people farmed, the local group who defended the common territory, and the local group within which one's family had to exist. There was a great incentive to maintain, alongside any regional languages used for trade, a form of speech peculiar to one's local group, which was used within it and which correlated with a commitment to it. As William Foley puts it, vernaculars were the "indispensable badge of a community's unique identity." This factor may well be enough to account for the maintenance of so many languages.

In his work among Selepet speakers, Ken McElhanon relates how villagers in one community decided at a meeting that they would be different from other Selepet-speaking villages by adopting a new word (*bunge*) for "no" to replace their usual word (*bia*) shared by all Selepet speakers. Other researchers report similar phenomena from other small communities showing how language is used as a way of marking distinctive local identities.

Traditional Papua New Guinea has been described as a country of *egalitarian bilingualism*. In other words people had access to several languages, but there was no overall hierarchy. For most people, foreign languages had their uses, but the vernacular (the *tok ples*, or "speech of [this] place," as it is known in Papua New Guinea's most widespread language, Tok Pisin) was the language of choice in local settings. People would have been able to expand their potential networks of communication by shifting to more use of lingua francas, but there would have been costs in terms of local solidarity if people opted out of the *tok ples* altogether.

Similarly, people could have increased their involvement in the wider economy, but there was little incentive to do so. The local gardens reliably provided for most basic needs. Specialist goods such as stone tools and pots were obtained through intergroup trade, but there is a limit to how many of these one wants. In general, the range of goods and services available outside the local groups was not sufficient to entice people to enlarge the scale of marketing and economic specialization. Such integration has costs and risks as well as benefits, and they were probably better off with local self-sufficiency, supplemented by intermittent intergroup alliances and exchange.

Viewing the country at a macroscopic scale, then, Papua New Guinea a few hundred years ago probably represented an example of what Bob Dixon has recently called a *linguistic equilibrium*. This means that the number of languages was roughly constant, and no one group or its language was rapidly expanding at the expense of another. The equilibrium is more a property of the whole country than of individual languages. There would always have been linguistic entrepreneurs at the boundary between groups, who perceived that one grouping was more desirable than another, and who started a trend of shift from one *tok ples* to the next. There are many historical examples of such shifts, which in small groups can happen very fast. On the other hand, new languages would from time to time be born as people fissioned out or established new settlements. There was, however, probably no overall trend of increase or decrease in the number of languages. The highland languages were much larger and grew more quickly than those below, but they were prevented from expanding down and annexing the lowlands by malaria and the different ecological conditions. Lower down, the balance of costs and benefits in local autonomy and self-sufficiency was favorable to that in aggregation and specialization; the social value of each *tok ples* was greater than the economic value of a language of wider communication. The possibility for linguistic homogenization was always there, but people had no good reason to pursue it. The coming of Europeans with their languages punctured this equilibrium.

The case of Papua New Guinea is really a perfect example of the idea that all human domains are interconnected. The extraordinary distribution of languages cannot be explained by facts of a linguistic nature. Rather, we had to understand both the ecological background, which favored small, self-sufficient, scattered local groups, and the cultural environment, in which a preference for local social capital kept a large number of local languages very much alive. Any change in either the cultural or biological environment could mean a dramatic change in the language map.

Most parts of the world have, for most of human history, been at or near linguistic equilibrium. This does not mean, however, that languages have not always been dying out. The equilibrium concept merely implies that the number dying out in a region roughly balances the number being created. Extinction has always been happening. In the next section, we consider the types of situation which produce it.

The ways languages die

A language dies out because an enduring social network to which people sought to belong somehow ceases to be. There are several quite different ways in which this may happen. For present purposes, we will identify three types of language loss, though we will also argue that there are cases which combine all three.

The first way a language can cease to exist is when the people who speak it cease to exist. This is language loss by population loss, and it has been extremely common over the last five hundred years. When Europeans expanded into the Americas, they unwittingly released a wave of epidemic disease which killed between 50 and 90 percent of native Americans. Countless languages were lost at this time, as whole groups succumbed, particularly to smallpox. The indigenous inhabitants of the Caribbean and Australia fared no better. We will take up their stories in the next chapter.

There are many cases, however, where language loss occurs without population loss. The Cornish have lost their language, for example, but they are still very much alive and have increased in number. Today they speak English rather than Cornish. This is a case of language death occurring by way of a shift from one language to another.

It may be useful to identify two subtypes of language shift. The first is where the shift is forced. Many times in history, dominant groups have forcibly broken up minorities. One way they have tried to do this is by making the dominant language compulsory. Interestingly, this unpleasant policy rarely seems to work. Stigmatizing a language can, under certain circumstances, make it even more valuable as a form of symbolic resistance and organization. However, dominant groups do force minorities into shift by other means, either by enslaving, by forcing them into a subordinate role, or by seizing the land and resources on which their communities are based. Recent examples of forced shift of this type include the disappearance of tropical rainforest peoples following logging and clearance. The forest storehouse is liquidated, and the very basis for the economic and cultural self-sufficiency of these peoples goes with it.

The fact that it is policies directed at the economic roles available to indigenous people—and not policies directed straight at the language—which kill minority languages is an important one. It confirms our view that language should not be seen in isolation but as one outcome of a more general ecological and economic matrix. The domain of language use is not entirely policeable or controllable, so political acts directed at it often fail. The key goods of the economic and social domains, on the other hand, can be seized and controlled, and without a socioeconomic basis a language will not thrive. This has important implications for language revitalization movements. To preserve a carnivore species, one must first preserve the species below it in the food chain so that it has an environment in which it can flourish. Language, too, can only be preserved where the communities which value it have some real basis.

The second type of language shift, and the third type of language death, is voluntary shift. This is where a community of people come to perceive that they would be better off speaking a language other than their original one. The important difference from forced shift is that the option of remaining where they are and who they are is, at least apparently, still open to them, as it was to the Cornish people, for instance. In her study of language shift in Austria, Susan Gal has shown how the newly available status of worker associated with German became available to a community previously monolingual in Hungarian. Choice of German, in particular by young women seeking German-speaking marriage partners, is an expression of their preference for the newer social identity by comparison with a more traditional one associated with Hungarian — which, in turn, is linked with peasant status and male-dominated subsistence agriculture.

Voluntary shift has presumably always been going on, as, in an area like Papua New Guinea, different local groups waxed and waned and people on the boundaries shifted allegiances. However, its pace and scope have greatly increased since the industrial revolution, when huge differences in the lifestyles of neighboring communities began to appear.

Where voluntary shift occurs, it can be gradual, with the incoming language replacing the indigenous one over a period of decades, or several hundred years. The indigenous language tends to disappear from some situations before others. In this context, we find it useful to distinguish between language death "from the top down" and language death "from the bottom up."

In top down death, the language retreats from official institutions and public domains like the courts, the church, and perhaps the worlds of commerce and politics first, so in the end it is restricted to use in the home and perhaps among friends. Many European minority languages, like Breton in France and Gaelic in Scotland, retreated in this way, lacking a role in government or religion, which were imposed from outside, but persisting as the home language of the peasantry. This pattern is also typical of immigrants in a new place, such as Panjabi speakers in Britain or Italians in the US or Australia. We generally find a range of individuals with differing degrees of proficiency in the ancestral language and varying degrees of bilingualism. Older speakers are usually the most fluent in the traditional language and may in some cases still be monolinguals, while younger ones who have not had the opportunity to use the language across the full range of functions their elders did may not have acquired full fluency. These younger speakers are very often more fluent in another language. As we saw in the previous chapter, they may not have as large a vocabulary in the dying language and they may also have simplified the grammar and made it more regular. They rely increasingly on the language to which the community as a whole is shifting in order to convey what they mean. The next stage may well be the fatal one in which the language will no longer be transmitted to the next generation. In this sense the last stage is abrupt. The language is tipped over the brink.

In death from the bottom up, a language has retreated from everyday use and survives primarily in ceremonial or more formal use, such as school. Such is the case with the language spoken by the Gros Ventres Indians on the Fort Belknap Indian reservation in Blaine County, Montana. Gros Ventres has not been anybody's principal language for at least 40 years. The last person believed to have spoken the language fluently died in 1981; his father was apparently the last monolingual speaker. Gros Ventres seems to be reserved for mainly ceremonial occasions and ritual purposes—church activities, feasts, and so on—which are often presided over by a knowledgeable older man. Most of the older people grieve for the loss of Gros Ventres. One older man, who left the reservation when young to work in the copper mines, has now come back and is trying to fill in his gaps in knowledge of the language. He visits other older people who have a better knowledge of the language than he does and records their conversations.

Other examples of this kind of death include spoken Latin in Europe, as well as Sanskrit in India. Sanskrit is a literary language and the liturgical language of Hinduism. As such it is transmitted, albeit in a rather restricted form, from priest to priest. However, it has almost disappeared as a spontaneous language outside of religious contexts. Spoken Hebrew was, at one stage, dying from the bottom up in this way. Hebrew was passed from one generation of Jews to another for over 2,000 years as the language of sacred texts, rabbinic writings, and formal prayer. In the nineteenth century it was hardly used in contexts beyond these. With the advent of Zionism and the creation of the state of Israel in 1948, Hebrew was, unprecedentedly, reinvented in the contexts from which it had disappeared. It is now the national language, and almost all Israelis speak it, perhaps over three million of them as their first language. Death from the bottom up and death from the top down present different problems and possibilities for revitalization, as we shall see in Chapter 8.

We have identified three types of language loss: population loss, forced shift, and voluntary shift. We must also recognize that the divisions between them are murky, and that many language losses involve some combination of all three. Many indigenous communities of the Americas and Australia lost some, but not all, of their population in the great epidemics. This left them too small to survive as independent communities. The survivors then underwent (or are still undergoing) language shift, either into the European language or into a more prosperous indigenous language.

We should also recognize a considerable grey area between forced and voluntary shift which is probably larger than either of the categories themselves. When agricultural peoples spread out into territory formerly occupied by hunters and gatherers, as is happening to the Shabo and Kwegu peoples in Ethiopia, for example, the hunters and gatherers might apparently have the option of retaining their lifestyle. However, the lands on which they forage will be marginal, as farmers clear the best lands for themselves, and the wide species base on which they depend may be depleted by the farmers' disruption of the local ecology. Their lifestyle can only be maintained at an ever-increasing cost; they will either have to move in larger and larger nomadic circuits to find resources, or switch to lower value food sources. These are exactly the factors that push people into farming, and so they are likely to adopt the farming system. This looks to all the world like the voluntary adoption of a good idea. Switching to farming has huge costs, however, and the voluntariness of the conversion is questionable.

There are many other examples of language shift which also illustrate the problem of distinguishing coercion from choice. Let us consider a relatively self-sufficient minority on the fringes of the national economy. As time goes by, one may detect increasing involvement in the cash system, and increasing use of the national language, which seems to be a simple choice. However, the national government's insistence on taxes paid in cash will force the minority workers to sell some goods or labor for money. But every good sold for money is one removed from the traditional system of barter, so households may need to start importing food to make up the difference. To secure imported food one needs money, which means selling more into the cash economy, which means less time and produce left for household production. This is a self-fueling cycle whose most likely outcome is integration of the minority into the national economy. It pleases government economists no end because total economic activity appears to go up. Household welfare is a different matter, however, since the shift stems initially not from economic choice, but from political domination. Yet processes of this kind are not untypical of the last five hundred years of history. They happened to the indigenous inhabitants of South America in the sixteenth century and to native Hawaiians in the nineteenth century and continue to happen in many developing countries now.

To take a concrete example, consider how in 1835, only 50 some years after Captain Cook had first landed in the Hawaiian islands, William Hooper was sent by Ladd and Company to Kōloa on the island of Kaua'i to establish the first sugarcane plantation. Within a year, the employment of native Hawaiians on the plantation had begun to undermine traditional society and the people's relationship with their land. Traditional Hawaiian society was a highly stratified one in which ruling chiefs allocated plots of land to commoners, who supported themselves from the land and in turn were required to pay tribute in goods and services to support their chiefs. The chiefs later redistributed these goods in order to secure their own status and prestige as well as the loyalty and welfare of the commoners. It was a social system similar to the one of accumulation and redistribution we described earlier for Papua New Guinean communities.

Although only 26 years old at the time, Hooper understood well the larger significance of his mission, which was, in the first instance, to secure a foothold for his company in a potentially lucrative business venture as the market economy of the mainland United States was advancing to its new Pacific frontier. An entry from Hooper's diary in September 1836 reveals how the plantation was developed "for the purpose of breaking up the system aforesaid [of chief labor] or in other words to serve as an entering wedge . . . [to] upset the whole system." Along with Christian missionaries, who had begun arriving in 1820, Hooper saw his task as one which would "eventually emancipate the natives from the miserable system of 'chief labor' . . . , which if not broken up, will be an effectual preventative to the progress of civilization, industry and national prosperity." In exchange for the labor of his workers, Hooper paid a fee to the ruling chief in return for his exemption of them from the tribute and services they would have owed him. Hooper also paid his workers in coupons which could only be exchanged at his plantation store. Thus, he managed to both pay his workers and make a profit from their purchases.

Taken away from the cultivation of their own lands, Hooper's native workers entered a new plantation community, where they lived in small houses Hooper allotted to them, while they worked and lived according to schedules he dictated. In the process, Hooper had created an entirely new economic system with both a wage-earning labor force and a consumer class dependent on a plantation-owned market which had to expand consumer needs constantly.

Off the plantations as well, radical changes were already taking place which further undermined traditional society. The fact that the Hawaiian islands were so conveniently situated midway on the route from the Pacific northwest to Canton, China brought an increasing number of ships with European trade goods such as clothing, china, tools, and firearms. The chiefs soon acquired a desire for these new things, and by 1826 became heavily indebted to foreign merchants, who took as payment most of the available sandalwood in the islands. Over its short duration the sandalwood trade wrought considerable hardship on the commoners, who were instructed by their chiefs to cut the wood; in doing so, people neglected the cultivation of the land on which they depended for food. Thus, the traditional relationship between chiefs and commoners was altered too. Under the old system the role of labor was part of a communal social system that supported extended families and chiefs. With the advent of European traders, the tax revenues went instead to satisfy the demands of the chiefs for material goods and to service their debt to foreigners.

The whaling industry, which began in earnest just as the supply of sandalwood was reaching its end, further enmeshed Hawaiians in the western economy. Honolulu (the present capital on the island of O'ahu) and Lahaina (on the island of Maui) became major ports, where the majority of ships stopped to restock and give their crews rest. These towns boomed with the infusion of millions of dollars as trading companies and other businesses such as bars and beer halls sprang up to meet the needs of the whalers. Between the years 1850 to 1860 thousands of ships, most of them American-owned, carrying some 18 million gallons of whale oil, passed through Hawaiian ports. Despite the efforts of missionaries to prevent prostitution and the sale of alcohol, the thousands of whalers at a time who passed through these ports had made them rough and rowdy places.

Ship captains also needed crewmen to replace those who had jumped ship or been lost en route. By the 1840s as many as a third of the crew on most Pacific whalers were Hawaiians; by the 1860s, that portion climbed to half. The migration of so many young men added yet more losses to the native population, who had no immunity to the new diseases brought by explorers, whalers, and traders. While the indigenous population declined dramatically to 70,000 in 1853 (from an estimated 800,000 to one million in the 1770s), the foreign population, mainly American at first, grew rapidly. A boom in the sugar industry, facilitated by a change in legislation allowing foreigners to purchase land outright, necessitated massive importation of 400,000 contract laborers from China, Japan, Portugal, and later, the Philippines. More commoners were dispossessed either because their ruling chiefs sold the land on which they lived, or because they had no money to buy the land which had become available for sale. A new constitution of 1887 forced on the then-king by his foreign advisers limited voting rights to land owners, in effect disenfranchising the majority of commoners. By that stage, the number of native Hawaiians had declined to a low of approximately 44,000, and no longer constituted half the total population.

As the planters continued to gain the upper hand economically and politically, they seized control of the government and overthrew the ruling Hawaiian monarch in 1893 in order to ensure the right to export sugar duty free into the US. The new provisional government banned the use of Hawaiian and in 1894 English was declared the official language of schooling. In 1898 the islands were finally annexed to the US, despite the signing in the preceding year of a petition protesting the proposal by more than half the remaining Hawaiian population. In 1959 voters were given a forced choice to continue as a territory of the US or to obtain full political incorporation into the union as the fiftieth state. On admission to the union, Hawai'i was removed from the United Nations list of Non-Self-Governing Territories, despite the fact that the US had not properly allowed the people to express themselves on the issue of self-determination as required by international law: return to independent status was never presented as an option. Thus, in the 200 years after the English language first reached Hawai'i's shores with the coming of Captain Cook, it became the preferred language of commerce, government, and education as society made the transition from communal to British-style monarchy to annexed territory to US state.

Major changes in culture and lifestyle, such as those seen in colonial Hawai'i — or indeed those seen in the transition from hunting to farming, from self-sufficiency to capitalism, or from extended families to nuclear ones — often have this problematic nature, so that it is hard to tell whether people are pushed into them or whether they jump. Choices often have unforeseen consequences over the long term. Certainly, the chiefs did not have to trade with foreigners, nor were the first Hawaiians who worked for Hooper forced to do so. They could have returned to the land. At that time, most Hawaiians continued to live in the traditional manner by farming and fishing. Hooper had accurately seen that as long as Hawaiians had the option of subsisting on their own land, and retained control of it, large-scale commercial agriculture would have difficulty gaining a foothold.

Nevertheless, the foreigners exerted increasing pressure. Planters like Hooper, along with the missionaries, complained repeatedly that the Hawaiians appeared uninterested in or were unwilling to work beyond what they needed to meet their needs. The missionaries envisioned large-scale agriculture as the salvation of the Hawaiian people and told them that their idleness was responsible for so much sickness and death. Ordinances were passed against idleness, indolence, and vagrancy in 1842 and 1846, the latter containing a provision which stated that "if a man be seen running about, or sitting idly without labor, or devoted to play and folly, he shall be taken before the judges." Persons found to be without valid employment were to be bound by the sheriff to an appropriate person for a period of one year's labor. As a result of a new law passed in

1850, commoners were required to pay a tax in cash, half going to the king or government, and half to the chief on whose land they lived. Rural villages became depopulated as people moved to the towns to earn money either by selling produce or their labor. The number of native Hawaiians dropped even further, to around 24,000 in 1920, by which time the majority of part Hawaiians and a third of pure Hawaiians lived in the urban area of Honolulu. As the plantation economy expanded, vast irrigation systems were developed which diverted water from the traditional lands people had farmed, pushing even more from the land into the city.

In effect, the demands of the plantations and other forms of paid work changed where and how ordinary people lived, what they produced and ate. By the turn of the century, these changes had completely altered the demography of the islands and shattered the linguistic equilibrium. Foreign travelers such as American Charles Nordhoff and Briton Isabella Bird, who published accounts of their respective visits in 1874 and 1875, tell us that it was hard to find natives outside Honolulu who understood more than a smattering of English. Today, it is hard to find Hawaiians who still understand and use their native language. Hawaiians lost not only their land but their language as their islands rapidly became the most acculturated in the Pacific. The replacement of Hawaiian with English was part of this process of intrusion of a new western-style political economy based on private ownership of land, and accumulation of wealth for individual consumption. An elite planter class came to dominate not only the physical means of reproduction but the symbolic means of reproduction as well.

The distinction between what is forced and what is voluntary, then, is a problematic one, but the terms are useful as idealized ends of a continuum, and we will continue to use them in our discussion of language death.

What has changed

We have considered the idea of linguistic equilibrium, in which a number of languages are maintained over time by the forces of local status and solidarity. We have also considered the ways that equilibrium may be broken by population loss, and forced or voluntary language shift.

All three of these modes of language loss support our general view that change in language use is a result of environmental change. In population loss, some change in the natural or disease environment causes a group of people to die out. In forced shift, the available social and natural environment is restricted by the coercive actions of other people. Finally, in voluntary shift, a change in people's practices, roles, and role models is brought about by changes in the human environment.

For most of the many millennia of human history, it seems likely that the world was close to linguistic equilibrium, with the number of languages being lost roughly equalling the new ones created. Indeed, there would have been periodic upsurges of diversity as new continents were settled. Locally dominant languages evolved and recruited new speakers, but the differences in size, organization, and technology between neighboring societies were never so great that the dominant relationships could not be reversed every few decades. The considerable benefits of autonomy and disaggregation kept at bay such incentives as there were for enlarging the market and crowding together, and therefore many small, culturally independent units thrived with their languages.

Something has clearly changed, for over the last five hundred years small languages nearly everywhere have come under intense threat. The equilibrium has been broken and the forces of homogenization seem to be rampant. What has changed so much in the human environment that such a massive transition could occur? We will argue that there have in fact been two great waves of change in the human environment which have spread from their centers of origin across the globe, and have endangered most of the world's languages as they spread. One of these was the industrial revolution, which created inequalities of technology, economic roles, and communications between neighboring communities which are unprecedented. This wave will be the subject of Chapter 6.

The other wave—the first wave, which made the second one possible—is the development of agriculture. This is a wave that began modestly around ten thousand years ago, and still continues today. We have argued that language loss began on a massive scale in the last thousand years; it therefore seems odd to trace it to a cause that began nine thousand years earlier. Agriculture, however, not only caused persistent waves of language disruption as farmer communities overcame hunters and gatherers, but set off the development of economic differences between human communities on a scale which had not existed before. When European farmers overcame Australian hunters and gatherers in the late eighteenth century, they were performing the final act of a drama which had begun nearly ten thousand years earlier in the Neolithic era. That drama is the subject of the next chapter.

Five

The Biological Wave

The white man made us many promises, more than I can remember, but they never kept but one; they promised to take our land, and they took it.

—Red Cloud

*I*n the previous chapter, we encountered the idea that for much of history, the number of languages in several continents was roughly constant. As in Papua New Guinea in recent historical times, the forces favoring localism and dispersal were, on the whole, just as strong as those that produce integration or domination of one location by another. One language group might have achieved preeminence over another, but this was a precarious affair which would be reversed in a few years. What was absent were massive, enduring differences between the expansionary potential of different peoples, of the kind which would cause the sustained expansion of a single, dominant language.

This equilibrium has been punctured forever. Some languages have, over the last few centuries, shown an awesome propensity to spread. By now, the speakers of the ten largest languages make up half the world's population, and this figure is increasing. The hundred largest languages account for almost 90 percent of the population, with the remaining 6,000 languages confined to 10 percent of the world's most marginalized people, whose communities have generally been on the retreat for several hundred years. This chapter and the next seek to understand how this great transformation has come about. We will argue that the rapid loss of diversity only really occurred in the last thousand years or so. It is a result of the emergence of massive differentials in the power which societies have to affect the environment. These differentials run in favor of Eurasia against the other continents—all of the ten giant languages are of Eurasian origin—and of large centers against small peripheries within Eurasia. We will seek to explain how this pattern evolved.

Such huge power differentials are mainly a modern phenomenon. However, they are not without prehistoric precedent. The origin of farming nearly ten thousand years earlier seems to have caused linguistic disruptions on a scale previously unknown; and, more importantly for our purposes, it began the process of divergent evolution, which meant that, millennia later, Eurasians were to overwhelm the indigenous inhabitants of several other continents. To understand the present predicament, then, we must trace its origins back to the Neolithic era.

One often encounters the argument that the spread of European languages and lifestyles over the globe was inevitable and perhaps desirable. This is because, the argument goes, Europeans developed a superior civilization by their great insight and industry, and so non-Europeans were bound to want the progress it represented.

We do not wish to duck the clear truth that the modern, industrial way of life has brought huge quality of life benefits which people all over the world want to share, and we will discuss the linguistic implications of this further in later chapters. However, we must take issue with the superiority argument, on two counts.

The first count is the claim that the Europeans earned their greater power by industry and insight. As we shall see in this chapter, the Europeans overwhelmed many indigenous peoples by spreading diseases. They had not "earned" these diseases (or their disease resistance) by their industry, and indeed they had no idea why they had them or, often, why native peoples were dying out. European diseases, and the European numerical advantage, ultimately stem from the creation of the very productive Eurasian farming package thousands of years ago. But even this was not a triumph of the European spirit. It was a biogeographical fluke. The heaviest-grained grasses, and the most appropriate medium-sized herbivores, were all in Eurasia, as it happens, and the process by which they were domesticated speaks less of brilliant insight and more of gradual, blind, and unconscious evolution.

The second problem with the superiority argument is that it assumes that all change from one way of life to another is in the direction of increased human welfare. This might be so if all choice were really free, but in fact undeniable disparities of power run through the whole history of language shift, and often distort choices, as we saw in the Hawaiian example we considered in the last chapter. The transition to agriculture, that key change, was not, as we shall see, a great leap forward in human well-being. It was a response to declining well-being which led to a drop in nutritional status and life expectancy. It had certain properties, though, which meant that once it was established it had a powerful tendency to expand—not by improving the lives of its new converts, but by radically altering their environments in a way which owed nothing to free choice. The integration of many marginal peoples into the modern world system has this character. They may or may not obtain benefits from membership in the long term, but the factors which bring them in are not those wished-for benefits but the lack of real choices in a changing environment. These points are worth bearing in mind as we discuss how the present dominance of a few languages has come about.

The Paleolithic world system

Let us consider the world ten thousand years ago, at the beginning of our present warm era, the Holocene. Modern humans, having originated, it seems, in Africa more than one hundred thousand years earlier, had by this point inhabited all the major continents. Of the countries which presently have a human population, only the extreme Northern latitudes, and some islands in the Pacific basin including New Zealand and Madagascar, were uninhabited.

The peoples of the time were, as far as we can establish, all hunters and gatherers. This meant they harvested the wild resources of their environments, which varied widely according to where they were. Large game were favored where available; fish and shellfish allowed dense coastal and riverine aggregations to develop; and fruits, nuts, seeds, small animals, and insects were gathered.

What we know of hunter-gatherer societies from recent history, which is not contradicted by anything in the archaeological record, is that they tend to be small, fluid, and relatively egalitarian. Hunters and gatherers rely on resources which occur at more or less their natural densities; unlike farmers and herders, they do not selectively breed up the species on which they rely in the space around them. This has several important implications for how their societies must evolve. Firstly, hunter-gatherer societies tend to be nomadic. Once a locale is gathered or hunted out, a new patch must be found, which entails moving on. The speed with which patches become depleted varies according to the ecological context. Some estuarine and coastal environments, such as those of the Pacific Northwest of America, were so bounteous as to allow their inhabitants to become sedentary. Others, such as the Western Desert in Australia, were arid and required foragers to move over huge ranges to secure adequate food. The constant movement inherent in most foraging lifestyles presumably explains why they gradually filled up the world. There would have been perpetual frontiers as groups exhausted local supplies and looked for new areas. Occasionally, these frontiers would reach a continental divide, such as the straits separating Southeast Asia from New Guinea and Australia or the bridge from Asia to America; even more rarely, a few groups would make it across. Each group would have moved only a few miles each year, but over the millennia, such a process produced the remarkable diaspora of homo sapiens.

The second important point about the hunting and gathering way of life is that it provides powerful incentives for groups to be small. The larger a group is, the more quickly it will deplete an area, and the sooner and farther it will have to move. This imposes heavy costs on all its members. Subgroups would thus have strong incentives to strike out on their own rather than remaining together. In historical hunter-gatherer societies, bands have indeed been very small, and their superordinate groupings fluid, fissiparous, and never immense.

A third and related generalization is that hunter-gatherer population densities are very low. The resources on which they depend are encountered at their unaugmented, natural densities. Though the range of species which can be used is very large, this sets a constraint on the number of people who can be supported in a given area. The level of this constraint varies from place to place, but the observed densities are rarely more than one person per square mile.

The combined effects of these constraints—the need to move, the incentive to fission, and the sparseness of population—have implications for the type of linguistic situation which must have obtained in the Paleolithic era. Most obviously, language groups would have been small. Language groups in aboriginal Australia consisted of no more than two or three thousand people at most, and this may not be an unreasonable model of most of the world before the origin of farming. More subtly, the hunter-gatherer way of life tended to preclude the emergence of dominant cultures or languages.

Hunting and gathering favors a relatively egalitarian political system. It is difficult to control people who are constantly moving around, and who have no farms or herds which may be seized, threatened, or taxed. Thus the emergence of a dominant political class is not possible. Military dominance is also difficult to establish. To become dominant, a group would have to become much larger than its neighbors, but because the subsistence system imposes severe costs on becoming larger than necessary, with land available, groups would have fissioned long before they could become mighty. Finally, economic dominance would also have been virtually precluded. With population so sparse and shifting, it would have been difficult to specialize economically to any great degree. Furthermore, nomadism without livestock makes the accumulation of capital items extremely difficult, as they have to be carried around. In fact, the accumulation of surplus suffers from terrible diminishing returns for hunter-gatherers. The more they gather above and beyond immediate requirements, the more quickly they will deplete the area and have to move, carrying their surplus with them or losing it in the process. The potential to exchange a surplus for anything else is limited by the fact that the people around are few and anyway are in the same boat. For this reason, hunter-gatherers in abundant conditions do not hoard; they can often provide their requirements in a short working week and have plenty of leisure time.

Under these conditions, it would be difficult if not impossible, for a dominant language or indeed a dominant group to evolve. Shifts of language would have been very localized, perhaps as one band was incorporated into a wider network. Local bilingualism could well have been common. The rise of any one language to global or even regional importance probably never happened. There were no empires, no armies, and no cities. In a moving world, centers and peripheries are hard to identify, and technological change and diffusion is localized and gradual. Thus, it is no surprise that when we examine the linguistic geography of a purely hunter-gatherer continent—aboriginal Australia is the only example we have—we find a multitude of small languages, not traceable to any particular dominant root, but showing evidence of considerable local fission and fusion over many centuries.

As long as the Paleolithic world system persisted, local autonomy and diversity would be high and the chances of any one language attaining dominant status in its region low. The duration of this half-forgotten period was immense. If the history of our species were compressed into a single day, then agriculture only appeared around ten in the evening. The walls of Jericho came up around the same time. Writing appeared nearer eleven o'clock, and the fall of the Roman Empire, which we call ancient history, was at twenty minutes to midnight. Most of the history of human languages, and the societies that spoke them, therefore took place on the localized, decentralized, oral, egalitarian stage of the Paleolithic. In some places, this system persisted into historical times. It began to be disrupted, however, as soon as agriculture appeared.

The Neolithic revolution

Agriculture appeared in perhaps half a dozen independent centers after 9000 BC (see Figure 5.1). The herding of livestock followed agriculture in some areas but not others. The earliest and perhaps best-known food production complexes are those that evolved in Mesopotamia and in Western Asia (based on wheat and barley, sheep and goats), and in China (based mainly on rice). These have been immensely influential and now cover much of the globe.

There were, however, several others, as the map shows. Parts of New Guinea had a transition to the cultivation of bananas and sugar cane as early as 7000 BC, though the sweet potato boom of the highlands, which we discussed in the last chapter, came thousands of years later through imports. The area of semi-arid savanna along the south of the Sahara Desert had its sorghum (guinea corn) farming by 5000 BC, and in moist, equatorial Africa, a separate complex based on the African yam was spreading by 3000 BC. The Ethiopian domestication of coffee and a grain called *teff* may have made it another independent center. After 4000 BC, at least three separate locations in the Americas developed food production, with no contact from Eurasia—Amazonia, which gave us the potato, Mesoamerica with its typical maize and beans, and the eastern US, with a complex based on goosefoot and sunflower. In a mere few thousand years hunting and gathering, which had been unchallenged for perhaps a hundred thousand years, was replaced by agriculture and herding as the dominant mode of human subsistence. Within a few millennia (one hour or so on our 24-hour clock) 99.997 percent of human beings came to depend on it. It had massive implications for all aspects of human life—not least the distribution of languages. To see why it had such a great impact, we must first consider its causes and consequences in the areas where it originated.

Causes

Since agriculture quickly spread to cover most of the world, it is tempting to see it as unconditionally superior to hunting and gathering. This was the perspective of much of the early archaeological writing on the subject. On this view, what has to be explained is not the adoption of farm-

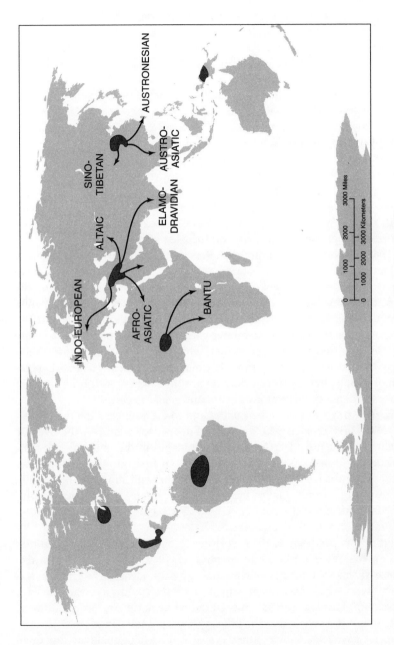

Figure 5.1   Centers of agricultural origin, and some associated language families

ing but the fact that it didn't get adopted much earlier — some time during the first twenty-two hours of the human day. The answer usually given to this puzzle was that humankind had somehow been too technologically primitive to make the breakthrough in earlier eras.

The problems with this view are twofold. First, it is unclear that the technology of primitive agriculture, which consists of simple digging sticks, among other things, is any more complex than the technology that was used by hunter-gatherers to catch fish and game. Second, and more generally, the archaeological evidence seems to suggest that farming, far from allowing a great leap forward in human well-being, was accompanied by a sharp decline in living standards.

Farming involves taking a few species and actively increasing their density in a concentrated area. The species involved are the descendants of what would for hunters and gatherers be very low-value resources, chiefly the grasses. Hunters and gatherers switch from high-value foodstuffs such as meat, fish, and nuts, to low-value ones as local availability changes, but grasses are very low on their list of priorities.

The question of why hunter-gatherers do not intensify the distribution of their food species can be stated another way: why bother? If a wide range of resources, often of high quality, can be simply gathered from the wild, the investment of energy in intensifying grasses or domesticating animals is unlikely to provide a good return. Both ethnographic and historical evidence suggest that hunter-gatherer populations have a highly diverse, balanced, and sufficient diet, which may be procured for a relatively modest investment of time. Farming would allow greater aggregation of people, but this is certainly no absolute benefit as it brings with it increased danger of infectious disease and social stresses.

Early farmers tended to be smaller and to die younger than the hunter-gatherers they replaced. In southeast Europe, for example, the average height of adult men decreased by seven inches in the millennium of the agricultural transition. Skeletal remains from first farming communities in the Americas testify unmistakably to anemia and shortages of protein, the results of a lower quality, narrower diet, perhaps in conjunction with increased infectious disease due to greater crowding. Such setbacks took thousands of years to overcome.

From this perspective, the surprising thing is the fact that agriculture was ever adopted at all. To understand why it was, we have to first recognize that agriculture is not a single step or idea. In fact, there was probably never a moment at which anybody could have said to have "invented" farming. It was a more gradual evolutionary process, during which both the people and the other species had to change.

As we have seen, hunter-gatherers switch from high-quality to low-quality resources when the former are scarce. If large game were becoming less abundant and wild grasses more so, people would switch to a greater use of the grasses. They would burn undergrowth and clear competitor species in order to harvest new shoots, and inadvertently spread the seeds of the grasses around camps which they frequented. The next step would have been the more deliberate sowing of these seeds and returning to the location a few months later to gather them. By choosing the plants with the heaviest ears, people caused gradual evolutionary change in the grass species around them, producing the cereals we know today.

A sequence of this kind may well have been at the heart of the origins of agriculture in the Near East around 8500 BC. Exactly why game was becoming less abundant and grasses more so is a difficult matter, but both over-hunting and climate change could have played a role.

Both farming and herding (which tended to follow the development of agriculture) are not simple human inventions but the results of a coevolution of human cultures and the biology of non-human species. Thus, they could only get going where the right candidates for domestication were available. Eurasia seems to have been particularly favored, having as it did 39 of the world's 56 heaviest seeded grasses. These went on to become the wheat, rice, and so on that now dominate much of the plant landscape. Eurasia also had the wild forerunners of the sheep, goat, cow, horse, and pig, while other areas lacked suitable large mammals and marsupials. This was another biogeographical accident that was to have profound long-term consequences.

Agriculture, then, rather than a brilliant insight causing a great leap forward in human welfare, was probably a gradual, mainly unconscious response to generally deteriorating conditions. If anything, the standard of living declined. How, then, can we explain its extraordinary success in ousting hunting and gathering?

Consequences

Farming had some negative consequences in terms of life expectancy and nutritional levels. It had another consequence, however, which far outweighed these drawbacks in determining its fate: the change in the rate of population growth.

Throughout the long diaspora of the Paleolithic era, the rate of population growth had been relatively slow. The first farming populations suffered from increased mortality, but they seemed to have enjoyed radically increased fertility, which more than offset it. Why this should be the case is not entirely clear. It may be that the high activity of nomadic hunter-gatherer women suppresses fertility. It may be that the difficulties of moving with several dependent children led hunter-gatherer women to control their fertility by prolonged breast-feeding or postpartum sexual abstinence. (On the other hand, prolonged breast-feeding may have simply been a response to a lack of suitable weaning foods in the hunter-gatherer diet.) Whatever the precise mechanism, the effects of the transition to agriculture are fairly clear. With the advent of farming and sedentism, populations in Eurasia increased their rate of population growth by about one hundredfold.

Waves of Advance

Once farming was established in its centers in the Old World—the Near East, the Yantgze and Yellow river valleys of China, and sub-Saharan West Africa, it began to spread out in a slow but determined wave. It is easy to see why this happened. Farming communities were increasing at up to one hundred times the rate of their hunter-gatherer neighbors. They also occupied the landscape much more densely, a side effect of specialized resource husbandry. This means their local groups could be many times larger than those of hunters and gatherers.

As they grew, agricultural populations brought more and more land from their frontiers into their orbit, spreading their crop species as well as themselves. Hunter-gatherers on the margins were thus faced with declining opportunities as more and more land was alienated from the species they relied upon. They were faced with limited options. Moving on was possible but would eventually lead to a piling up of refugees into an ever-smaller, non-farming periphery. Military resistance was unlikely. For perhaps the first time in history, there were now massive differences in the size and density of societies confronting each other over how resources were to be shared. Finally, they could simply become farmers, responding to the deteriorating environment as their neighbors had already done. Whatever they chose to do, the spread of farming was the most likely outcome.

There is a paradox about farming. In its primitive form, it has deleterious effects on the standard of living. These costs are so high that throughout most of history, individuals who made steps toward farming achieved no benefit, and so societies did not cross the Rubicon. However, some groups were clearly impelled, probably by a deteriorating situation, into the transition. One imagines that their situation would, for a long time, have been grim, before the new practices had been refined and while the crop species were still only partly improved. Once a group had made it through the transition, however, it was bound, by a simple Darwinian logic, to spread as far as the environment would allow it. For the first time, one society had a massive advantage over another in terms of its power to people and appropriate the landscape.

We can say, then, that hunting and farming are separated by an *equilibrium trap*. That is to say, in a world of hunters and gatherers, people who move toward farming do not do better than their rivals, and so hunting and gathering will not usually be replaced by farming. On the other hand, in a world of farmers, hunters and gatherers cannot displace them, because of their slow rates of reproduction. However, where one or a few societies are forced through the equilibrium trap from hunting to farming, they will cover the rest like a flooding tide.

As farming spread out from its centers of origin, languages were pushed out with it. It is not entirely clear whether the hunters and gatherers on the periphery were incorporated or ousted, but in either case, the wave of farming people carried with it the language that they happened to speak. We know this because many of the great families of languages with which we are familiar are the daughters of an ancestor spread out in this way. Some of these families, with their relationships to agricultural centers, are shown on Figure 5.1.

According to one theory, Indo-European, the large family which includes English, spread from an origin in the Near East all the way to the Atlantic over the course of about 4,000 years. It also spread in the other direction into India. Another family, Elamo-Dravidian, had descended from Iran into India before Indo-European, giving us contemporary South Indian languages such as Tamil. The aboriginal inhabitants of India were swept away by these two waves, and survive only in isolated hill tracts and on islands in the Indian Ocean. The Sino-Tibetan family, of which Chinese is one modern representative, swept from north China into south China and Southeast Asia; in time, other language families originating in south China, such as Tai-Kadai and Austroasiatic, overran the rest of Southeast Asia. Austronesian, from a base on Taiwan, spread out into the Pacific basin, and it was one branch of this family of spreading farmers, the Polynesians, who achieved the colonization of New Zealand and Madagascar, which the Palaeolithic peoples had not been able to do. In Africa, the Bantu family spread from a heartland in Cameroon all the way to South Africa, covering most of the continent over the course of three and a half millennia, to be halted only at the Fish River.

Farming and language spreads were stopped only where the ecology became unsuitable for that type of farming, or where natural barriers intervened. Bantu, for example, which was a farming complex adapted to the moist tropics, could not spread north toward the Sahara, and could not get all the way to the temperate Cape. It filled up almost all of the space in between, however. Neither the west Asian nor east Asian spreads were able to get into the extreme north of Eurasia for similar reasons. Dense patches of forest and mountain ranges also presented checks to farming spreads. Where there were such impediments, the two systems existed side by side and even developed a kind of symbiosis, but over open country farming won out.

On the margins of the great language families today, where the farming juggernaut was finally stalled, or in mountain or forest refuges it could not overrun, we see small societies whose presence hints at the now-lost diversity of the Palaeolithic era. On the fringes of Indo-European, pressed against the Atlantic or walled in by mountains, are Basque, the languages of the Caucasus, the languages of interior Siberia, and, now long extinct, the Pictish language of Scotland. In Africa, there are some small groups on the margins of the Bantu spread, such as the Hadza, Sandawe, and San Bushmen, with their unparalleled click languages. There are also the Pygmies, in the dense forests of the center of the continent, who have forgotten their language in favor of that of the Bantu incomers. There are fragmented groups in the rain forests of Southeast Asia, India, and the Philippines, and on the Andaman Islands in the Indian Ocean. All of these peoples show a similar profile. They live in some inaccessible refuge which the farming spread passed by, or reached only recently. They speak small languages, belonging to very small families (sometimes with no living relatives at all), with a structure and vocabulary quite different from those around them. These groups only hint at the great linguistic diversity which must have existed everywhere before the farming spreads.

The Neolithic era, then, was the first great linguistic homogenization of history. However, it was in one respect very different from the extinctions which have gone on the last few hundred years. As farming groups spread, they broke up. They were still economically simple, small-scale societies, and they soon fragmented into a local mosaic in which diversity immediately began to re-evolve in the time-honored way. Bantu may have homogenized much of the African continent, but by now it has produced five hundred different daughter languages. These daughter languages are relatively close to each other in structure and in lexicon, since the time span of their separation is modest; over another few thousand years, however, if other processes had not intervened, the diversity of Africa might have been back to its Palaeolithic levels.

After the shock of the Neolithic homogenization, diversity began to evolve again and continents returned to some kind of linguistic equilibrium. This is in marked contrast to the more recent spreads of European languages. The alert reader will have noticed that all the great linguistic spreads we have described occurred in Africa and Eurasia. What about the other continents? Here we see the beginning of the different pathways which were eventually to mean that it was European languages which spread to the Americas and elsewhere, and not American languages which spread to Europe. The Neolithic took very different courses in the Americas, New Guinea, and Australia.

The Americas had, as we have seen, at least three separate agricultural innovations. However, these did not produce the waves of advance seen in the Old World. Why this should have been so is not entirely clear. Perhaps the crop complexes did not produce the same increases in population growth as their Eurasian counterparts. Livestock species were certainly lacking; the only major domestications made in the Americas were the llama family, the guinea pig, and the turkey, and even these did not spread to all areas. The geography of the continent did not favor diffusion. Eurasia is a vast plain, arrayed on an east-west axis at temperate latitudes; the dominant axis in the Americas is north-south, giving it many different ecological zones, which require different production systems. Thus the three different agricultures never met up. Whatever the reasons, no population wave was unleashed in the Americas comparable to the magnitude of that unleashed in Eurasia. By the time of European contact, the population of the Americas was dense in a few locations, such as the central Andes and Mexico, but sparse elsewhere, and many Americans were still hunting and gathering.

New Guinea, as we know, had an early conversion to banana farming. This produced no major population wave. Into this century, New Guineans were still mixing farming, hunting, gathering, and fishing, and living at very low densities. New Guinea's many-leveled mountain ecology does not favor waves of advance. The importation of the sweet potato to the highlands produced a population boom capable of starting a farming spread, but this was checked from spreading downward by ecology and disease.

Finally, Australia never had a Neolithic transition at all. It was still peopled entirely by hunters and gatherers in the eighteenth century. Exactly why this should be is difficult to say. One factor was almost certainly the mainly arid and uncertain climate; appropriate species for domestication may also have been lacking. The population density of Australia remained fairly low, and it may be that no shock or pressure ever forced any Australian group through the equilibrium trap into the farming way of life.

Whatever the reasons for these differing conversions to farming, they were to give rise to varying courses of development after the Neolithic era. These, in turn, gave rise to the dominance of a few languages in the last five hundred years. We will now examine how this happened.

Different trajectories after the Neolithic

Weight of numbers

The most important single component of the different courses of human history in the last five thousand years is the difference in population between the different continents. A small difference in average growth rate can, because of the exponential nature of population growth, lead to a huge difference over a few millennia, and this seems to be what happened. Numbers are very difficult to estimate, of course, and become more difficult as we go further back in time. According to one estimate, by the time of Christ, Eurasia and North Africa could count around 227 million inhabitants, with just twelve million in each of sub-Saharan

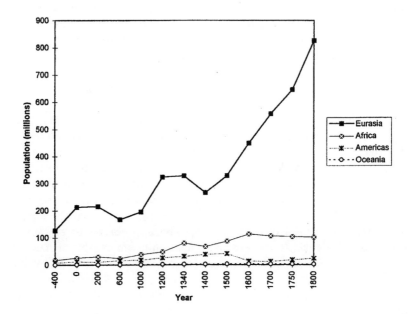

Figure 5.2   Estimates of world population by continent, 400 BC–AD 1800

Africa and the Americas, and less than one million in the Pacific Basin. Thus 90 percent of all people were in Eurasia. Such estimates as we have for the trends after this time show the imbalance widening (Figure 5.2), with the Eurasian population soaring, especially after AD 1000, while the other continents remained stagnant.

By AD 1000, the continents were on very unequal footings. In Eurasia, productive farming had unleashed waves of population growth which had covered the continent with farmers from coast to coast. The pockets of the interior had gradually been filled; the North Chinese had begun the long colonization of their own interior, displacing tribal peoples as they went. Russians were soon to begin pushing into interior Siberia. The continent was teeming and nearly full, while Australia, the Americas, and Africa were relatively empty.

Technology and social organization

The greater population of Eurasia affected its social organization and technology. In Australia, the inherent cost for hunter-gatherers of gathering together in large groups or accumulating surplus prevented any departure from a fluid, small-scale, egalitarian social organization. Disputes were addressed by small-scale warfare, which often led to one party moving away or dissolving.

In Eurasia, the picture was quite different. Growing populations provided an incentive for the invention of ever more intensive ways of extracting food from the land. The groups confronting each other over living space were ever larger and denser, leading to runaway demand for technologies of large-scale war, in which Eurasia has specialized for several millennia. Where there were keystone resources, such as land or irrigation systems that could be appropriated, powerful elites came to control them—sometimes for the benefit of the people, but always for the benefit of themselves. They needed systems of administration and transport to secure their interests. States were formed earlier and were larger in Eurasia than anywhere else. Economic specialization followed from both the dense population and the needs of elites, which further bolstered technological change.

Eurasia's population boom in the Neolithic era had set it on a new path. Eurasians not only outnumbered other people ten to one; they were also better armed and more hierarchically controlled. They had one other key attribute that was to determine the fates of many human societies, although they were unaware of it: they were prone to illness.

Disease

The infectious diseases that have been the great killers of humans in modern times are mainly those referred to as *crowd diseases*. They can only thrive where their hosts are packed together densely, so that they may always have somewhere to live. Where people are sparse, such as they were in Australia and the Americas, such diseases as measles and smallpox cannot be sustained.

The Eurasian preference for surrounding themselves with livestock also meant that many parasites originally found in other animals passed to people. Measles, smallpox, tuberculosis, and influenza all have such an origin. These diseases all became major presences in the environments of Eurasia.

The unceasing presence of these diseases killed many Europeans, but it also allowed them to develop some resistance. In the Americas and Australia, yellow fever, smallpox, mumps, measles, flu, typhus, and tuberculosis were unknown until European contact, and so people's immune systems were unprepared. Africa, with its livestock and its intermediate densities, was also an intermediate case in terms of disease. These differences in disease levels and immunity were perhaps the decisive factor which, added to difference in numbers, technology, and social organization, determined that dominance flowed in one direction only when the two hemispheres collided.

The Neolithic aftershock

Europe and Asia

Waves of post-Neolithic population growth had filled Eurasia with communities whose origins, linguistic and biological, were in the farming centers. The process of European expansion in this millennium was really just a continuation overseas of the process which had been going on at home. As such, its occurrence is perhaps not that surprising. One of the great puzzles of history, though, is why Europe expanded (and later industrialized), and not the greater centers of Eurasia, China, and India.

In 1500, the population densities of China and India were around three times that of Europe. The Chinese, in particular, had the technology and social organization to mount a major expansion. They had already colonized much of their own interior. In the early fifteenth century, they were sending fleets of hundreds of large, heavily armed ships, with total crews of up to 28,000, as far afield as East Africa and India. They never settled, however, and after 1433 the voyages stopped. Why this was so, and why the Chinese never reached the Pacific Northwest of America, which was well within their reach, is a mystery.

For whatever reason, it was not China or India but Europe which became the center of expansion. Europe was poorer in people but seems, for reasons which historians continue to debate, to have been better at mustering investment in expansionary activity. The European expansions of 1492 are well known, but in fact expansion had begun much earlier. Europe's first overseas colony was Greenland, which was founded by Erik the Red in the tenth century. The Norsemen probably visited North America around the same time but failed to establish a foothold. In the other direction, the crusades pushed thousands of Europeans south and east from the most densely populated areas into the Levant, where they set up kingdoms.

The European economy was depressed by the population crash that followed the Black Death in the fourteenth century (which is visible on the graph in Figure 5.2). Oddly enough, this gave a further impetus for the discovery of new lands, as landowners suffered declining revenues at home and sought to tap the rich overseas trades. The late fifteenth century and the first years of the sixteenth saw the great voyages of exploration and the establishment of European trading posts in West Africa and the Americas as well as Asia. As population recovered at home, outposts which had been established for trade quickly became attractive as sites for the spread of the colonizers, which was in all cases bad news for the indigenous peoples. Thus the great migration of Europeans to other continents began.

The Americas

Columbus "discovered" America in 1492; by the follow-up voyage of the next year, colonization was firmly in view, as he carried with him 1,200

Figure 5.3   Colonists land in Virginia, early seventeenth century

[After John White. Courtesy of The Mansell Collection, London].

men including artisans and agricultural laborers. The next forty years were to see the establishment of the Spaniards in the Caribbean, with a first colony on Haiti, and then, after 1540, the rapid occupation of mainland South America. The Portuguese, meanwhile, had discovered Brazil in 1500, and established a number of trading posts along the coasts.

The original motive for these early American settlements may have been trade. However, the rationale quickly changed, first to political domination, and then, as the potential of the overseas possessions for settlement was realized, to occupation. There were early attempts at permanent settlement by the Spanish and Portuguese in Latin America and the Caribbean, which were matched by English settlements in the north, where the East Coast colonies were founded in the early seventeenth century. By the end of that century, around four hundred thousand English people had gone to North America, with about the same number from each of Spain and Portugal settling further south.

The settlements in South and Central America spread into the interior, moving along open plains and river valleys. In the north of the continent,

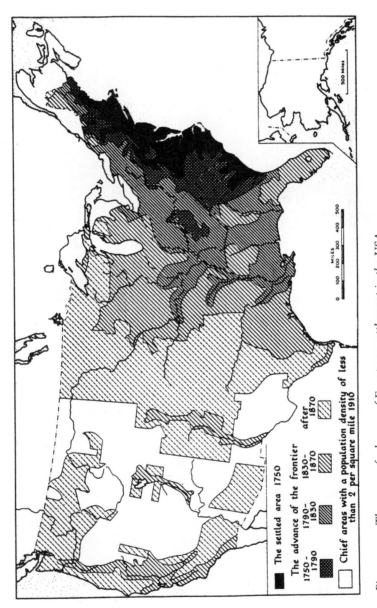

Figure 5.4   The wave of advance of European settlement in the USA

[Adapted from D.K. Adams, S.F. Mills and H.B. Rodgers, An Atlas of North American Affairs, 2d edition, New York: Methuen, 1979] as the great migrations of the eighteenth and nineteenth centuries gained pace, the frontier pushed implacably westward (Figure 5.4). The same pattern of displacement would repeat itself along this frontier again and again for over two hundred years. Fighting broke out between the indigenous inhabitants and settlers in newly settled areas, which continued until Indians had been killed or persuaded to move out beyond the frontier. Treaties were signed offering the area to the west as permanent Indian country, and the surviving fragments of native tribes were driven out into it. Almost as soon as the treaties were signed, however, they were broken by the uncontrolled wave of settlement, which meant a new round of conflict and displacement further west, until the frontier eventually leapt across the Great Plains to reach the Pacific coast.

In 1850, California joined the Union and America was European from the Atlantic to the Pacific. The remaining Indians, perhaps as few as 300,000 in number by this time, were hemmed into the midwest region by a staggering 30 million settlers and their descendants. Forty years of war were to follow, in which the remaining Indians, though by this time skilled with horses and firearms, were to lose more and more of their land and liberty. After the battle of Wounded Knee in 1890, the whole of North America was effectively controlled by settlers, with the indigenous peoples confined to reservations whose sites they had not chosen. "The white man made us many promises, more than I can remember," chief Red Cloud of the Sioux was to comment, "but they never kept but one; they promised to take our land and they took it."

The important thing to understand about the settlement of the Americas is that it was not just a movement of people. It was the expansion of one whole ecosystem into the domain of another one. Europeans brought their sheep and goats, horses, cattle, and wheat to the Americas in a wholesale attempt to divert that environment into an extension of their own. The number of sheep and goats in Mexico rose from zero to 8 million in the period between 1500 and 1620, during which time the number of indigenous inhabitants fell by 90 percent. There were 1.3 million cattle in Brazil by 1711; and those same beasts were to replace the indigenous wild bison on the great plains of America. Wheat, other European cereals, and weeds pushed out native vegetation, wild and farmed. This was a process of ecological succession in which the species on which the European production system was based ousted those on which traditional societies depended, and often became wild and spread in advance of the Europeans themselves. The species spread included, most crucially, those microorganisms that make their living in human beings, and whose lifestyle has the unfortunate side effect of producing infectious disease.

The effect on the hitherto unexposed indigenous population was dramatic. Up to 95 percent of all native Americans died from successive epidemics of smallpox, measles, malaria, and yellow fever that ran riot around the continent. The indigenous population of the Caribbean more or less disappeared. The population of central Mexico—the densest in the Americas—fell from perhaps 25 million in 1519 to 2 million in 1580. The decline elsewhere, though perhaps not quite as rapid, was almost as significant. Thus, the popular perception that the Americas were empty, virgin soil just waiting for industrious Europeans to work it was a consequence not of the real pre-contact situation but of a fearsome tide of microorganisms that Europeans neither intended nor understood.

In the early period of contact, particularly in South America, Europeans had ambitions for the natives. As well as trade, there was tribute to be extracted to serve the interests of the elites who financed early overseas expansion. The empires of the Aztecs and the Incas, rocked by disease and internal division, and lacking horses and firearms, were captured early in the sixteenth century and brought under Spanish sovereignty. The tribute exacted was so high that natives complained they were having to work seven or eight months a year for this alone, leaving them no time to farm their own lands. They were also forced to switch from maize to European wheat (in which tribute was to be paid), a crop that they neither liked nor knew how to farm. Later, they were to be forced into the colonial money economy by a demand for taxes in silver. Thus, native American participation in the spreading economic system was less a matter of economic choice and more a matter of political domination.

There were widespread attempts to bring native Americans into forced labor. The increasing land-per-person ratio in Europe meant that by the end of the middle ages labor was no longer the scarcest factor of production. Internal slavery, a key feature of earlier epochs in Europe, had disappeared and feudalism had dissolved. In the colonies, however, things were different. New land had opened up at a much faster rate than Europe could produce people to fill it. Spain, for example, increased its effective acreage by 400 percent between 1519 and 1540; overall, the amount of land available to Europe per capita increased from 24 to 148 acres as a result of the discoveries. Development of this vast "ghost acreage" therefore required new sources of labor.

Natives were enslaved everywhere in Latin America and put to work on these ghost acres. Religious orders of almost military efficiency were sent to "pacify" the natives, which meant making them suitable for labor by establishing some ideological dominance over them. In close contact with Europeans, however, native Americans had a dramatic tendency to die, and so proved unsatisfactory as a labor force. Thus the infernal mechanism of importing one set of tropical peoples—Africans, with their Old World disease resistance—to work the lands appropriated from another was born. A consignment of African slaves reached Haiti by 1505. Perhaps 10 million more were to follow them.

Native American reactions to contact were tremendously varied. In many places, they resisted fiercely. At first, the simple technologies of warfare, developed in an entirely different context, proved hopelessly inadequate. Much later they were to obtain horses and firearms, and the picture was somewhat different. By this time, though, the balance was entirely with the settlers, and the demand for land had become more militant than ever, its militancy being variously expressed in violence and duplicity. The depleted natives had no real chance of stemming the tide.

Often the reaction to contact was one of utter dislocation. Losing such a high proportion of the population completely undermined traditional social networks, just as the changing environment, which was now full of wheat and cattle where the bison and maize had been before, undermined the basis of the economic system. "Let us die, then, let us die, then, for our gods are already dead," went one response to the destruction of the Inca way of life. This dislocation continues into the present day. The Kaiowa, Nandeva, and Terana tribes of Brazil, for example, have been stripped of their lands and are now crowded into a tiny reservation, with just a third of a hectare of space per person. They have no real economic options and no power to choose their social roles. Inside the reservation no fewer than five Pentecostal churches and a German mission compete for their souls. Over the past three years the National Indian Foundation has recorded 69 suicides among the 24,000 remaining Kaiowa people—a rate 25 times the average suicide rate for the Brazilian population. The religious leader Atanaio Teixeira explains the suicides as a reaction of despair brought on by cultural disintegration: "The whites take away our land and bring us their God, their food, their music, their cachaca (strong sugarcane rum). We have our own religion, our own customs, but many want to live like whites. When they become half Kaiowa, half white, they regret it. They want to go back to being Indians, but they cannot, so they decide to die." Many of the suicides are committed by young people who drink rat poison or hang themselves from trees. Given huge upheavals such as these, the surprise is not that the indigenous languages have declined, but that they survived at all—which, with varying degrees of success, many have, right into the twentieth century.

The native American population stabilized and rallied in the seventeenth and eighteenth centuries. By this time, though, the number of Europeans in the Americas far exceeded the number of natives, and the landscape was almost a European one. European crops such as wheat ousted indigenous ones. Any niches the natives could find in this new world order were likely to be on the margins and at the bottom of a European-defined heap. Native Americans had had their environment radically changed, and their social groups have had a hard time to recover.

A thorough survey in 1962 found around 210 native languages still in use in North America, but only 89 of these had speakers of all ages. Furthermore, 86 had fewer than one hundred speakers. It is probable that nearly all of those 86 have by now gone the way of the Californian language Cupeño, which disappeared forever when its last speaker, Roscinda

Figure 5.5   Luiseño women in a government-run (English language) school in California, 1904

[Courtesy of National Museum of the American Indian, credited to Edward H. Davis]

Nolasquez, died in 1987 at the age of 94. Another 75 languages had between 100 and 1,000 speakers in 1962, and their situation appears grim. Only a handful of indigenous languages—Navajo and Dakota in the US, Cree and Ojibwa in Canada—seem promisingly viable, with thousands of speakers and schooling projects.

The situation in Latin America is more varied, but scarcely more encouraging. Most of the languages are gravely endangered, and there are none at all left alive in Uruguay and the Caribbean. On the other hand, there are parts of Latin America where indigenous communities have been less completely overrun than in the north. Several larger indigenous languages are still very much alive. Aymara and Quechua, which both have over one million speakers, have obtained some official status in Bolivia and Peru. These are the exceptions, however. Most of the languages of the Americas are in pressing danger of joining the legion of legendary voices which, like the Mohicans and the Huron, the Pentlatch and the Miami, can be heard no more.

Australia and New Zealand

The first European settlement of Australia was in 1788, in New South Wales. There is some argument as to whether the decision to exploit Captain Cook's discovery stemmed from the need to find a place of settlement for convicts, who could no longer be shipped to newly independent America, or the wish to enlarge trading interests in the Pacific basin at this time. Whichever motive was important, the colonies, after a slow and shaky start, multiplied and became a center for free as well as convict migration. Within one hundred years of that first landing, most of the vast continent had been brought under British control and settlement.

As in the Americas, British occupation was an ecological transition. Aboriginal Australia had no domestic animals. By 1805, there were 500 horses, 4,000 cattle, 5,000 goats, 23,000 pigs and 20,000 sheep. By 1860 the sheep had multiplied exponentially to a total of 20 million. Today, just two hundred years after their first arrival, their number has reached 161 million.

Relations between settlers and Aborigines were always uneasy, though not initially hostile. As Europeans and their livestock began to fill more of the landscape, conflicts ensued as Aborigines tried to maintain their traditional lifestyles. Like some native Americans, the Aborigines were nomadic, and seemed to Europeans to be absent from areas of land and to be making no use of them. They would return on their circuits of migration to find the best areas appropriated for livestock grazing and crops, and the species they depended on hunted, removed, or grazed away.

Conflict over resources led to increasing open violence by the year 1800, and indeed what followed has been described as a "150 years war." Aborigines, in their small groups with simple technology, were always at a disadvantage in confrontation and were pushed back to marginal lands. The settlers, for their part, were not in the least interested in sharing the grazing land with the indigenes, whom they regarded as below the level of moral consideration, and had no qualms about using genocidal tactics. Indeed, in this respect the Aborigines were accorded even less consideration than the Native Americans or the Maoris. In those cases, Europeans made notional treaties with the indigenes, which they invariably broke. In the Australian case, the settlers did not even bother to do this. Aboriginal rights were not even considered to exist, as most of Australia was declared unclaimed land and therefore open to indiscriminate appropriation. Any remaining aborigines were simply pests to be removed. One Reverend John West wrote, of the Tasmanians, "their appearance is offensive, their proximity obstructive, their presence renders everything insecure. Thus the muskets of the soldier, and those of the bandits, are equally useful; they clear the land of a detested incubus."

The Tasmanians were shot where they were found, or rounded up into prison camps, where the survivors languished in miserable conditions. The last of them, a woman called Trucanini, who had been raped by white convicts and then used by the authorities as a pawn to bring her people in, died in 1876. Tasmanian, a unique branch on the tree of the world's languages, was thus destroyed along with its people.

*Figure 5.6   The last
pureblood Tasmanians*

*[Courtesy of The National
Library of Australia,
Canberra]*

Throughout the rest of Australia, the inhabitants were hunted and killed, poisoned, imprisoned, or driven from their lands. By 1847, a settler of Western Australia could boast that "we have seized upon the country, and shot down the inhabitants, until the survivors have found it expedient to submit to our rule." With habitual pomposity, Europeans managed to find divine legitimation for their actions. The Presbyterian clergyman J.D. Lang preached in 1856 that "God, in making the earth, never intended that it should be occupied by men so incapable of appreciating its resources as the Aborigines of Australia. The white man has, indeed, only carried out the intentions of the creator in coming and settling down in the territory of the natives." And this sermon was to an organization called the *Morton Bay Friends of the Aborigines.*

As in North America, diseases played a key role in the collapse of the indigenous population. It has been estimated that one third of all Aborigines died of smallpox in the century following contact. The slaughters, the diseases, and the loss of resources combined to mean that the aboriginal population slumped from a 1788 total which may have exceeded three-quarters of a million to just sixty thousand in 1888. By 1960, it had scarcely changed, while the white population of Australia moved toward four million.

The history of Australia, then, was that of a moving frontier along which an aggressively expanding Neolithic population and its associated species gradually pushed back a less dense, slower-growing set of hunters and gatherers, using disease and simple violence. Those Australian Aborigines who survived were faced with the age-old hunter-gatherer choice: resist, flee, or be incorporated at the bottom of a farming society.

Aborigines are very much at the bottom of Australian society, even today. Surrounded by one of the richest economic systems in the world, their life expectancy is so low as to be matched only by that of India and Central Africa. Aboriginal deaths from preventable infectious diseases still exceed the white average three hundredfold, and Aboriginal infant mortality in Western Australia is higher than the level found in Bangladesh. A few publicized land tribunals which have accorded Aborigines some consideration have provoked a backlash from racist politicians, but are in reality almost insignificant. The appropriation of land from Aboriginal communities by mining and farming interests, and the consequent poverty and disease, continues today.

So too does the attempt by Europeans to break up Aboriginal communities by force. A Human Rights and Equal Opportunities Commission report in 1997 revealed a systematic campaign of abuses against Aboriginal families which lasted most of the present century. Between 1910 and 1970, up to a third of Aboriginal children, perhaps 100,000 in all, were forcibly removed from their parents in an orchestrated attempt to destroy their societies. They languished in white missions, cattle stations, and foster homes, often in terrible conditions, with no access to friends or relatives, who had not been told where they were. Elsewhere, Aboriginal women were forcibly sterilized to stop the multiplying of what the professor of anthropology at Sydney in 1930 still called "the lowest race."

Almost all of the Aboriginal languages did, amazingly, persist in some form well into this century, but, disrupted and displaced, they were unable to recruit new speakers or even keep their old ones. Of the 260 or so unique languages of precolonial Australia, at least 100 have already died out. Another 100 are close to extinction, and fewer than 20 are now being learned by children.

The history of New Zealand is in some ways a similar story. By 1840, there were 2,000 white settlers sharing the island with 100,000 Maoris. By 1854, the whites had increased to 32,000, and the Maoris decreased to about 60,000, a level which they were not to exceed for one hundred years. Meanwhile, the European population continued to grow. The causes of the shift are much the same as those in Australia. The Maoris, a Polynesian farming people, had no domestic animals except small dogs. Indeed, New Zealand had no native mammals except a species of bat which had flown there and dogs and rats brought with the Maori. Nor did they have any exposure to the diseases of the crowd. They soon succumbed to epidemics of European disease.

The New Zealand experience was also one of a spreading European biota. European weeds spread into the hinterland faster than Europeans themselves. European crops and animals annexed the landscape. The Maoris knew what was happening. "Is not the land already gone? Is it not all covered with men, with strangers, foreigners—even as the grass and herbage—over whom we have no power?" asked Tamati Waaka Nene in 1840. They signed treaties with the crown to protect their territory, but their assessment of the honesty of the foreigners proved too generous and in the second half of the century they took to fierce and well-organized military resistance.

In the end, they were unable to reverse New Zealand's conversion to a European landscape. In 1981, New Zealand was filled with 2.7 million whites, 70 million sheep, 8 million cows, and fields producing 326 thousand tons of wheat. These are all European species, and they are controlled by a population speaking a European language.

The state of Maori, though still perilous, is not as bad as that of many other indigenous languages. Unlike Australia's Aborigines, New Zealand's 100,000 indigenes all shared a common language before European contact, although there were sizeable dialectal variations. Thus Maoris have a single resource under which they can unite. Maori is still spoken by at least 50,000 people. There are over 400 Maori schools, and the language is widely written and used in the law. Indeed, Maori took its place alongside English as an official language of New Zealand in 1987. These are all promising developments for the language. The danger is not past, however. The retreat of Maori as a language of the home has not been reversed, and without that achievement its position will remain precarious.

The untouched world

The wave of European biological expansion which spread European people, crops, diseases, and languages into the Americas and Oceania were in many ways just an extension of the waves of advance that had spread agriculture within Eurasia thousands of years earlier. It was as if the wave that brought Indo-European farmers to the coasts of England and Portugal had merely been blocked for five thousand years, before finding an appropriate maritime vector for their continued expansion.

Just like the Neolithic waves, the European expansions were disastrous for the less densely settled peoples along their margins. The terms on which they confronted their environments were changed radically by the expansion of foreign peoples and species into their vicinity. If they did not die, they had little choice but to move or become assimilated. Languages were part of this ecological package, and native varieties were driven out. The difference between this wave and the earlier one was that the earlier one had at least created new diversity, as spreading farmers fragmented into local groups. The expanding Europeans, by contrast, were tied together by modern communications, writing, and states to such an extent that theirs was a wave which remained largely homogeneous.

Like the Neolithic waves, the European expansions were ultimately constrained by geography and ecology. As Alfred Crosby has shown, the European system expanded best into areas which were like Europe itself, with temperate climates to suit the European suite of species. They also had to be reasonably empty; Asia, with the vast Chinese and Indian populations already there practicing intensive farming, was not an option. Moist equatorial climates, with no summer-winter cycle, did not favor European agriculture. In these areas, the European immune system had the same trick worked on it that it worked on Native Americans. Attempts to settle the "white man's graves" of tropical Africa and the Pacific were attended with huge mortality rates; half the Englishmen sent to West Africa in the eighteenth century, for example, died within a year. The only exception was temperate South Africa, more hospitable to Europeans than the rest of its continent, where a sizeable presence was established by the Dutch and British. It could never spread, however, into the tropical environment above it.

Thus it is that there are populations of European descent in Australia but not New Guinea, South Africa but not Zaire, and more white faces in Argentina than Ecuador. The European expansions created "neo-Europes," with primarily European peoples, landscapes of European crops and animals, and, of course European languages. These neo-Europes were mainly around the latitudes of Europe itself, on either side of the equator. They could not cover the whole world.

By the end of the nineteenth century there was a sharp division between the Eurasian environment, now extended to cover most of the Americas, Australia, New Zealand, and South Africa, and the "untouched world." The untouched world covered tropical Africa, the Southeast Asian islands, New Guinea, some of the Pacific islands, and a few other tropical refuges. In these places, the spreading Eurasian giant languages had almost no toehold. Trading posts and even political domination had been established, but these were of a completely different character from the European occupation of the neo-Europes. The demographic and agricultural impacts were minimal, and to a large extent, the traditional linguistic equilibrium still reigned.

As it happened, the untouched world also contained a large fraction of the world's linguistic diversity—perhaps two-thirds of all languages. As European expansion slowed, it seemed that these areas might be safe. But this is not so. Another kind of process, following hard on the biological wave, is now spreading giant languages into new territory: we call this the economic wave.

Six

The Economic Wave

The [Native American] tragedy illustrates the larger dilemma of modernization: change or lose; change and lose.

—David Landes

We have seen how European populations, their crops, and their languages have replaced indigenous peoples in most of the New World, Australia, and New Zealand over the last five hundred years. We also saw that this expansionary wave was ultimately limited by geography. Most of non-European Eurasia was already full of

dense farming populations. The moist tropics were unhealthy and difficult for Europeans to colonize. Thus these areas do not have major populations of European descent, and Europeans, whose population is now
stable or declining, are no longer expanding their geographical range.

We might assume that the remaining indigenous languages of the rest
of the world—Africa and the tropical Pacific, for example, both rich in
linguistic diversity—are safe from encroaching domination. However, a
glance at the language situations of these areas shows that this is not so,
for there are many examples of shifts to dominant languages which occur
without a corresponding movement of people.

Consider again the villagers of Gapun, Papua New Guinea. When
Don Kulick studied the village a shift was underway from Taiap, the traditional vernacular, to Tok Pisin which is one of Papua New Guinea's
national languages. This shift was not occuring because Gapun was
being overrun by land-hungry Europeans, or even land-hungry people
from another part of New Guinea. Nor was it the case that the people of
the village were dying out, or moving away. Indeed, their subsistence
occupations and lifestyles were at that time relatively unchanged.

What was changing was something much less concrete and less easily
observable, but equally powerful. People had come to associate Tok Pisin
with the economic possiblities of the modern world, which seemed to
them fantastically attractive. By shifting their language, they were
attempting to gain symbolic association with, and entry into, the sphere
of the developed economy, much in the same way that young women in
Oberwart, Austria chose German over Hungarian because they perceived
the former to be of greater economic value. For Gapuners, this economy
is as yet a mere idea, something they encounter through occasional visits
to towns (several days distant by canoe), through migrants and the things
they bring back, and through information which filters back to them. Yet
it seems this idea is powerful enough to cause a change in language use. In
less isolated parts of Papua New Guinea, people see English as the language which will secure their economic future. In remote Gapun, however, English plays almost no role in villagers' perception of development,
and Tok Pisin is the expanding language.

As another example, we could take a small European language like
Cornish. Cornish was once the thriving language of the southwest of
England, but since the seventeenth century, it has scarcely been spoken.
This is not because the Cornish people died out or were displaced. On
the contrary, they stayed in their traditional habitat and boomed in number, but gradually adopted a different language—English—to the exclusion of their original one. Much contemporary language loss has more in
common with the Cornish or Taiap cases than that of the Brazilian Indians, who were wiped out by disease, or the Tasmanians, who were exterminated by genocide. This is clearly a different process—a subtle shift of

language that happens while the people remain constant, rather than an expansion of people spreading their language as they go.

Language shift of this kind is not a biological transition in quite the same way as the European colonizers brought about. If there were a biological analogy it would be this: rather than a suite of species from the core (people, crops, livestock, diseases) spreading to the periphery, the indigenous species of the periphery stay where they are, but take on some of the characteristics of the species of the core. Such a process is not found in species other than our own, since it is a product of our almost unique ability to transmit norms and practices culturally.

The process that took Cornish and appears to be taking Taiap is distinct from that described in the previous chapter, and must be separately explained. It began in the present millennium and has spread a few large languages over vast areas—most obviously, but by no means exclusively, European ones. Like the biological expansion, it has produced a wavelike motion, and the forward momentum of the wave is a product of different levels of power of the people in front of and behind it. In the biological case, those behind the wave had ecological power, greater numbers, a better suite of crops and livestock, greater population growth rates, and, above all, greater disease resistance. This power pushed them forward, and pushed those on the other side of the wave back into oblivion.

In the language shift case, the power differential is different, though related. What pushed English into the Celtic-speaking areas, and Tok Pisin into Gapun village, was primarily an economic advantage that allowed speakers of the metropolitan language not just to dominate the economic game, but to define the very rules by which it was played.

The rise to dominance

The difference between English and Cornish, or between Tok Pisin and Taiap, may be captured by the opposing terms *metropolitan* and *peripheral*. Metropolitan languages are associated with a dominant economic or social class, such as the English in industrializing Britain, or the urban elite in any developing country. They are also associated with economically leading central places such as London or Port Moresby. Peripheral languages, by contrast, are restricted to economically less developed areas, and also to a smaller range of economic roles and functions. For example, English is used in international finance, aviation, computing, religious texts, television, the international legal system, and many other domains. Compare this with the scope of a small tongue such as the Nigerian language Hórom. Hórom is used by a small, fairly autonomous community whose only major economic activity is farming. If people from Hórom wish or are obliged to take on economic roles in any other domain, such as teaching, organized religion, long-distance trade, or the law, they are obliged to use another language in which to express themselves. On the other hand, English is used in many parts of the world by farmers. There is thus an asymmetry between the set of roles available to English and to Hórom speakers; the former include all the latter and add many more. In this sense, Hórom is peripheral and English, Nigeria's national language, is metropolitan.

As we explained in Chapter 2, when we introduced the idea of layers of diglossia, the metropolitan/peripheral distinction is a relational one, and a language that is metropolitan in one context is peripheral in another. Many schools in Kenya and Tanzania, for example, use Swahili as the language of instruction, so people from other ethnic groups wishing to reach a certain educational level must adopt Swahili. Swahili is thus metropolitan compared to, say, Maa, the language of the Maasai herders. However, in university level education, English is essential because so much of the available printed material is in English. Swahili is thus peripheral to English at this level.

It is crucial to stress again that there is no intrinsic attribute of any language which makes it metropolitan or peripheral. Tuyuca, as we saw in Chapter 3, would offer certain advantages as a medium for legal proceedings, but it is never used for this function, just as Hórom and Taiap have never been developed as languages of education and science. Any language can in fact be turned to any purpose, perhaps by the simple incorporation of a few new words. What determines peripherality, then, is not the language itself, but differences in the economies and societies of the people who speak it.

Europe and North America clearly have a kind of global centrality that makes everywhere else peripheral. At a more local scale, almost every country has its cores and peripheries, and at the boundaries of almost all of these, peripheral languages are on the retreat. We must therefore ask where core-periphery inequalities come from.

Such inequalities have been present in incipient form for several millennia. Large states and empires began to be established in the fourth millennium BC in Western Eurasia, in the second millennium BC in China, and somewhat later in Africa and the Americas. When this happened, the ruling classes would often manage to extend their dominions to encompass peoples speaking several languages. Within such empires, the metropolitan language-peripheral language distinction was already present.

The metropolitan languages were the languages of central places and of elite classes. Local, egalitarian bilingualism, of the type we saw in Papua New Guinea, had always been common. The rise of metropolitan languages meant a slightly new type of bilingualism in which people had radically different economic roles: not equal, like two groups of forest foragers, and not complementary, like a coastal gatherer meeting an inland hunter, but in which the prospects of one party were a superset of the prospects of the other. Of course, it would be foolish to claim that there had been no power differentials between adjacent societies in earlier phases of human history. There would have been local dominance, and indeed local shifts of language reflecting it, but the rise of politically complex societies with large numbers of people radically increased the sizes of such disparities.

We have traced the opposition between metropolitan and peripheral languages back to the origin of multiethnic state societies as much as five thousand years ago. However, this does not mean that peripheral languages have been retreating for five thousand years. In epochs prior to the present one, peripheral vernaculars seem to have shown a great degree of resilience. Two factors explain why this is so.

First, for ordinary people, the need for local community solidarity has still been the primary one, whatever the political situation. Secondly, the integration of cores and peripheries has until recently been rather limited. All over the preindustrial world, the percentage of the population in nonagricultural activity remained low until the present era, usually less than 10 percent, and despite the splendor of many elite constructions—one thinks of the Pyramids—no appreciable economic development for ordinary people followed from their participation in the state economy. Their interaction with the elite would be limited for the most part to an occasional extraction of tribute, and perhaps sporadic fighting or laboring. There was often need for interface groups between farmers and elites, or local headmen, servants, and tradesmen, and these people would have had to be bilingual. These groups remained quite small, however, and the mobility between the classes was extremely limited. Being subsumed under one empire or another thus made little difference to everyday communication in the country. At most it made people add a new dimension to their repertoire—the regional lingua franca—but they did not lose the vernacular.

Not only did elite classes fail to change the tongue of their subjects, but they sometimes even lost their own. This was the case with the Fulani overlords in West Africa and, closer to home, the Norman aristocracy in England, to give but two examples. Thus, in what remained a rural economy operating near to the level of subsistence, elites were rarely influential enough to cause language loss among their subjects. The few obvious exceptions to this pattern include the Roman Empire, which succeeded in Romanizing parts of Southern Europe, and perhaps China, where the prolonged dominance of Mandarin has led to great uniformity in writing, if not quite in speech.

The situation is very different today. Metropolitan languages are advancing staggeringly fast, at the expense of peripheral ones, almost everywhere in the world. The event that has tipped the balance, we believe, has been economic takeoff, which has occurred this millennium in a few of the world's societies. Like the origins of agriculture, this is another great singularity in world history. Having shown no sign of happening for the first twenty-three hours of the human day, it has happened in the last twenty minutes in such a revolutionary and uneven way that the shock waves are now resounding through the world's languages.

Economic takeoff

The transformation of the economies in the developed world over the last few hundred years is a remarkable one. Societies have produced surpluses of goods ever since the Neolithic era, but those surpluses tended to be consumed by small elites in ultimately fruitless ways. The elites never constituted more than a tiny percentage of the population, and for the great majority, there was a limited choice of economic roles. Life expectancies remained low, and though incomes fluctuated with the seasons and years, they had no general tendency to rise.

By the end of the industrial revolution—which took place mainly in Europe during the present millennium—the picture in the developed economies was quite different. Enormous gains in productivity had released many people from the land into a far greater diversity of occupations. Surpluses were shared far more widely and contributed to radically improved housing and nutrition, which gave rise to unprecedented life expectancies. New technologies were developed at an ever-accelerating rate. Above all, the long-term expectation for most people (though still not all) had been changed from stasis to growth in real incomes and opportunities.

Exactly how this transformation can be explained is still a subject of controversy among economists. Certainly, the dense population of Europe is a factor, since populousness encourages economic specialization and intensification. However, both India and China were far more densely populated than Europe, and failed to undergo the transformation. Other conditions must therefore be necessary. Competition between Europe's many small states may have been a beneficial stimulant, in marked contrast to the monolithic hand of the state in China. Stability is also important: though Europe continued to suffer devastating and destructive famines and disasters well into the nineteenth century, these may have been less marked than in Asia, allowing greater long-term investment and accumulation. Finally, we must not discount the huge flows of capital into Europe after 1500 from the newly exploited colonies overseas. This flow had implications for both parties: it swelled the coffers of the metropolitan areas, while making the peripheries ever more dependent economically. Masses of people and resources were thus caught up in a social, political, and economic cycle which was remaking the entire world.

There are two sides to the coin of economic takeoff and both will be important in understanding its effect on the fate of languages. On the one hand, the developed economies have a strong pull factor, offering as they do the apparent possibility of wonderful new technologies, more profitable occupations, and a rising standard of living. On the other hand, economic takeoff gives the elite classes extraordinary power, by furnishing them with ever-better weapons, larger armies, and many other technologies for controlling and brainwashing people. Such elites have a strong interest in compelling people to join their sphere of economic interest — a larger sphere of interest means more profits — and they often do so. This "push" factor is just as significant as the intrinsic "pull" of economic development in understanding subsequent history. Indeed, one must not forget that improving people's standard of living was not the motive force in economic takeoff. Such improvements were an unpredictable and incidental side effect. The engine driving growth forward was blind, dumb competition between capitalists for economic power. Economic takeoff was thus no more noble of motive or sublime in its genius than the origin of agriculture. Rather, an age-old pattern of human interaction, when played out in geographical circumstances which happened to be right, brought about an unforeseen transformation.

We are prone to equate economic takeoff with the Industrial Revolution of the eighteenth and nineteenth centuries. In fact, the economic growth trajectory had been transformed much earlier, probably around AD 1000. At that time, in the metropolitan economies of Europe, there was an increase in agricultural productivity, investment in technologies such as water- and windmills, and increasing market participation and economic specialization. With the end of feudalism and the emergence of efficient labor markets in the late Middle Ages, the capitalist economy was essentially in place. By the fourteenth century, almost 15 percent of the population in France, Britain, and Germany had risen above peasant status and did not work the land. This percentage is roughly the same in Papua New Guinea even today, and in China was as low as 2 percent in the 1880s. The general trajectory of the European economy, whether measured by incomes or by quality of life indicators, shows a jerky but sustained increase over nearly a millennium to the present day.

The great transformation occurred in a spatially uneven way. Most obviously, it happened within Europe but nowhere else, at least initially. Even within Europe, a few metropoles — southern England being a good example — passed the watershed while their neighbors languished, and it is this inequality of development that was one of the conditions for the resulting wave of language loss.

Economic takeoff vastly heightened the differentials between metropolitan and peripheral languages. The metropolitan economies did not just take surplus to prop up small elites; they were able to offer a variety of new economic roles and opportunities, an expectation of higher living standards, and impressive technologies of production and control. Thus began in earnest a process that we now see on every continent. Those around the margins of the metropolitan economy began to be sucked in, adopting its money, its terms of trade, and—crucially for our purposes—its language, undermining the economy and language of the periphery. Whether this process should best be seen as one of free choice ("pull" factors) or one of coercion ("push" factors) is a complex question. There is no escaping the fact, however, that what drove seventeenth-century Cornishmen to adopt English is the very same phenomenon driving the people of Gapun to Tok Pisin today: the huge difference in economic power of the metropolitan and peripheral societies.

First casualties: the Celtic languages

The Celtic languages were once spoken in much of Europe, and on the eve of economic takeoff, they still dominated Ireland, western Britain and northwest France. Welsh was spoken not only throughout present-day Wales but in the English counties of Herefordshire, Gloucestershire, and Shropshire as well. Irish had been expanding militantly, a splinter from it having colonized western Scotland. This splinter would give rise to the Scots Gaelic language. The Irish language had been enjoying a golden age of scholarship and literature, rooted in numerous monasteries. Celtic tongues were also spoken throughout Cornwall, the Isle of Man, Brittany, and the northern tip of England.

Over the next nine hundred years or so, all the Celtic languages were gradually pushed backward as English and French advanced. Cumbric, which was spoken in northern England and is now known to us only by its distinctive numerals, was already gone by perhaps the early twelfth century. The retreat of Cornish seems to have begun as early as AD 1000, when its domain was nearly one hundred miles long. By 1700, there were only around 5,000 Cornish speakers, clustered around Penzance at the very toe of England. The last known native speaker, Dolly Pentreath, died in 1777. The date of her birth is unknown; she was probably in her late eighties, though she sometimes claimed to have been over a hundred, and it is said she learned no English until she was twenty.

Manx, spoken for 1,500 years on the island midway between Scotland and Ireland, was already coexisting with English there by the seventeenth century. It too retreated in the face of its larger rival. It held on longer among the peasantry than the upper classes, and longer in the

Figure 6.1   Map of the Celtic countries

[*Reprinted from Maryon McDonald,* We Are Not French. *Routledge, 1989, p. 323*]

country than the town, but by the second half of the nineteenth century it was clearly moribund. There followed the long twilight typical of moribund languages, as the last cohort of speakers grows old and dies. The last native speaker, Ned Maddrell, died in 1974 at the age of 97, having watched nearly a century of cultural shift go on around him.

Scots Gaelic disappeared from the southern lowlands of Scotland as early as the year 1400, or perhaps before. It persisted in the holds of the highlands and islands, but here too it has given way over the last two centuries. In 1891 it could still muster some quarter of a million speakers. By 1971 this had declined to less than eighty thousand, all situated in the remoter parts of the north and west, with a few tiny pockets along the east coast of Sutherland.

*Figure 6.2   The grave of Dolly
Pentreath, last speaker of
Cornish.*

*[Courtesy of St. Pol-de-Léon Parish
Council, Paul, Penzance, Cornwall]*

Irish Gaelic was unchallenged as the language of ordinary people in
the island of Ireland before the seventeenth century. English was
restricted to a small enclave on the eastern seaboard ("the pale"), and all
beyond the pale was Irish-speaking. Settlements in the seventeenth century established English-speaking colonies (mainly of lowlands Scots,
whose forefathers had shifted to English from the other branch of Gaelic
a few generations earlier) in the northeast of the island. From around
1800, a spectacular linguistic collapse began pushing the Irish language
back toward the peninsulas and islands of the western and southwestern
seaboards, into narrow glens, and up the sides of mountains. By the first
detailed census in 1851, Irish was nearly absent from the eastern half of
the country and was losing ground everywhere except the far western tip.
The number of speakers declined from 1.5 million in 1861 to around
600,000 in 1901. It has stayed at around this level ever since, now supported by the state in the independent Republic of Ireland, and widely
taught in schools as a second language to those whose native language
has long been English, but gaining no ground as a mother tongue.

Welsh, for its part, lost its eastern flank fairly early, but held on firmly
as the language of the principality into and through the nineteenth cen-

tury. By 1901, half of the population of present-day Wales spoke Welsh (with 15 percent speaking no English). Over the next seventy years, a catastrophic collapse was to follow. The 1971 census shows just 20 percent of the population speaking Welsh, mainly restricted to the far west. The trajectory of decline has slowed and even reversed since then; even at its nadir, Welsh had half a million speakers. It is unquestionably in the strongest position of any Celtic language today.

Finally, Breton, in northwest France, shows a pattern of retreat similar to its sister languages. French censuses do not record matters of language, but it is clear that the French-Breton frontier was moving westward by the thirteenth century and that the present Breton-speaking communities are huddled on the very extremity of their peninsula (Figure 6.3).

Why, then, have we seen this sustained movement of the metropolitan-Celtic frontier over nearly a thousand years? And why always in the same direction, west or north, away from the main economic centers and into the sea and oblivion? What seems clear is that there has been a pattern of asymmetry in language transmission which has endured for the whole period and is found in the several Celtic areas. Where a parental generation was monolingual in the Celtic language but near to the English (or French) frontier, the children tended to become bilingual. Where the parents were bilingual, the children tended to become monolingual in the dominant language. This is the classic three-generational pattern of language shift that imperceptibly makes children strangers to their own grandparents: generation 1 is monolingual Welsh, generation 2 is bilingual, and generation 3 is monolingual English. The process can sometimes stretch out over more generations, with the bilingual phase longer and more gradual, but the end point is almost always the same.

When the three-generational pattern is played out in space and time, a moving frontier is created. Monolingual communities on the edge become first bilingual and then monolingual in the invading language; their neighbors to the west then acquire bilingualism from them, then their neighbors in turn, and so on. The result is a slow but implacable cultural wave, moving steadily west over the decades, lasting longer than any one life span, and in which each generation plays only a small part. As long as the bias to acquire English persists, so will the wavelike movement, and the fate of Celtic shows that such a bias was a persistent fact of life. We chose to illustrate Cornish and Breton in Figure 6.3, but we could have chosen any Celtic language (or indeed, many others elsewhere) to see the same pattern.

The wave was not uniform; towns were always ahead of the country, as the metropolitan way of life penetrated them first, and pockets of greater and lesser resistance made the linguistic map a complex mosaic; however, the overall trend was seldom reversed. Today, no Celtic language has secured a major urban area in which it is predominant. The

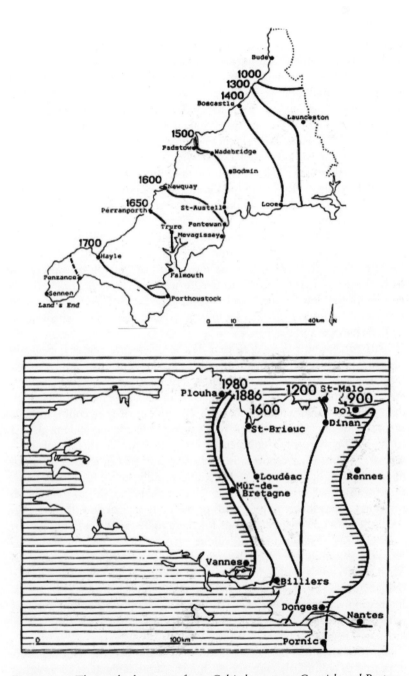

Figure 6.3   The gradual retreat of two Celtic languages: Cornish and Breton

[Adapted from Hervé Abalain, Destin des Langues Celtiques. Paris: Ophrys, 1989, pp. 170 and 205]

Isle of Lewis in the Hebrides is the major stronghold of Scottish Gaelic with over 85 percent of the population speaking the language. However, Stornoway, its capital, is in no sense a Gaelic town. In effect, this means that Gaelic does not claim a town of even 12,000. The same is true of Welsh, Irish, and Breton. These languages also show an uneven social distribution. Agricultural workers and manual laborers provide the numerical stronghold for Scottish Gaelic much as they do in Ireland (and Brittany), while English (or French) monolingualism is associated with the white collar and professional classes.

How is this greater propensity to acquire English to be explained? The metropolitan economy certainly offered roles, opportunities, and prestige that the Celtic economies could not muster; the young and ambitious would either migrate east to work or orient their production toward the center, like the Cornish who took up tin mining and the Welsh during and after the industrial revolution. English was certainly perceived in many cases as the language of the future and of possible advancement, while the vernacular according to Gregor was "rustic, stagnant . . . familiar, emotional, and comic," and "synonymous with poverty and social inferiority." Children flocked to English role models, often encouraged by their parents and teachers to do so.

This perception ran so deep that by the nineteenth century, it was in some areas difficult to persuade people to accept education in the vernacular. The Edinburgh Gaelic School society reported in 1839 that "it is difficult to convince [the parents] that it can be any benefit to their children to learn Gaelic, though they are all anxious, if they could, to have them taught English." In Wales, too, some parents deliberately neglected to speak Welsh to their children in order to improve their English. A school commissioner reported in 1847 that any school teacher attempting to conduct his school in Welsh would rapidly starve for want of customers. Another commissioner concluded that "so far as the Welsh peasantry interest themselves at all in the daily instruction of their children, they are everywhere anxious for them to be taught in English."

There was certainly a real economic basis to the perception of the differential possibilities of the metropolitan and peripheral languages. Michael Hechter's studies have shown a significant and persistent gap in real incomes and possibilities between the English and Celtic zones. Interestingly, it was only in the late twentieth century, when this gap was narrowed and nearly closed, that any stabilization or revival of the Celtic languages began.

Our discussion so far has stressed the extent to which Celtic speakers appeared to voluntarily embrace the metropolitan language as a passport to social and economic advancement. Should we, then, see the decline of Celtic as the consequence of benign free choice, of real progress and economic development? We do not believe the picture is so simple.

There are, as we have stressed, two sides to the coin of economic take-off. On the one hand, it provides new economic opportunities for ordinary people; but on the other, it allows elite castes unprecedented opportunity for domination by providing them with technologies and institutions that they can use to promote their own influence and control. We must not forget that all the Celtic-speaking areas came under metropolitan political and military dominance early in the process of language shift. Cornwall was incorporated into Wessex by AD 802; Wales was annexed in 1536; the Union of Scotland was achieved in 1701 after prolonged hostilities and with the complicity of the Scottish aristocracy; and Ireland was formally absorbed into the kingdom in 1801. In all cases, English elites seized the commanding positions of the social and economic heap more or less by force, and diverted economic production to the advantage of themselves and their own kind. This was important because it meant that young Celts were deprived of positive models of economic and social success who came from within their own speech communities. Indeed, both the English and the French went to some lengths to ensure that no such models existed. Here we see symbolic domination accompanying political and economic domination.

Nonelected elites are generally interested in enhancing their own spheres of influence and control, rather than meeting the desires of their people. As such, the English and French were hostile to any form of indigenous social organization or power, and perceived the vernacular languages as dangerous expressions of just this kind. Over the hundreds of years of political domination, they consistently enacted policies which directly or indirectly sought to undermine the positions of the languages and force people into the mainstream society where they could be better controlled.

Examples of such policies are not hard to find. The penal laws of Henry IV, in force in Wales through the fifteenth century, specifically denigrated Welsh speakers and debarred them from economic or social progress. The laws included the following provisions: In the border areas, Welshmen were forbidden to acquire lands; if stolen goods from a border town were not recovered in one week, residents could retaliate against any Welshman they could seize; Welshmen were prohibited from acquiring lands within boroughs, nor could they hold any municipal offices; Welshmen were forbidden from the carrying of arms, the fortification of any house, or the holding of responsible office in the service of any English lord; Welshmen were denied freedom of assembly without special permit.

The Act of Union of 1536 specifically prohibited Welsh speakers from holding office, and imposed English judges and the English church. No policy could have been better calculated to undermine the social basis for the transmission of the vernacular language.

Similar policies were pursued in Scotland and Ireland. Henry VIII attempted to assimilate the Irish directly with his Act for the English

Order, Habit and Language, which began by claiming that there was "nothing which does more contain and keep many of his subjects in a certain savage and wild kind and manner of living than the diversity that is betwixt them in tongue, language, order and habit." The act thus decreed that the Irish "to the utmost of their power, cunning and knowledge, shall use and speak commonly the English tongue and language." The clergy were obliged to see that English be imposed in religion and schools in the furtherance of this aim. The coup de grace for Irish, three hundred years later, was economic rather than political, with the collapse of agricultural society in the west of the country and massive migration to areas where Irish was not known.

In Scotland, James VI (of Scotland; in England he was James I) tried to undermine indigenous social organization by imposing Anglophone churches, outlawing the bards, and forcing clan chiefs to send their children to the lowlands for an English education. All high-status indigenous role models were thus suppressed, paving the way for anglicization. The same king's Act for the Settling of Parochial Schools of 1616 was quite explicit that this was the aim, indicating that it was desired that "the vulgar English tongue be universally planted, and the Irish language, which is one of the chief and principal causes of the continuance of barbarity and incivility amongst the inhabitants of the Isles and Highlands, may be abolished and removed."

Attitudes and policies such as these continued into surprisingly recent times. In 1846, government education commissioners attacked the Welsh language as a "disastrous barrier to all moral improvement and popular progress in Wales," and claimed that it "distorts the truth, favours fraud and abets perjury." In nineteenth-century schools, pupils who were caught speaking Welsh were forced to wear a wooden badge called the "Welsh Not." The wearer was in turn allowed to transfer the badge to any of his or her peers overheard speaking Welsh, and so it passed from child to child. At the end of the week, whoever had it in his possession was punished by flogging. The practice of the Welsh Not largely disappeared in the 1880s, though in some areas it persisted into the twentieth century.

The French campaign against Breton was even more determined, and was sustained until even more recently. The revolution of 1789 had stressed the need for a national language for the united and indivisible republic it envisioned. The committee on public education quickly advocated the removal of France's regional languages by stating that "it is more important that you politicians realise to extirpate this diversity of vile dialects, which prolong the childhood of the mind and the old age of prejudice."

Local education officers thenceforth insisted, well into the post-war period of the present century, that "it is absolutely necessary that we destroy the Breton language." Newly appointed junior school teachers in

Figure 6.4   The Welsh Not

[Courtesy of The Museum of Welsh Life, St. Fagans]

Brittany were left in no doubt as to their task: "Above all remember, gentlemen, that you are here for no other reason than to destroy the Breton language"; and, later, "We need French people to make them French, they won't do it for themselves." As recently as the 1970s, France refused birth certificates and identity cards to children with Breton names. It is only in the last thirty years that any concession has been made to Breton, and even that is in most cases largely rhetorical.

The Celtic languages were systematically undermined in an attempt to bring their speakers into cultural and political compliance. When this process was frustrated the metropolitan elites were quite prepared to forcibly remove them and replace them with an amenable work force—as when the north of Ireland was forcibly settled by anglicized peasants from the mainland, or in the clearances of the Scottish highlands in the 1800s in which Gaelic speakers were brutally evicted from their lands and forced north, west, and east to more marginal areas.

On closer examination, it seems that while the speakers of Celtic languages, when faced with the conscious or subconscious choice between the metropolitan and peripheral language, did often favor the metropolitan, this can hardly be called a free or benign choice. Like the Hawaiians whose case we examined earlier, they were choosing within a framework defined and overcast by systematic political and cultural domination. It is not surprising that by the nineteenth and twentieth centuries many people wanted little association with their past, given the institutions which had been working to alienate them from it. What is surprising is not that many people chose to abandon the Celtic languages, but that so many people chose for so long to maintain them in the face of enormous external degradation and policies designed to forcibly assimilate both the peoples and their languages.

Within Europe itself there were disparities in status and development similar to those between Europe and its overseas colonies. Europeans who belonged to the ruling elites in their respective countries looked down upon the various minorities within their borders and spoke of them in terms of contempt. Lord Salisbury, a Conservative leader in the late nineteenth century, said that the Irish were as unfit for self-government as the Hottentots. At least one sociologist has pointed out that the British occupation of Ireland for four centuries was certainly as "imperialistic as anything the great powers have done anywhere in the world; and if the word *genocide* cannot be applied to British policy in Ireland, then it has little legitimate use." As early as the fourteenth century Scotland was described in similar terms of two opposing peoples. In his 1387 account of Scotland, John of Fordun depicts the Lowlanders (of Anglo-Saxon origin) as being "of domestic and civilised habits, trusty, patient, and urbane, decent in their attire, affable and peaceful." The Gaels, however, are characterized as a "savage and untamed nation, rude and independent, given to rapine, ease-loving . . . hostile to the English people and language . . . [and] exceedingly cruel." These attitudes were used to justify the Highland Clearances of 1800–1850: the forcible evictions of tenants, referred to euphemistically as "improvements." One historian drew an analogy between the fate of the Scottish highlanders and Australian aborigines in describing how the population was removed very much against their will from lands their ancestors had cultivated from time immemorial, without right of redress or appeal.

The dictum that people make history, but not under conditions of their own choosing, has never been more true than in the case of these languages. People did choose English, repeatedly and consistently, but did not themselves generate the conditions under which they had to choose. Clearly, the Celtic territories were always going to be attracted to the incidental benefits of the economic takeoff that was going on in the neighboring economy, but had a more equitable political system been in place it is far from obvious that the linguistic decline would have happened. Where significant use of the Celtic languages was allowed to develop in religion and particularly in education, the tide was stemmed. This factor may partly account for the better position of Welsh than its sister languages today.

Indeed, now that a more accountable political system has evolved alongside a reduction in the economic disparities between the European core and the Celtic fringe, the resurgence of interest in the languages has been striking. Unfortunately, only Welsh, and possibly Breton, retain the demographic strength to really exploit this upsurge.

The relative contributions of the pull of economic advancement and the push of political domination varied at different times and between the different Celtic languages. Celtic speakers were seldom allowed the autonomy to generate their own institutions, however. The Celtic case—the first of many cases of tongues threatened with submergence by the economic wave—is one from which many lessons are to be learned.

The spread to the developing world

The dynamic we have just described for the Celtic languages is a complex one. Members of an economically powerful metropolitan society seized the controlling heights of economic production and social influence in peripheral societies, and a shift of language followed this asymmetry. The same dynamic has been a persistent feature of the last few hundred years of history not just in Europe but across the globe, as the shock waves of the hugely uneven course of economic development have made themselves felt.

The larger western European societies and their former colonial outposts have, by virtue of their early industrialization and technological lead, been the main winners in this process. Thus, smaller languages like Livonian, Saami, and Basque have lost ground to their larger neighbors. Russian has pushed back many of more than two hundred indigenous languages of the former Soviet Union, many of whose names, like Circassian and Tartar, recall earlier phases of our history when the geography of power was quite different. There too, a "melting pot" ideology played a critical role. One of the widespread beliefs of communism was that there would never be any ethnic or linguistic conflicts between nations and ethnic groups and the central government once the "national question" had been solved once and for all by assimilation.

The metropolitan expansion in Europe has not stopped at the continent's boundaries. European powers were able to take effective control of large parts of Asia and the Pacific, and almost all of tropical Africa, for much of the last few hundred years without any sustained settlement of those regions, merely by implanting a small but extremely powerful metropolitan caste. That caste also made its language—though demographically insignificant—the key to the gateway to positions of influence and affluence. Thus English, French, and Spanish are still the languages of government, industry, and the law in almost all the countries of Africa, the Americas, the Caribbean, and in parts of South and Southeast Asia. The role played by language in England's changing conceptions of itself can be seen in both the construction of a glorious past for the language as well as in ever increasing prognostications of a bright future as world language. English, like England, was to have its conquests. As Dean Trench wrote in 1855, "What can more clearly point out our ancestors' native land and ours as having fulfilled a glorious past, as being destined for a glorious future, than that they should have acquired for themselves and for those who came after a clear, a strong, a harmonious, a noble language?"

The period since the second world war has seen the decolonization of large parts of the world. However, the cultural division of labor that began under colonialism still persists. The elites of the newly independent countries were in general raised to their positions through the colonial system. They were highly westernized, and generally users of the Western languages. Furthermore, the political framework of colonialism was never undone. Colonially imposed national boundaries are still in place; colonial bureaucracies, education systems, and institutions are unaltered, though now controlled by an indigenous rather than a colonizing elite. Furthermore, the economies of many developing countries are still controlled by the same interests, living on in scarcely changed guises.

These factors have meant that the linguistic structure of colonialism has seldom been undone. The colonial languages English and French, for example, have scarcely been challenged as the languages of power and aspiration in Africa, and their spread is leading to the top-down displacement of numerous other tongues.

In countries where English, French, or Spanish have not themselves taken up the dominant position, one local language has often managed to achieve vicarious metropolitan status. This is usually that most associated with the colonial or post-colonial elite, found in the capital or used by the army, or otherwise able to muster greater influence. Each of these locally dominant languages has started in its own area the battle which went on between English and Celtic in Britain three hundred years earlier. Thus, Thai in Thailand is encroaching on small languages like Ugong. Bahasa Malaysia and Bahasa Indonesia, which are the national languages of their respective countries, are rampant in Peninsula and Island Southeast Asia. Tagalog or Pilipino has the same role in the Philippines. Tok Pisin, the English-based Creole which is the most widespread language in Papua New Guinea, threatens Taiap and countless other vernaculars.

In India, English retains its place as a key official language alongside Hindi, which is the vernacular of the Delhi area. Fourteen other languages have obtained official status in their respective states, making Indian democracy the most multilingual administration in history. But even this great concession to local expression scarcely scratches the surface of the subcontinent's diversity. The 850 million inhabitants of India belong to at least 1,700 historic communities, sharing around 405 living languages among them.

In Africa, English and French have had great influence, but there are other languages which are locally dominant. The Bantu language Swahili threatens many smaller languages such as Zaremo in Tanzania and Alagwa in Kenya. In Nigeria, the Chadic language Hausa overshadows languages such as Fyem, Hórom, and Anaguta.

All over the world, then, a few languages have made themselves metropolitan by being lucky or powerful enough to become associated with economically powerful groups. Other languages have been consigned to peripheral status, and their speakers have often faced up to a stark choice between retaining their traditional identity and seeking to get on in the world.

Surveying this recurrent scene, the same question always arises. Is it not a good thing that people are joining the mainstream of the metropolitan economy? Isn't it progress that ever-larger groups of people can speak English, French, or a few other international languages? And if people want to give up their language, is not that their sovereign choice?

Here the lessons of the Celtic case might be recalled. People did often choose to give up their mother tongues, but the circumstances under which they did so were rarely what could be called free, and it is far from clear that the decline would have been inevitable under a more equitable political system. The same conclusion can be transferred to the modern developing-world cases.

Linguist Peter Ladefoged has pointed out that many members of small Kenyan communities such as the Dahalo are proud that their children will speak the national language, Swahili, and feel that this provides them with promising future prospects in that developing nation. For the moment, at least, they see this as a positive change that outweighs any regret at the loss of their tribal languages. Furthermore, people in these groups are not under any obvious coercion to switch their language. It appears to be more of a free choice.

Even if his interpretation were accepted, for every case of the kind Ladefoged describes there are plenty that are less benign. One can hardly call the decline of the Timorese languages voluntary. In twenty-five years of bloody occupation, the Indonesian invaders of East Timor have killed one-third of the population. All indigenous forms of social organization have been ruthlessly suppressed—including the languages, which are banned. The choice not to uphold one's traditions under these circumstances is hardly a free one. Nor was it a freer one for the indigenous inhabitants of El Salvador after many of those identifiable as Indian were exterminated in the massacres of 1932.

Another striking example is that of the Kurds, one of the oldest peoples in the Middle East. There are somewhere between 5 and 10 million speakers of Kurdish, a language spoken in Iraq, Iran, Turkey, Syria, and parts of the former Soviet Union. One of the largest groups lives in Turkey, where they account for close to one-fifth of the country's population. Yet the Turkish census does not count Kurds because the government denies their very existence. Kurds have been sent to prison even for saying they were Kurds, and the Kurdish language is banned. Insofar as the Turkish government takes any official notice of Kurds at all, they refer to them as "mountain Turks." Consider these chilling extracts from the testimony of Esref Okumus, a Kurdish journalist working in Sweden, who testified at a conference on minority rights in Copenhagen in 1990:

> As a Kurd in Turkey you are born in a village or a town the name of which is not valid, because names of nearly all Kurdish villages and towns I know are today changed into Turkish.
>
> If your parents wish to give you a Kurdish name, your name will not be registered by the authorities. It will be changed into Turkish. If your parents still insist to keep your Kurdish name, they will be prosecuted . . .
>
> When you . . . go to school, you won't be able to communicate with your teachers . . . if you . . . have parents who do not speak Turkish.
>
> . . . you are not allowed to claim that your mother tongue is Kurdish. The third section of law no. 2932 tells you what your mother tongue is: "The mother tongue of Turkish citizens is Turkish." You are not allowed to speak Kurdish in public places . . . you can be sentenced to a maximum of two years of imprisonment. . . .
>
> If you "build or attempt to build an association" to strengthen your culture and language, you can be sentenced to a maximum of 15 years of imprisonment. . . .
>
> Thousands of Kurds have been sentenced according to these laws. If you try to explain this situation abroad, exactly as I am doing at this moment, you can be sentenced to 10 years of imprisonment for "damaging the reputation of the Turkish state."

We could multiply such examples. Across the developing world, because access to the goods of the metropolitan economies is so uneven, governments have been established that are ruthlessly authoritarian and little tolerant of local autonomy and diversity. Developing-world elites often have more of an interest in forcing peripheral regions into the mainstream economy—so that they can be controlled, and so that their resources and labor can be turned into cash for the mainstream elite—than those regions have in coming in voluntarily. Aid policy has merely accentuated this trend. Donor countries have been mainly interested either in generating business for their industries (mainly their defense industries, since much so-called aid actually consists of incentives or credits to buy weapons) or else in maintaining a strong but compliant puppet nation, ensuring access for the West's transnational corporations.

Thus the West's long-term support for President Mobutu of Zaire, and for Saddam Hussein before he became troublesome, Britain's thirty-year arming of Suharto's genocides in East Timor and West Papua, and the United States' wars against democratic movements in Latin America, have all sustained strong, antidemocratic and antilibertarian centers in the developing world. These centers have continued to suppress their linguistic and economic peripheries.

It might be argued that a strong centralizing power, however unpalatable in the short term, is ultimately necessary to turn developing areas into modern and prosperous nation states, and that this would be to everyone's advantage. Neither ethics nor economics support this conclusion, however. Good development involves local community involvement, control, and accountability. It also involves—perhaps may even be defined as—giving local people real choice.

We feel the same about language policy. If there are real economic advantages to having access to a larger language, as some claim, people will discover this for themselves. Attempts to "modernize" people by force are thus at best misguided, and at worst conceal other agendas. We accept that the modern world economy will require many more people to use English and the other global languages, but this does not mean that they have to lose their mother tongues if they choose not to do so. It is not an either-or choice. Where people are given a real opportunity to set the parameters of development for themselves, they often find win-win strategies in which they retain the autonomy of their local communities, along with appropriate strategic involvement in the wider economic and political system. In linguistic terms this may result in a thoroughly multilingual community with a recognition of the complementary, but all-positive, values of the different languages in the repertoire.

During these long conflicts between metropolitan and peripheral languages, people on the periphery have very often not been given a real choice. Such choice is not only good in itself, for reasons to do with human rights, but it can have beneficial effects on both economy and society.

Double dangers

We have described how a wave of dominant languages has spread out from the industrialized areas into less developed ones. It is spreading faster than ever today. This wave travels fast with only minimal movement of people, as it is propelled by language users shifting from peripheral to metropolitan languages.

We have treated this wave as an entirely separate phenomenon from the biological expansion of Europeans. This was an analytical convenience. Although the two events are logically distinct, in fact the two waves have often hit vulnerable communities at the same time, or at least so close together as to constitute a double danger. The Native Americans, native Hawaiians, and Aboriginal Australians, for example, were first overcome by the biological expansion of Europe, but once this had leveled off much of the remaining damage to the languages was done by language shift, as the remnant indigenous communities became confined to the bottom of the economic and political scale and many of their young people opted out.

The Celtic case, on the other hand, although basically a cultural replacement, had biological elements too. Both Ireland and the Scottish highlands were settled by English-speaking immigrants who ousted elements of the indigenous peasantry. And part of the collapse of Irish Gaelic was undoubtedly related to the demographic crises of nineteenth-century Ireland, in which much of the population either starved or emigrated to America.

The two waves can often combine to form an implacable flooding tide, as we saw in our example of Hawai'i. This is what is faced today by the minority peoples of West Papua and East Timor in Indonesia. These islands are being systematically settled by Indonesians from the more crowded islands of Java and Sumatra. At the same time, Indonesians hold all the political and economic power and are converting the indigenous peoples by force where necessary.

The twentieth century has been the most uneven in human history. A few communities have enjoyed extraordinary progress in technology, which has given them absolutely unprecedented power. This power takes many forms. It is not simply a matter of military dominance; it is the power to dominate the flow of information through radio and television, and to dominate local politics in all parts of the world through the weapon-rich, money-rich game of international relations. Above all, the metropolitan communities have the power to change the environment, which they often do in their ever-increasing quest for material resources.

Many communities, however, have not been empowered to this extent. Recall that 90 percent of the world's languages are spoken by less than 10 percent of the population. That 10 percent consists of small, vulnerable, often poor societies scattered around the world. There is no doubt that these peoples will want to increase their participation in the world economy and enjoy some of the material benefits it brings. The question is under what terms they will be allowed to do this. Will they be forcibly dispossessed of their lands, broken up, or massacred? Will they come under the cultural tyranny of nation-states intent on controlling them and turning them into a docile proletariat? Or will they be given a real chance to set their own courses?

The answers to these questions are not yet clear. As we have seen, the dangers facing small communities are greater than ever, and this is reflected in the increasing number of languages which die out each year. On the other hand, there are many recent developments which offer them hope. There has at last been some real technology transfer between the different regions of the world, especially between Europe and Asia. Computer technology means that books, newspapers, discs, and websites can be produced in small languages at minimal cost, and these technologies are quite democratic. In East Timor, for example, the liberation movement takes the internet very seriously, with resistance leaders using laptops in the jungle. Through their web site they make available for public consumption reports on their situation and the actions of the Indonesian military. In the words of Nobel Peace laureate José Ramos-Horta, "the Internet is hard to intercept and almost impossible to censor . . . [It] has revolutionized the fight for human rights. It has broken down the barriers erected by dictatorships, and put an end to the silence and isolation felt by the victims of oppression."

There is also some sign of a shift toward more people-centered policies in development programs and a climate of public opinion sympathetic to cultural pluralism and human rights. Government foreign policy, however, so long defined by the goal of creating strong, often brutal client regimes in the developing world, has a long way to go.

Seven

Why Something Should Be Done

Wisdom is better than strength;
Nevertheless the poor man's wisdom is despised,
And his words are not heard.
—*Ecclesiastes 9:14–16*

W e have seen how the changing face of linguistic diversity in the
modern world is the story of how a few metropolitan languages expanded very rapidly at the expense of the rest, as
smaller communities have been pulled into the orbit of more powerful
ones. Must we accept the demise of the world's small languages? Or

should we try to support them, and if so, what might really be achieved in practice?

We hope we have made clear that the reasons most non-Eurasian languages are in danger of dying out have nothing to do with the intrinsic properties of those languages—which are just as complex, expressive, and creative as any others—nor with the greater intelligence, virtue, or industry of their speakers compared to speakers of other languages. If the tale of the Eurasian rise to global dominance were told as a tale of human motives it would be a shabby one indeed, with more than its share of greed, dishonesty, cruelty, and sloth. But the rise to dominance cannot be explained at this level. It instead requires an understanding of the deeper, complex, structural conditions obtained in Eurasian societies and not elsewhere. Eurasia had by far the world's most productive farming and livestock complex. This was no more than a fluke of biogeography, but it allowed Eurasians to boom in number and eventually expand beyond their shores. It also made them hosts to the great killer diseases, which, paradoxically, gave them an edge over other peoples when the continents collided. Finally, the dense population and the high agricultural productivity, in Europe at least, unleashed a process of diversification and specialization that set those economies on the path to industrialization. Thus, a world of small-scale societies more or less equal in wealth and power has become a world of nation-states, some far wealthier and stronger than others, with ruling classes and minorities within them.

Intricate sets of interacting factors are required to bring about any historical transition. Although the present is the outcome of a series of acts of human intent, the participants never had any real idea of what the long-term results would be—but these results have allowed a few metropolitan groups a virtual stranglehold upon global resources and global power. Britain's empire, for instance, was said to have been acquired absent-mindedly, but by 1914 Europe held a grand total of 85 percent of the world as colonies, protectorates, dependencies, and commonwealths. No other set of colonies in history was as large, so totally dominated, or as unequal in power as this western metropolis.

It may seem as if present circumstances are outside human control, with this power differential now an inevitable fact of life. One might even be tempted to argue that while it may be true that the metropolitan languages and their speakers did not particularly deserve their status, having achieved it by a combination of historical accidents and unsavory oppression, it is more realistic to focus our efforts now on getting everyone else's standard of living up to the undeniably high standards of the metropolitan societies. This means aiding the spread of English and other world languages as part of the modernization process, and gently letting the remnants of other languages wither away, as they inevitably must do. Another variant of this type of argument says we shouldn't intervene to

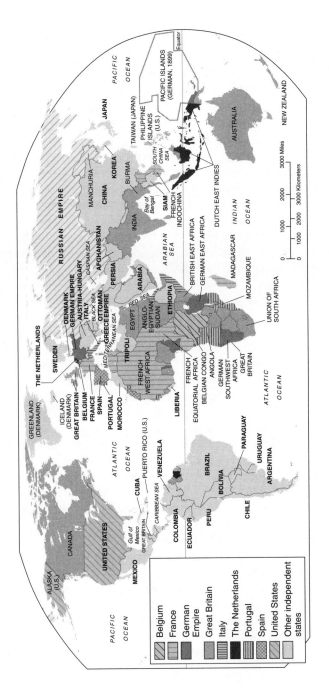

Figure 7.1   *French equatorial Africa in 1914*

[Adapted from Major World States and Colonial Possessions, 1914 in front matter of T. Walter Wallbank et al. Civilization Past & Present. Vol. 2. Harper Collins. 6th ed.]

save languages (or species) because extinction is simply a fact of life. There have always been massive extinctions, so why should we be concerned about the prospect of another?

Here we will seek to undermine this argument, which we will term the *benign neglect* position. We will also counter other arguments mounted against language maintenance efforts. Some, for instance, would say that other problems, such as eliminating poverty or protecting the environment, are more pressing concerns than the loss of languages. We will make the case that the need to preserve languages and the need for economic development in the world's peripheral societies are not opposing ones, as widely supposed, but complementary aspects of the same problem. The idea that linguistic diversity should be preserved is not a sentimental tribute to some idealized past, but part of the promotion of sustainable, appropriate, and empowering development. The problem of language death is thus a "good" problem, in that solving it would mean solving many other urgent and interrelated problems at the same time.

Why bother?

The benign neglect position points out that languages are abstract systems that are constantly changing anyway, and whose trajectory is beyond the control of any one person or institution. Language death, the argument goes, occurs because speakers have voluntarily chosen to shift to a metropolitan language. Since this means people are moving from their traditional poverty to the greater quality of life and range of possibilities which the developed world system offers, it is no bad thing. It may be sad to see the heritage of the past disappear, but this is just an inevitable side effect of progress.

Furthermore, as an advocate of benign neglect might point out, it is hardly fair for someone from the industrialized countries, who lost most of their languages centuries ago, to try to persuade developing-world peoples to cling to the past for heritage reasons when these peoples quite reasonably have more pressing concerns, such as improving their economic prospects. This parallels the argument about biodiversity: why should the South be expected to preserve its forests for the sake of the heritage of the world? The North ransacked its own environment to fuel its development, and so now its moralizing about conservation scarcely seems fair. The South has enough problems without Northerners loading it with demands that they themselves did not fulfill and that would debar it from the immediate economic benefits which it justifiably craves.

This is a very important argument. Western culture has thought about traditional societies in a very schizoid way. Either they have been seen as backward and morally deficient, or they have been idealized as representing something timeless, harmonious, and self-contented, which should be preserved intact. Obviously, the former of these standpoints is a way to justify dispossessing traditional societies. However, the latter standpoint is also a way of disempowering them, in that it denies them a claim to participation in economic and political progress. We must be careful in presuming that people in traditional societies were in a state of primitive harmony, contented with their lot, and would just continue in this happy state if left untouched. However, we will make an argument in favor of supporting traditional languages that does not draw on this idea. Traditional peoples have the same wants and needs as anyone else, and they will be quick to take a route out of the poverty and squalor that has undeniably accompanied much of human existence if they can. As we will argue, though, the very policies which will best support their languages are likely to be the ones which will offer them such a route. This is because the benign neglect position, reasonable as it might sound, depends on a series of incorrect assumptions.

Making choices

According to the benign neglect position, language death comes about because people make a free choice to shift to another language. As people are rational beings who may reasonably be expected to know where their self-interest lies, we, as outside observers, cannot condemn such choices. Seen from an economist's perspective the arena of languages is just another free market, and as economists are fond of pointing out, it can be shown that a free, competitive market in any activity should produce an optimal distribution of that activity for all concerned. The wane of some languages is simply a side effect of countless individual choices, and thus is no more or less morally significant than a change in the price of fish.

Our earlier examples have undermined the basis of this argument. We have shown that in many cases of language death, the shift occurred not because of an increase in the available choices, but because of a decrease in choice brought about by the exercise of undemocratic power. Such power is almost always wielded by denying access to resources from which communities make their living. Aboriginal Australians, for example, or Native Americans, can hardly have been said to have exercised free choice in coming to live in white society. They were dispossessed by groups exercising a greater power over the environment (because of their crops, diseases, and technology), such that the natives' options were reduced rather than increased. Even in cases where the shift seemed more voluntary, as we have seen from Ireland, the choices were not made under ideal conditions, but in a political framework which diverted resources to the metropolitan economy and inhibited the social and economic success of the smaller community.

As well as showing that competitive free markets produce an optimal allocation of activity, economic theory points out that when the market is distorted, the allocation resulting is seldom optimal. Distortion arises wherever the activities of one group interfere with the possibilities of action of the other group. In these cases, an efficient solution often involves the legal or political system stepping in to mediate between different interests.

The market of competing languages has been distorted, over the long term, by the material, political, and symbolic domination of the world by a few communities. This has meant people losing languages that they valued and community structures which would have still had benefits for them. And, most notably, it has often meant that though the world's wealth has increased, the poor have remained just as poor.

Language, development, and sustainability

An influential article on language diversity written at the beginning of the 1970s concludes by claiming that "a planner who insists on preserving cultural-linguistic pluralism had better be ready to sacrifice economic progress." The author, Jonathan Pool, believed that the fantastic diversity of languages and peoples in developing countries was fundamentally at variance with the prospects for their development. The diversity could be preserved by keeping people locked in what Marx called the "idiocy of rural life"—or that idiocy could be escaped by modernization. It was an either-or choice.

Pool's conclusion is interesting because it reflects many of the tacit beliefs about economic development which were in circulation at the time and have continued to influence policy until very recently. The central assumption is that the route out of long-term poverty for tropical countries was to become as much as possible like the northern industrial countries. This meant having a single national language and a centralized nation-state to go with it. In other domains, similar beliefs led to the clearing of forests, imposition of European monocrop style farming, the enforced settling of nomadic peoples, the introduction of western-style education in European languages, and the concentration of resources on a large industrial sector.

If Pool's conclusion were correct, it would put those interested in language preservation in a very dubious position. We would like to see the Fyem, Hawaiian, and Ma'a languages survive into the twenty-second century, but we also believe that people, and their quality of life, are more important than linguistic heritage per se. We would not therefore support measures to preserve a language which consigned its people to economic disadvantage and political marginality. Fortunately, as we shall show, there is no such conflict. The measures most likely to preserve small languages are the very ones which will help increase their speakers' standard of living in a long-term, sustainable way. This is because many assumptions about development have been shown, over the last three decades, to be wrong.

The world has seen significant growth in wealth over the half century, even in wealth per capita, which is striking given that the population has been rising so fast. However, there are two large areas of concern which prevent us from rejoicing at this growth.

The first is that while the rich have got much richer the poor have also become poorer (or, at best, have not increased their standard). There are stark contrasts between income per person (and related measures of well-being such as life expectancy and rate of infant mortality) in developed countries, most of them in the temperate zone of the northern hemisphere, and developing countries in the tropics and semitropics. The proportion of people below the poverty line in most developing countries has remained around the same, and the standard of living of the bottom quarter of humanity is stagnant. In 1992, the richest 20 percent of the world's people had 150 times the income of the poorest 20 percent. The bottom 20–25 percent of the world's population includes the bearers of most of the linguistic diversity—small communities, mainly in the tropics and semitropics, generally away from the main centers and capital cities where most investment occurs. Fifty years of "development" has had little positive effect, and plenty of negative side effects.

The second area of concern about contemporary economic growth is that it is not "sustainable." This term, which has attracted much publicity, if less action, means that the growth does not leave the environment at the same value as it was found. One of the goals of the 1992 United Nations Conference on Environment and Development in Rio was to get nations to commit to a declaration of principles for sustainable development. At the heart of the problem is bridging the gap between rich and poor nations by curtailing the activities of the rich. Industrial nations, with 25 percent of the world's population, consume 70 percent of all its resources and produce the most pollution. The big seven industrialized nations produce 45 percent of greenhouse gases such as carbon dioxide, which many scientists believe is responsible for global warming. This means that the ecological and economic impact on the global ecosystem of a citizen of a developed country is far greater than that of one person living in a developing country. Those causing the greatest change to the environment owe the biggest debt.

An obvious example of unsustainability is deforestation. The world's tropical forests are being felled at a far faster rate than they can replenish themselves. Throughout the 1980s the average yearly rate of loss was around 150,000km^2, or almost 1 percent of the world's total, and the rate has sharply increased during the 1990s. If this damage continues, many of the endemic species contained in the forests will become extinct, which means that those ecosystems will never be able to replenish themselves at all.

The felling of the forests swells economic statistics for the short term, since the valuable woods they contain and the land they occupy suddenly come into circulation; that extra value, however, once converted into cash, can never be called on again. Future generations will inherit an environment without the potential that forests provide for fuel, fruits, honey, medicines, tourism, and so on. Furthermore, the role of forests in absorbing carbon dioxide and in preventing soil loss will no longer be fulfilled. The value of the environment to people in the future is thus permanently diminished by a little economic growth now.

This is currently happening in Papua New Guinea, where industrial logging has increased 400 percent in the last year, with one Malaysian company controlling 80 percent of the over 1 billion dollar industry. These same multinational timber operations have already destroyed the rain forests of the Philippines, Thailand, Malaysia, and much of Indonesia. While highly industrialized countries such as the US and Canada protect their remaining forests, logging companies turn to cash-poor developing countries for cheap wood to meet the developed world's growing need for wood and pulp products. Industrial logging totally clears the forest of all growth, resulting in massive erosion and nutrient loss, which in turn leads to the demise of the soil's fertility, loss of animal life, and reduction in water quality.

Resource extraction on an industrial scale usually follows a boom-bust pattern of activity with few long-term benefits to local owners. Following a brief period of access to jobs, money, and commodities, villagers are left with the consequences of a devastated environment, unemployment, and displacement from their homeland when the resource runs out. Yalaum Mosol, a Bemal villager who lives at the site of a recent clear-cut, summed up the results this way: "We have no water to wash in, and hardly any water to drink that is not polluted. We have no good ground on which to grow food, we have no mushroom ground, no good trees for fruit, no clay pot ground. Our secret places and wild animals are gone, and all our ancient trees are being destroyed."

Mosol's statement illustrates how the price the logs get in the international market is not linked to their full local use-value, their cultural significance, or the role of the forest in complex ecosystems. Once old-growth forests such as these have been harvested, it is virtually impossible to recover the same ecosystem in all its diversity. Experts estimate that full regeneration after large-scale logging can take as long as 600–1,000 years. If reforestation is undertaken, however, it usually involves planting pines, eucalyptus, or other introduced species rather than indigenous ones.

Deforestation is not the only example of unsustainable development. Many contemporary global problems—the biodiversity crisis, the loss of land through soil erosion and pollution, global warming, the loss of livelihoods through environmental change—can be seen as symptoms of a general unsustainability in the way economic growth is being realized. The unequal distribution of wealth and resources, along with soaring population, is the cause of what Niles Eldredge calls the "sixth extinction." We are causing a catastrophic loss of biolinguistic diversity, and because we are causing it, only we can stop it. The only way to do this is to alter our behavior.

We have, then, two pressing global concerns. The first is that economic growth is achieving little or nothing for the poorest quarter of humanity, the rural poor in the developing world. The second is that the growth is unsustainable, meaning that it threatens to seriously impoverish us over the long term.

Why have these problems come about? There are, unfortunately, no simple answers to this question, for if there were we could more easily put a stop to the some of the outrages of contemporary life. However, there are some easily identifiable contributory factors, and the marginalization of minority groups, which is the main cause of language death, is bound up with all of them.

As the more perceptive development economists have pointed out, the biases inherent in the development process are huge. Over the last fifty years, investment has consistently been directed toward the urban elite and their needs. New roads have been built to whisk them from city to city; universities and airports, which reflect their interests and prestige, have been produced at vast cost. Subsidy and investment have been directed to the industrial sector, which makes goods for the elite, often by taxing the rural economy. This is in spite of the fact that most poor people depend on farming, not industry, and that it was increases in farming productivity that lay behind the improvements in living standards seen in the history of the developed countries. Moreover, there is no evidence that concentration on the capital-hungry industrial sector produces superior economic growth.

Another bias has been toward resource liquidation rather than preservation. Across the developing world forests have been logged, coral reefs dynamited, fisheries emptied, and meadows cleared at an alarming rate. This unsustainable outcome represents precisely the same privileging of metropolitan elites over peripheral cores as the urban

Figure 7.2   Yonggom villagers inspecting damage caused by mine tailings from Ok Tedi mine

[Courtesy of Stuart Kirsch]

bias. When a forest is logged, as we have seen in the case of Papua New Guinea, the flow of income from the concession does not go to the people who formerly lived in the forest but is instead absorbed by the national government, who usually see to it that very little filters back to the rural areas.

The same applies to other forms of resource extraction. It was the inequitable distribution of mining revenues which prompted a civil war in Papua New Guinea, lasting from 1989 to 1997. The Bougainville mine at Panguna together with the Ok Tedi mine in the highlands are two of the world's biggest copper mines. Just before the war, the Panguna mine generated nearly half of the country's export revenue. According to the 1966 Mining Bill, however, only 5 percent of government royalties went to local landowners. Landowners revolted at this inequity by shutting down the mine and demanded compensation for the environmental damage done to the island. Metropolitan centers thus take the full benefit of resource liquidation. Very often they rely on this benefit, as in the case of the government of Papua New Guinea, which is entirely dependent upon mining concessions, or the government of Nigeria, which is largely paid for by the oil industry.

However, it is not the people in the metropolitan centers who pay the cost of unsustainability. That cost is paid by the peripheral poor, whose fisheries are empty, whose farms lose their soil, who can no longer gather forest products. Western assessments of the impact of large-scale resource development projects on indigenous peoples have emphasized the economic costs and benefits. Anthropologist Stuart Kirsch has shown how inadequate these are in acccounting for the experiences of the Yonggom people whose communities have been disrupted by the Ok Tedi mine. The annual releasing of 30 million tons of mine tailings and 40 million tons of waste material into the local river system has resulted in deforestation, destruction of garden land, and the disappearance of birds and other wildlife; it has also introduced unknown chemical hazards. Once self-sufficient, now the Yonggom must rely on compensation payments from the mine that are scheduled to continue only through the remaining 10 to 15 years of production.

Meanwhile, the Yonggoms' relationship to their land has been irrevocably altered. Clan names link groups of people to particular landscapes that have now been transformed, and with them their connections to places where they emerged as a people.

If local communities had control over resources, they would be much more likely to conserve them. This is not because traditional peoples have some mysterious essence that keeps them in harmony with nature, while modern people always seem to be fighting against it, as some romantic portrayals of indigenous society imply. It is for the more practical reason that it is the traditional people who will have to stay around in the environment and make their living there after the loggers have gone, and so they have much more incentive to preserve its structure and value.

Related to the bias toward resource liquidation has been a bias toward global homogenization. Millions of acres of formerly mixed traditional farming with local varieties has given way to monocultural production of wheat or cattle for export. As well as being a loss of diversity in itself, this has led to increased erosion and soil loss and a vastly increased demand for energy and chemical fertilizers, since the same varieties are not optimal for every setting.

These biases in world development — in favor of urban elites, in favor of resource liquidation, in favor of homogeneity — are in no sense the outcome of a benign free market, operating to provide the most efficient distribution of resources. They are instead the symptom of the domination of resources and opportunities by a small group of colonial and post-colonial elites. These elites have been able to use the political system, the legal system, and often actual force to help themselves to the resources belonging to peripheral peoples, in the ostensible interest of national development. National development, though, tends to do little for the rural poor, whose resources are actually funding it, since the urban elites have a habit of diverting the income gained into the things they want rather than the things that would alleviate rural poverty. Land is turned to gaining the most dollar income possible for the few rather than providing the long-term best yield for the many.

In the Niger Delta region of Mali, for instance, over one hundred million dollars has been invested in cattle ranching and rice growing schemes, none of which has benefited the local residents who practiced a system of multiple land use based on fishing, farming, and pastoralism. Every newly created acre of rice paddy results in four acres of flood plain reverting to desert. During the drought of 1984 over 600,000 well-watered cattle died for lack of pasture. The people's plight was worsened by the conversion of 20 percent of the delta from grazing land to rice polders that produced no rice that year. Teetering on the edge of survival, people were diversifying their activities: fishermen started farming, farmers turned to fishing, and everyone tried to graze a few cattle. This pushed the land and water resources to the limit. Taxes in Mali are levied on means of production, such as boats, plows, nets, and carts, regardless of their earnings. If the taxes are not paid, the goods are impounded. In 1984, during the worst drought in recorded history, the taxes and fines assessed on unpaid taxes taken out of the area by the Service des Eaux et Forêts were twice those of 1973, and more than two-and-a-half times as much money was taken from the local people as they received in the local budget. Thus, the delta was financing a state bureaucracy that gave it very little in return. Meanwhile, at the national level Mali and most of the rest of Africa have negative trade balances, which means that they pay out more than they earn or receive in aid.

Where indigenous people disagree with elite agendas, like the Brazilian Indians, the Ogoni in Nigeria, or the natives of Bougainville, they can be depicted as dangerous and primordial terrorists, and suppressed or relocated with the tacit or direct assistance of international organizations. A case in point is that of two Kayapo Indians from Brazil who attended a rainforest conference in the United States. They later met with members of the US Congress and World Bank officials to explain the reasons they opposed the construction of hydroelectric dams that would flood their lands and force them to move. When they returned to Brazil, they were charged with committing subversive activities. The government feared the Indians would obstruct a 500 million dollar loan that the country needed to pay some of the interest on its foreign debt.

Elites in the developing world have not achieved their complete distortion of power and resources unaided: they are backed up by a huge system of subsidy from the North. Aid policy (much of which actually consists of direct and indirect subsidies to the arms trade) increases the military strength of elites so that they can more completely dominate their peripheries. Which elites are supported is dictated by perceived international relations issues such as trade and access to natural resources such as oil, and not by any humanitarian concerns.

Meanwhile, such bodies as the International Monetary Fund and the World Bank have often served to underwrite the stripping of resources from peripheral areas. The World Bank is partly responsible for the near extinction of Rwanda's mountain gorillas, for example, through its financing of pyrethrum plantations, which involved chopping down all but the most inaccessible part of the gorillas' habitat. The same institution is also the major agent in the promotion of monoculture forestry on an industrial scale. The turning over of land in Latin America from mixed forest and indigenous farming to large ranches producing beef for export, mainly to American hamburger chains, received 10 billion dollars in World Bank and Inter American Development Bank support in the 1970s. The humid tropics do not sustain intensive ranching, and the long-term environmental prospects are poor. The settlement of Indonesians from Java to the peripheral islands received 350 million dollars in funding from the World Bank, despite concerns over both the fate of indigenous diversity and the extent to which this would solve the undeniable problems of Java. The Brazilian government's development plan for the northwest, which threatens both indigenous people and biodiversity, received 443 million dollars in 1981. Between 1979 and 1983, almost half a million people were resettled as a result of projects approved by the World Bank.

From the 1960s to the 1980s, development policy and practice were seriously flawed. The industrial governments and related organizations such as the World Bank were working to their own agendas, which had relatively little to do with sustainable poverty reduction and much to do with international relations and creating economic growth back home. Even when motivations were more obviously altruistic, as in the case of nongovernmental organizations, the policies pursued in the name of development often failed the tests of both sustainability and poverty reduction.

In Africa, for example, the bulk of rural development effort until very recently was directed toward changing the production system. African communities traditionally practiced forms of farming in which different crops are interspersed in small plots which are themselves interspersed with trees. Where rainfall is too scant for this system, people are mainly nomadic animal herders. Both of these systems were judged by European agronomy to be inefficient. It was determined that farmers would achieve greater economies of scale by having large, clear fields of a single crop, while herders would achieve more calories per hectare by settling down with their animals, or by farming cash crops such as peanuts.

Development organizations were engaged in the task of reforming "backward" African production systems for several decades, before the lack of improvement in yields, and in some places the obvious degradation of the environment, led some of them to question their assumptions. Subsequent research has shown that the traditional systems far outperformed European-derived alternatives on the criteria of security, yield, and sustainability. This is because the dynamics of the tropics are completely different from those of Europe, and the land resists the imposition of European technologies. High temperatures mean that, unless subtly protected, soil will break down more quickly than the decay of organic matter can form it. In most parts of the continent, rainfall is a limiting factor with plant growth, and so the moisture in the soil must be protected. Furthermore, the range and danger of pests is quite different from Europe, and food must be protected from these. Plowed by tractors, fertilized chemically, and sprayed with herbicides and pesticides, the land may yield more for a period of a few years than a plot traditionally farmed, but the situation is soon reversed as the topsoil washes away, leaving hardpan and gravel. Mechanized farming has been a miserable failure in Africa. The best way to clear a tropical rainforest for planting is still by hand, leaving the tree roots in place and growing crops among the trees.

It turns out that many traditional systems of production which were more diverse than in more temperate climates, did all this and more. Putting different types of plants together allows adjacent stands to exploit the moisture available at different levels, and crops which are scattered are less vulnerable to pest swarms than monocrop fields. Mixed cropping involving plants of different heights retains moisture and creates a productive microclimate, and keeps down weeds. Finally, mixed cropping responds to what local people actually want, which is a spreading of both the work input and the food yields throughout the year so that they do not face periods of slack and shortage while waiting for a single crop.

Nomadic herding, for its part, is quite rational under certain circumstances. Periodic movement of herds avoids overstripping the delicate soils in the semi-arid parts of Africa. Where herds have been settled as a result of well-intentioned schemes, the land has been overgrazed. This leads to a vicious cycle: land covered in vegetation gives off warm, moist thermal currents, which cause seasonal rainfall; once the land is bare, the thermals are reduced, reducing rainfall, making it more difficult for vegetation to get back. This is a one-way trip, and the destination is desert.

Where pastoralists have been turned to farming cash crops, the results are no better. It is not without reason that Africans did not traditionally farm in the Northern Sahel, for example. A series of development schemes has forced them to start doing so, and as a result the farm output per hectare in the republic of Niger is now only three-quarters of what it was in 1969. The African example was repeated on every continent. Development policies failed to make progress on the front lines of rural poverty reduction and sustainability, because they were so often inappropriately driven. They either directly served the interests of metropolitan elites, or while trying to help peripheral peoples, they used inappropriate metropolitan knowledge and priorities.

Educational policy is another striking example of misguided strategies imported from the West into developing countries. Believing that tribal languages stood in the way of unity and were not suitable as languages of education and technology essential for western-style development, most newly independent countries did not develop their own languages, but continued using the languages of their former colonizers even when most of their citizens did not know them. Western aid policies and practices have generally reinforced European languages. France continues to tie its economic aid package to its former colony, Vanuatu, to the maintenance of French-medium education in the country. Development agents sent into the field rarely bother to learn the local languages, which leads to communication problems. The World Bank and International Monetary Fund seldom make reference to the possible role indigenous languages might play in development. The use of western school curricula in developing countries tends to devalue traditional culture and excludes formal study of traditional knowledge systems. Younger members of the culture are educated to believe that traditional knowledge is not worth learning because it will not lead to a job.

J.S. Furnivall, one of the earliest observers to make a comparative study of formal western education in tropical colonies, concluded that educational policy developed along similar lines in these places, produced similar types of schools, and encountered similar difficulties. Repeatedly, the results have been directly contrary to the ends proposed: "For the repeated failure there would seem to be one sufficient explanation: they disregard the environment." Furnivall was especially critical of the single-minded view that schools are economic institutions, and went on to say that

> [s]chools, teachers and textbooks may try to sow the seed of Western civilization, but pupils are content to pluck the fruit. They see the fruit; they see that export crops are more profitable than food crops; that the motor car is speedier and more comfortable than the bullock cart; and . . . they learn that education is a way to make a living. . . . From the beginning of the nineteenth century, missionaries and humanitarians have expected education in the tropics to change the character of the environment, but in the event the environment had changed the character of education . . . where schools teach children how to live, the more who go to school the better; but when they teach them merely how to make a living, the more who go to school, the less they earn.

Disappointment with the results of projects has led to something of a reorientation in development thinking, with the beliefs of the 1950s, 1960s, and 1970s challenged and a renewed emphasis on appropriate, environmentally sustainable schemes which involve local people much more. As recently as 1957, for example, a Geneva convention concerning indigenous and tribal populations set itself the goal of softening the impact of the global assimilation process without questioning its inevitability. In 1989, however, it was revised, with the stated goal of preserving indigenous cultures and peoples. This shift in emphasis was marked by UNESCO proclaiming the decade from the mid 1980s as the decade of cultural development, and 1993 was declared the Year of Indigenous Peoples.

What has all this to do with saving peripheral languages? The answer is a great deal. For, as we have shown, languages are tied up with local systems of knowledge and ways of life. Ways of life can only persist where the community has control over its resources and activities. Development practices have tended to suppress indigenous ways of life and the languages that they sustained, by displacing people, liquidating their resources, and changing their patterns of production and exchange, rather than sustainably improving their standard of living. Furthermore, these practices have been based on outsiders' knowledge, outsiders' crops, outsiders' languages, and outsiders' priorities. Indigenous systems of knowledge and languages have been downgraded, or treated as backward relics to be erased by western-style education. All this means that if we want to save languages, we would have to change some development priorities. But, as we have seen, we would do well to reassess these priorities anyway.

What then are the major development objectives we face as we pass the millennium? First, human population growth must stabilize. Second, we must raise the living standards of the rural poor in the developing world, and those poor who exist in pockets in such developed countries as Australia and the US. Third, we need to conserve the world's biolinguistic diversity. This diversity is concentrated in the tropics, in and around the vast forests, along the coasts and islands, in pockets on the great savannas. To have any hope of conserving precious diversity we must enlist the people who live in those environments and thus are stakeholders in their preservation. Their interests must be upheld against asset-stripping elites with unaccountable power.

The striking thing about these three laudable objectives is that the parties who must be empowered if they are to be met are the same in all three cases: it is peripheral rural communities, mainly in the tropics, who are in the environments where the biodiversity is, who are poor and marginalized by unsustainable development, and who are the stewards of most linguistic and cultural diversity. To a very significant extent, common cause can be made among development, biodiversity, and linguistic diversity. It is not just that the historical causes of the problems are the same, but also that the solutions are likely to come from the same place: empowering local people.

When it was founded in 1948, the International Union for the Conservation of Nature and Natural Resources (ICUN), a consortium of 500 government and environmental groups, began employing a variety of traditional measures for protecting plants and animals. Although it originally thought about conservation in terms of individual species, it soon realized it needed to think in terms of environments. Only belatedly have they realized that they also need to think about people. Plants, animals, peoples, and their languages need to be put back in a social matrix to see what people do with their natural resources and how they benefit from conserving them.

There is now widespread agreement that the problem of sustainable development is more likely to be solved if indigenous systems of knowledge and languages are valued and brought into play. As we saw from the African example, imported Western knowledge often leads to inappropriate and unproductive schemes, and outsiders' objectives may not be compatible with sustainability. The African continent is littered with failed attempts to transfer technology from the northern to southern hemisphere—fish packing plants that have never seen a fish, for example, and vaccination programs that when discontinued result in epidemics. These technofixes have failed repeatedly, either because the technology was wrong for the culture or the technology itself was faulty. The solution lies in adapting ourselves to the environment rather than expecting the environment to yield to us. What might be appropriate for one area will be disastrous in another. Delicate tropical environments in particular must be managed with care and skill. It is indigenous peoples who have the relevant practical knowledge, since they have been successfully making a living in them for hundreds of generations. Much of this detailed knowledge about local ecosystems is encoded in indigenous languages and rapidly being lost.

Indigenous knowledge systems

We will give just a few examples of the extent and value of local knowledge. The first comes from the Philippines. This is a classic example of a moist tropical area of high biolinguistic diversity, but also extreme ecological delicacy. Simplistic importation of ranching or monocrop intensive agriculture could be a human and ecological disaster.

The Haunóo are a group of around 12,000 people living on the mountainous and heavily forested island of Mindoro in the northwest of the Philippine archipelago. They practice a system of mixed swidden cultivation that in the 1960s and 1970s would no doubt have been dismissed as primitive. Yet seen as a knowledge base of their environment, the claim of primitiveness is absurd. The Haunóo distinguish more than 450 types of animals and 1,500 plants. Their categories for the plants of the area exceed those of Western science by around 400. Over a thousand types are gathered from the wild for various practical purposes, which gives the Haunóo a strong incentive to preserve the wonderful diversity of their surroundings. Some 430 plants are cultivated in their gardens. Haunóo farmers recognize ten basic and thirty derivative types of soil. They have four different terms for soil firmness, nine color terms which distinguish different soil types, five classes of land topography, and three different ways of classifying slope. This information would be absolutely invaluable to anyone interested in understanding or preserving the ecosystem, and its specificity and subtlety must lie at the heart of initiatives to improve rural output in a sustainable way.

The second example of a local knowledge system comes from Africa. It is not widely known that African peoples had been producing carburized steel for tools and weapons for hundreds of years before colonial contact. The ores were local laterites and other minerals. Furnaces were charcoal-fired and used ingenious combinations of shape and leather bellows to achieve the necessary flows of air. The industry of the Kpelle people of Liberia was particularly advanced, since iron was mixed with other ores (mainly manganese) to produce a rust-resistant, high-strength product. Traditional African steelmaking is either extinct or on the decline in most areas, with metals now imported from abroad. The scholarly literature on the industry reflects a belief in both the backwardness of indigenous techniques and the inevitability of progress—whether it is Marxist in bent, in which case it is viewed as an example of the domestic mode of production making way for the capitalist mode, or economistic, in which case it is an example of a more efficient technology driving out a less efficient one through free competition.

But the extent to which this is free market development is extremely questionable. Colonial authorities in some areas deliberately suppressed indigenous metallurgy, fearful of competition for their imports and the production of weapons. Elsewhere, trade was disrupted and prices were controlled in a way which artificially favored imports, while other measures such as hut taxes and forced labor distorted the economy in such a way that—quite predictably—people were pulled out of self-sufficiency and into dependency. The colonial system was based on monopoly capitalism. It was arguably the traditional African system which represented the efficient free market.

Africa now needs more steel tools, and, given its exchange rates and terms of trade, it needs to get them more cheaply than it can from the industrialized North. Indigenous steelmaking could well fill the gap. What is more, indigenous products are adapted to local needs. Being also farmers themselves, traditional smiths produce dozens of different types of hoes, for example, each suited to particular types of crop and soil. These designs are in greater demand than the imported products. Traditional African smithing relies on an unformalized, orally transmitted system of knowledge which, like a dying language, is no longer being transmitted. If it disappears, the economic loss to the continent will be significant.

Our third example of a valuable indigenous knowledge system comes from the Indonesian island of Bali. The Balinese are largely dependent on rice farms, which must be irrigated from the many streams and rivers that flow down the flanks of their volcanic island to the sea. This is done by the construction of weirs high upstream, which divert water flow into complex systems of tunnels, canals, and aqueducts. These in turn pay out at the summit of rice terraces, where the water flow can be routed appropriately and any block of fields can be flooded at any time.

This complex system of engineering—itself a major achievement—has been gradually developed over more than a thousand years. However, more remarkable than the physical infrastructure the Balinese have made to control water flow is the social system they developed to regulate it, as recent studies by anthropologist Stephen Lansing show.

Rainfall is not continuous in Bali. The year is divided into a wet and a dry season. During the dry season, water flow is not sufficient to supply all farms simultaneously. An interruption in the flow is not fatal to the rice crop, provided that an appropriate schedule is maintained so that the fields do not become too dry and the cycle of planting, growth, and harvest is synchronized with water availability. With several hundred farms often dependent on a few weirs using the same stream, this coordination is no mean feat.

In fact the cooperation required among the different farmers is more complex still. The long-term productivity of rice fields is optimized not by continuous flooding but by strategically interspersed floodings and dryings, which keep the algal, bacterial, and mineral contents of the soil in balance. Rice fields can become infested with numerous pests, such as rodents, insects, bacteria, and viruses, which greatly decrease the yield. Farmers can locally control these pests by leaving an area fallow, and either flooding it or drying it out accordingly. The best timing and duration of the fallow depends on the pest species to be dealt with. However, the fallow system is ineffective if adjacent farmers do not coordinate their actions. If one block of fields is left empty and dry to counteract an infestation, but the next block is flooded, the pest will simply migrate next door and thrive, to return to the original block as soon as it is next planted. Neighboring farmers must thus synchronize their plantings, fallows, and water supplies in order to combat pests.

Balinese farmers were traditionally successful in their attempts to coordinate water supply, to judge from the high rice yields they achieved without chemical pesticides. Lansing has shown that the key element in their irrigation management was the system of water temples. Every major weir has a temple, to which the groups of farmers downstream form the congregation. At temple meetings, farmers coordinate their plantings and the routing of the water, sharing their knowledge of local pest densities and laying out a series of traditional rituals which will accompany their agriculture. This ensures the right schedule of irrigation for every farmer. The computation involved in regulating the system is impressive; there may be dozens of sluices, hundreds of blocks of fields, and each block needs to receive an allotment of water appropriate for its crop and phase in the cycle, all within the available water supply.

The agreed schedule is regulated by an indigenous calender, the *tika*, whose complexity dwarfs anything found in Western culture. The *tika* does not measure absolute time; the Balinese have a separate, lunar calendar much like our own for doing that. The *tika* is for tracking the concurrent cycles relevant to the management of many separate farms. The period of the *tika* is 210 days. Within this period there are ten different sets of weeks, varying in length from one to ten days, which all run concurrently. For example, today could be the third day of the second seven-day week, that is Tuesday of *landep,* and the second day of the three-day week (*beteng*), and the last day of the ten day week (*raksasa*), all at the same time.

The *tika* is used in calculating when different blocks should be flooded. Vegetables may need flooding one day in five for 105 days; this is easily done by directing water to them every time it is *kliwon*, the last day of the five-day week. Longer cycles can also be accommodated, using the intersection of different weeks. Thus the third day of the three-day week falls on the fifth day of the five-day week every fifteen days, and the first day of the five-day week falls on the first day of the seven-day week every thirty-five days. Any interval or cycle can thus be maintained simply by stipulating that a certain sluice be opened whenever the day is both *duka* and *kajeng*, or whatever the appropriate case may be.

The traditional cyclical planting system began to be challenged in the 1970s by modernization schemes undertaken first by the Indonesian government, and later by the Asian Development Bank. New strains of rice from the International Rice Research Institute in the Philippines were introduced, along with the chemical fertilizers to which these strains responded. More significantly, the Bali Irrigation Project, launched in 1979, set out to change the indigenous water management system. Weirs were reconstructed to increase water flows, and farmers were instructed to abandon the traditional cyclical patterns of planting in favor of year-round, continuous cropping.

The result of these changes was a breakdown of coordination between farmers. As soon as one crop was harvested, another was sown, and the cycles of neighbors began to drift apart. In the rainy season everyone had water, but during the dry season the supply became unpredictable. Furthermore, populations of pests exploded as the coordinated fallows which had traditionally suppressed them no longer occurred. The solution was found in artificial pesticides, which, within a few years, had pervasively polluted the island's soil and water resources without solving the problem.

By the late 1980s, faced with declining rice yields and increased pollution, the authorities in Bali bowed to increasing pressure to allow farmers to return to their traditional cropping and irrigation cycles. The temples now informally control water management again in much of Bali. Meanwhile, Lansing's studies have shown that the traditional system optimizes the overall yield of the farms, way outperforming either a free-for-all in which every farmer negotiates water access independently, or a centralized system with a single controller.

This example, like the preceding ones, shows very clearly that indigenous systems of knowledge and ecosystem management can be both highly sophisticated and incredibly useful, and this alone is a reason for valuing minority languages and the cultures which are tied to them. Improvements in the well-being of the Balinese are just as likely to come from the traditional culture as from powerful outsiders. Indeed, faced with complexity of the *tika* and the culture it represents, it is almost laughable that it is the Balinese, rather than outsiders, who should be dubbed "backward." The most telling evaluation of the whole Balinese fiasco comes from the Asian Development Bank itself when it stated that the "cost of the lack of appreciation of the merits of the traditional system has been high. Project experience highlights the fact that the irrigated rice terraces of Bali form a complex artificial ecosystem which has been recognized locally for centuries."

Our examples have shown how indigenous knowledge has served and could continue to serve as the basis for sustainable development. This does not mean that indigenous knowledge is already perfect—to assume that would be as absurd as assuming a priori that it was worthless—but it does mean we should use it as a starting point. Local people know what they need and know a lot more about what works than outsiders do. The path they will follow need not be that which the Northern countries followed two hundred years earlier. That path was notably inefficient, polluting, and expensive. The best new technologies will now allow the creation of wealth more cheaply, efficiently, and cleanly. These need to be transferred to the South, but must be coupled with local knowledge and local priorities.

For similar reasons, indigenous peoples should also be seen as essential allies, and not obstacles, in the struggle for conservation. Such peoples are not "natural" conservationists, any more than Northerners are. However, they have more of a long-term interest in their environments than outsiders do, and both their decisions and their knowledge reflect this.

Once again we might ask, what does all this have to do with language? Different languages evolved in the web of different communities

Figure 7.3 *Women supplying timber for a village-run sawmill in Papua New Guinea. Such locally-controlled, small-scale enterprises are now providing sustainable alternatives to multinational logging operations in many parts of the country.*

[*Photograph by Suzanne Romaine*]

with their own resources and practices, and languages disappear when these practices are banned or the resources appropriated. All over Africa, for instance, the languages of small groups of pastoralists are giving way as the traditional lifestyles that supported them are disappearing. If we allowed indigenous peoples much more participation in decisions about resource use and styles of development, more elements of traditional practices and structures would be retained, and it is much more likely that languages would survive. Looked at the other way, the study of traditional knowledge systems and the languages in which they are encoded will help us solve problems of sustainable development. This is what we call the win-win approach—good for biolinguistic diversity, good for people. It is not about setting indigenous peoples aside in isolated reservations, or expecting them to go on completely unchanged. It is merely about giving them real choice about what happens in the places where they live.

In Palau, for instance, whose fishermen we discussed in Chapter 3, chiefs in some villages have restored some of their traditional conservation practices after a period of 15 years in which the fish population had declined rapidly. In one area, fishing was banned for a year while local

Figure 7.4   Women fishing with handnets in Chuuk, Federated States of Micronesia, following the lifting of a closure placed on the reef. Periodic closures function as conservation measures.

[Courtesy of Craig Severance]

people together with marine biologists such as Bob Johannes monitored the situation. In 1991 the Palaun Congress enacted a new set of fishing regulations empowering local people.

Language rights and human rights

Our view, then, is fairly clear. We believe that people should be given control over their environments at the local level to the greatest extent possible. We also believe that where this is done many people will choose, as Palauans have, to retain elements of their cultural heritage. In the Ombessa area of Cameroon, for example, people have set up village development committees; at the top of their agenda is the promotion of the local language, Nugunu, and research into village history and folkore. Moreover, this choice is their right.

True development of a political, economic, or social nature cannot take place, however, unless there is also development of a linguistic nature. Unless the populace has access to information, they will be controlled by a small elite minority who have access to the dominant language—in most cases, a metropolitan European one. Democracy is severely limited when people cannot use their own languages. Looked at the other way around, if political domination by elites is lifted, the reasons for giving up a language are also weakened, and the benefits of keeping it increased.

The right of people to exist, to practice and reproduce their own language and culture, should be inalienable. A guarantee of their rights is what many people need most urgently. A number of indigenous peoples have begun to assert their rights. The Kuna Indians of Panama, for instance, have recently set up the world's first internationally recognized forest park created and run by indigenous people. They control access to research sites and require scientists to submit reports on their experiments. They also require each scientist to hire a Kuna assistant. This provides training opportunities for Kuna people and allows them to retain control over the forest. They also obtain revenue from the sale of research permits to the scientists and from tourists who come to learn about the rainforest. Another example can be seen in Colombia, where a group called CRIC (Regional Indian Council of Cauca), comprising 56 Indian communities, was formed in 1971 in order to protect Indian lands and culture in an area where forests have been destroyed by miners and cattle ranchers. In 1984 they began a forestry program with tree nurseries run by local communities. They supply seedlings to groups that agree to plant a minimum of 1,000 trees. Their aims are to reforest the area.

Preserving linguistic diversity does not mean that language repertoires and cultures must remain unchanged. It is obvious that more and more people will require a knowledge of English and the other world languages, as they seek to tap into the exciting and profitable services that the global economy offers. This need not necessarily conflict with the maintenance of diversity. Languages have coexisted in complementary functions since time immemorial. Furthermore, bi- or multilingualism supplies the advantages of a strong local identity *and* a global communication network at almost no cost, since children's capacity for spontaneous language learning is almost limitless. The negative attitude to multilingualism often voiced in the press in the US and Britain reflects more the dominant class's resentment of any form of knowledge or organization they do not control than any real problems associated with it.

To choose to use a language, is an act of identity or belonging to a particular community. We believe the choice to be who one wishes to be is a human right. Identity goes beyond the choice of a language or a name; it is also an economic freedom. Apolu Nakero, a Turkana pastoralist, when asked if there was anything she'd rather do than keep her family herd, said, "No, because if you don't have animals, you don't know what you are." For the Turkana, economy, society, and language form a single matrix which they desire the freedom to sustain.

The principle of self-determination has been often expressed in liberal thought for centuries and might seem uncontroversial. However, the practice of governments has hardly followed the theory in this respect. Taking the right of choice seriously would mean decentralizing power and knowledge to a much greater extent than national governments have generally been willing to do. It means, for example, allowing the language and even the content of educational curricula to be devolved to the smallest appropriate level. Such policies can be pursued to a certain extent within existing political structures, though legal, administrative, and educational reform are all necessary, as is a change in general priorities. Ultimately, they may require a rethinking of the nation-state itself.

For the last two hundred years or so, nation-states on the European model have been the dominant loci of decision making all over the world. Such states have typically had strongly centralized cultural, linguistic, and land-use policies. We must remember, however, that there is nothing inevitable about our present political bodies. For 99 percent of our history they did not exist (recall our description of stateless New Guinea).

The nation-state form of government arose in Europe in a particular historical context. The standard national languages—English, French, Spanish, and so on—all developed in a climate of intense political nationalism. The peculiar conditions of early modern Europe fed the need to create prominent ideological symbols of common origin, shared purpose, and modern nationhood. As Dr. Samuel Johnson wrote in his *Journal of a Tour to the Hebrides*, "Languages are the pedigree of nations." The linguistic models selected for codification and spread in education systems were those current in capitals such as London and Paris, seats of the court, centers of trade and finance, breeding places of the aristocracy. Those wanting to join such classes or to liaise with them would have to learn the metropolitan language. The spread of these new standard languages was made successful by the printing press and the rise of the newly literate middle classes who adopted them eagerly as a means of social advancement and mobility.

The modern European nation-states that emerged in the nineteenth century were based on the principle of one national language. Due to the identification of national entities with linguistic integrity, linguistic diversity in Europe has tended to be limited to the border regions. In the carving out of national boundaries and subsequent reshiftings as a result of war, some people ended up on the wrong side of borders (such as the Hungarian speakers in present-day Austria), or found themselves parceled out across a number of nation-states (such as the Basques in Spain and France, or Macedonians in Greece, Bulgaria, and the former Yugoslav Republic of Macedonia). The extension of Greek national sovereignty over parts of the territory of Macedonia was accompanied by particularly aggressive measures aimed at Hellenization of the Slavic-speaking population, among them the prohibition of the use of any language but Greek in public. People were fined, sent to prison, or forced to drink castor oil, and children beaten at school, if they were caught speaking their own language.

Although 25 of the 36 modern European nation-states are officially monolingual, most have minorities, both indigenous and nonindigenous, whose languages do not have the same status and rights as those granted to official languages. This can be seen as a form of internal colonialism, with the onus being on those occupying the periphery to be bilingual.

This model—the centralized nation-state, based around one language—was subsequently exported to the rest of the world. This model does not reflect how the world is naturally. Nor did it arise spontaneously, or outcompete indigenous alternatives; it was imposed by the force of monopolistic colonialism. International policies in this century have always defended nation-states, by arming and subsidizing their central elites and turning a blind eye to what they do to their peripheral peoples. This reflects the desire of Northern governments to have world resources controlled by a small number of docile clients. It does not always reflect the needs and aspirations of ordinary people, since the borders of many tropical nations are completely lacking in historical legitimacy or economic sense. The rise of nation-states in Africa, for example, has imposed parasitic bureaucracies on ordinary people and weakened the most successful strategy for survival in marginal parts of the continent—the ability of nomads to move hundreds, sometimes thousands, of miles in search of water and pasture for their animals. Meanwhile, government taxation policies have pushed people toward cash cropping at the expense of crops based on local needs, and government schools have forced children to learn in western languages rather than their own vernaculars.

If the triple goals of rural development, sustainability, and cultural-linguistic pluralism are to be pursued, then forms of decision making both above and below the existing nation-state will have to be developed. This will be a major challenge for the twenty-first century. Ideas such as these are never popular with the powerful, who are always uneasy about losing domains of control. However, for the reasons we have outlined, we believe that they would be good for languages, good for the environment, and good for people. Putting them into practice, however, is complex, and requires different strategies in every case. In our final chapter, we look at examples of the efforts that have been and can be made to preserve languages, and we consider their prospects for success.

Eight

Sustainable Futures

A language cannot be saved by singing a few songs or having a word printed on a postage stamp. It cannot even be saved by getting "official status" for it, or getting it taught in schools. It is saved by its use (no matter how imperfect) by its introduction and use in every walk of life and at every conceivable opportunity until it becomes a natural thing, no longer laboured or false. It means in short a period of struggle and hardship. There is no easy route to the restoration of a language.

—*Ellis and mac a' Ghobhainn*

W e have spent most of this book examining how the world's biolinguistic diversity has come to the brink of a new extinction crisis because we believe that only a better understanding of these historical processes will allow us to change them. International, regional, and national policies that empower indigenous peoples and promote sustainable development are the key to preserving local ecosystems essential to language maintenance. The preservation of local ecosystems is, in turn, critical for the preservation of the global ecosystem, which is the intersection of all local ecosystems. Because it is in local ecosystems that the game of life is played out, it is these individual habitats all around the world which need support. As the environmental slogan tells us: think globally, act locally.

We must apply an ecological bottom-up approach to language maintenance as well. Action needs to begin at the most local level in two senses. First, most of the work will have to be done primarily by small groups themselves rather than by any of the international agencies and networks that exist today (though their support also has a role to play). Second, it is necessary to concentrate on the home front (i.e., intergenerational transmission) before resources are expended at higher levels (school, work, government, and so on). Without transmission, there can be no long-term maintenance. We examine some case studies of language maintenance and revitalization to illustrate some of our arguments.

We also take up in more detail some of the themes in Chapter 3 concerning the value of biolinguistic diversity and its meaning to our continued existence on earth. In addition to utilitarian values (such as the indigenous knowledge the many languages of the world contain), the continued healthy existence of the world's ecosystems and languages is needed for our own long-term survival as a species. However, there is another argument of a different kind: we should preserve our biolinguistic diversity for moral, ethical, and aesthetic reasons. We must view the earth's languages as natural resources to be managed carefully, part of each group's rightful inheritance, and part of our collective human cultural legacy. We outline some guidelines for international, regional, and local policy makers in line with these sentiments.

Bottom-up approaches to language maintenance: some case studies

How are we to proceed in this enormous task of ensuring the transmission of as many languages as possible? Like the many problems surrounding the promotion of sustainable development, the question of language preservation appears daunting because so much needs to be done so quickly, and there are too few resources available to do it. Setting realistic priorities is therefore of paramount importance. The immediate one is to identify and stabilize languages under threat so that they can be transmitted to the next generation in as many of their functions as possible. This means assessing which functions are crucial to intergenerational transmission and have a reasonable chance of successful revival and continuation.

To measure the degree of disruption and shift a community has experienced in the use of its language, Joshua Fishman proposes an eight-stage scale, with the highest representing a community whose language is no longer being spoken by younger community members. The more disadvantaged a language is, the more unproductive and often less feasible high-level planning can be. Some languages have already disintegrated to such an extent that the first step must be piecing together what is left. When a language is no longer being passed on at home, efforts to promote it outside that domain — in church or school, for instance — usually end up being symbolic and ceremonial.

Most language policy deals with national or international levels rather than local usage. Too much attention focused on official policy statements can be counterproductive in the absence of other lower-level activity. In 1974 a largely decorative amendment to the Maori Affairs Act "officially" recognized the Maori language as "the ancestral language of the population of Maori descent." While it enabled the Minister of Maori Affairs to take such steps as were considered appropriate to the encouragement of the learning of the language, it became clear in 1979 that this statement meant nothing in the courts and required no government action on behalf of Maori. This came as a disappointment to those activists who had seen legislation as a way of strengthening the position of Maori. In any case, these acts fall short of what is required in practical terms if a language is to survive in spoken everyday use. Survival cannot depend on legislation as its main support.

Although control over the language of the workplace, government, and education may be ultimate goals of language revival and maintenance efforts, they should not be the first priorities. Without safeguards for language use at home sufficient to ensure transmission, attempts to prop the language up outside the home will be like blowing air into a punctured tire. It will be impossible to achieve a steady state based on the incoming air due to the continual losses resulting from the unmended puncture.

Many groups are in this unenviable position of having outflow exceeding inflow for many generations, yet at the same time have spent large sums of money on dictionary and grammar projects without sufficient justification. This plan of action is similar to the behavior of some of the international development agencies we examined in the last chapter, who poured vast sums of money into the African continent in top-down fashion without due consideration of local ecologies. Grammars and dictionaries are artificial environments for languages. They reflect only a fraction of the diversity of a language in its everyday use and cannot capture the ever-changing nature of language. It is like arguing that we should concentrate our efforts on preserving the spotted owl by building museums where we can display stuffed owls, but do nothing to preserve the bird in its natural habitat or guarantee that it can reproduce. While salvage operations aimed at recording a language for preservation in books are worthwhile endeavors and may be all that can be accomplished for some severely eroded languages, they do not address the root causes of language decline, and without further action they do not contribute substantially to language maintenance efforts in the long term.

Much of the campaign about the spotted owl was rightly about its habitat, the forest it needed to survive. People's sympathies could be more easily aroused about the plight of the owl than about the forest, even though preservation of the owl's home was a prerequisite to the owl's continued existence. Unfortunately, much of the professional linguistic literature on language maintenance has been concerned with preserving the structures of individual languages in grammars and dictionaries, or has directed its attention to education programs in the threatened language or to campaigns for official status. The preservation of a language in its fullest sense ultimately entails the maintenance of the group who speaks it, and therefore the arguments in favor of doing something to reverse language death are ultimately about preserving cultures and habitats. In the following case studies we show how successful language restorations are invariably part of this larger cultural goal, but efforts must first be focused at the grassroots level.

Case study 1: I ka ʻōlelo nō ke ola; i ka ʻōlelo nō ka make

Belief in the traditional power of the Hawaiian language is expressed in the proverb *I ka ʻōlelo nō ke ola; i ka ʻōlelo nō ka make*, meaning "in language rests life; in language rests death." In Chapter 4 we examined some of the historical and political factors that led to a decline in the use of the Hawaiian language, chief among them population loss, loss of political autonomy, and cultural and physical dislocation.

As a result, Hawaiian is presently a severely endangered language. Within the space of 200 years it went from being the lingua franca and the language of government, education, and religion, to being the home language of only a few hundred Hawaiians (most of them living on the privately owned, isolated island of Niʻihau, westernmost in the island chain shown in Figure 8.1). Here we see a top-down pattern of language shift similar to the one that pushed the Celtic languages to the periphery of western Europe. Outside Niʻihau, there are another few hundred Hawaiian speakers on the neighboring island of Kauaʻi plus another few hundred mainly elderly speakers scattered across the remaining islands, but they do not live in Hawaiian-speaking communities and are surrounded by English in their everyday lives. For most people living in today's multiethnic society, in which Hawaiians and part-Hawaiians

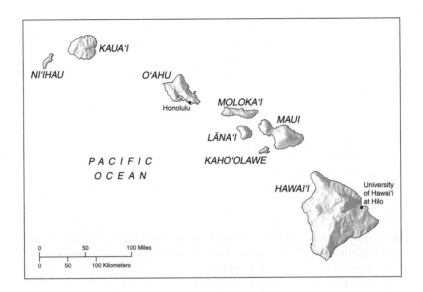

Figure 8.1   Map of the Hawaiian islands

comprise about 20 percent, the main reminders of the once ubiquitous presence of the Hawaiian language as a living force are street signs, place names, and Hawaiian music.

In the 1970s, however, a cultural and political Hawaiian renaissance took hold. Concern for the Hawaiian language went hand in hand with increased activism for land rights, sovereignty, a heightened interest in traditional art forms intimately connected with the language such as hula, and other activities relying on traditional knowledge such as canoe-building and long-distance canoe voyaging without instruments. In the photograph in Figure 8.2 people are clearing the land in Waipi'o Valley for planting of dry and wet taro. In addition to its importance as the traditional staple food source, taro is culturally significant. According to Hawaiian accounts of their origins, Wākea and Papa, the primal parents who gave birth to the Hawaiian islands, later gave birth to the taro plant and the taro's younger brother, Hāloa, the first Hawaiian. Thus, taro links Hawaiians intimately with their islands, lands, and ancestors.

In 1984 a program of Hawaiian immersion preschools was set up called *Pūnana Leo*, modeled on the New Zealand program *Kōhanga Reo* ('language nest') begun in 1982 and now serving some 14,000 children. The Hawaiian program was the first indigenous language immersion program in the US, operated under the auspices of a grassroots

Figure 8.2   Replanting of Waipi'o valley, island of Hawai'i, with traditional wet and dry taro

[Courtesy of Ellen Okuma]

Figure 8.3   Students in Maori immersion program

[Courtesy of Art Wolfe]

organization 'Aha Pūnana Leo, Inc., with initial funds provided by tuition paid by parents, small grants from private foundations, and community fund-raising activities. Upon a child's acceptance, the parents must attend language classes as well as assist in the school's maintenance.

These efforts undertaken on behalf of the Hawaiian language rightly concentrated first on the youngest generation in an attempt to create a sheltered environment in which they can learn the language. The philosophy of Hawaiian medium education is based on the recognition of the people's right to conduct full lives in their native language and the basic right of a language to flourish in its homeland. The movement reached a critical point, however, when it decided to expand immersion education vertically rather than horizontally in order not to lose any students. There were legal barriers to using Hawaiian as a medium of instruction in public schools, as a result of earlier legislation making English the official language of instruction. Even though the 1978 constitutional convention declared Hawaiian and English official languages, it was not until 1986 that provision was made for the Hawaiian language to be used in special Department of Education programs. The first elementary immersion programs began in 1987.

An outside evaluation of the program commissioned by the State of Hawai'i's Department of Education in 1988 concluded that the schools' instruction in Hawaiian had been successful on a number of grounds. It had been conducted with no apparent loss to the children's English language skills, an area of major concern to critics. Parental support and involvement were also exceptionally high. The evaluators recommended that the program should be extended. Parents who enrolled their children in the program did so because they were convinced of the importance of maintaining Hawaiian language and culture. One parent said, "My kids already understand that without the language, we'll die as a people, without the language we'll lose our culture and history." Another mother commented that her daughter's grandfather recovered his Hawaiian through talking to his granddaughter. And another wrote, "This is only the beginning of what can be a very successful and innovative program for Hawaiian people, culture, and language."

One of the biggest problems faced by teachers of languages similar in status to Hawaiian is a lack of teaching materials and qualified teachers. This was particularly acute for Hawaiian because the language had not been used in education since the nineteenth century. At one school the teacher borrowed library books, translated them, and pasted Hawaiian print over the English text—a practice which continues today. In 1989 the State Legislature established Hale Kuamo'o at the University of Hawai'i at Hilo, which acts as a support center for Hawaiian language and culture in the medium of Hawaiian. It provides a wide variety of

Hawaiian language materials, coins new vocabulary, and coordinates in-service training programs for teachers.

Despite many setbacks and a continual struggle for funding, immersion opportunities continue to expand and demand for immersion education grows steadily. In 1993 there were 162 children enrolled at all seven Pūnana Leo schools in the state. In that same year Niʻihau parents living on the neighboring island of Kauaʻi requested Hawaiian-medium education for their children through the sixth grade. Parents boycotted a local school when their request was denied. In 1994 they received funding from the Office of Hawaiian Affairs to start a public immersion kindergarten through the sixth grade. By 1995 immersion preschool enrollment climbed to 181 at nine preschools throughout the state. In that same year an intermediate/high school program began at Nāwahīokalaniʻōpuʻu school on the island of Hawaiʻi, and there are currently about 60 students there in grades 7 through 11. Despite the lack of a library, science lab, and a range of course offerings equivalent to what is found at nearby Hilo High School, each student scored above the statewide average on college admission tests. In 1996 the state Board of Education approved a site on Oʻahu as the state's first total immersion school from kindergarten to high school. In 1999 around 1,600 students participated in public school immersion programs, and eleven students graduated from the state's two immersion high schools, the first to have been educated entirely in Hawaiian for over a century. Enrollment in Hawaiian classes has also increased steadily in high schools and universities, with about 2,500 students at each level studying Hawaiian as a second language. At the University of Hawaiʻi numbers have increased 500 percent over the past ten years.

In 1997 the state legislature approved the establishment of a Hawaiian Language College at the University of Hawaiʻi at Hilo which will strengthen and expand the Hawaiian Studies Department, already the most highly developed program in an indigenous language in the US. In 1998 the new college admitted nine students for the degree of M.A. in Hawaiian language and literature, the first graduate program in an indigenous language in the US. There are plans for an M.A. in immersion teacher training.

Case study 2: Lessons from the rain forest

Our second example comes from the Karaja people, who inhabit small villages on Banalal Island, some 50 miles wide and 240 miles long, in the Middle Araguaia River in central Brazil. They first came to the attention of Europeans in 1684 when pioneers came from Sao Paulo to open up the Brazilian interior. From 1776 military outposts were set up in the Karaja area. Since the time of these first contacts the population has declined. Until 1958 their language was unclassified. Their island location has provided natural boundaries and has proved a buffer between them and the outside world. They maintained a semi-nomadic lifestyle up until around 1970. Although they obtain food by hunting and fishing, they now cultivate fields near their villages where they grow sweet potatoes, corn, bananas, and rice. Just a few decades ago they had only intermittent contact with the outside world in the form of occasional passing boats and planes. Now there are weekly commercial flights landing on paved runways built near some of the villages.

The first formal schools to be set up in this area taught in Portuguese, but in 1972 the Brazilian government passed legislation which stated that any minority group having a linguistic barrier to education in Portuguese had the right to study initially in their own language. The National Indian Foundation began bilingual-bicultural programs with four tribes, one of which was the Karaja. In these new schools the study of local history and culture is an integral part of the curriculum.

Because the Karaja language was unwritten, a writing system had to be devised for it so that teaching materials could be created. Although the first primers produced were written by outsiders, they tried to make them sensitive to local traditions and lifestyles. The drawings and characters in the stories look like Karaja people rather than European Brazilians, and many of the stories in the books were taken from tape recordings of Karaja oral myths. Later, the Karaja began to write their own textbooks.

At the beginning of the bilingual-bicultural program adults were taught to read first, and some Karaja from each of the three major clans were trained as teachers. Rather than bringing the teachers to some central location, however, the training was conducted in local villages. Initially, 50 students were taught by the first group of teachers to complete this course. By 1987 the number of children in these schools was around 300. In this way, the responsibility for Karaja education has been placed in the hands of the people themselves. Indigenous leaders are involved in the education program, and Karaja teachers and students use the men and women of the village as an oral library of traditional knowledge. The entire community is involved in this new kind of education just as it was in traditional culture. The development of their own literature enhances the Karajas' sense of the value of their own culture. The oral knowledge provided by the people themselves has proved a rich resource for the schools. The Karaja have the first social studies book written by indigenous people in Brazil.

Another example from the Amazonian rain forest is the Shuar people, who live in the remote rain forest of Ecuador's Amazon region. They have learned to adapt new technologies and ideas from the outside while also preserving their own culture, language, and way of life. They have formed the Shuar Indian Federation, one of the strongest indigenous organizations in Latin America. Knowing that in order to maintain their community they had to retain control over their children's education, but realizing at the same time the need for access to the knowledge of western society, they have set up a radio education program. Each village has its own receiver and a trained teacher's assistant. Thus, the children can stay at home in the village where they are best able to maintain their own customs and language. They study Shuar history, resource management, and science in their own language at the same time as they meet Ecuador's formal education requirements. The radios are also used to provide adult education and news.

Case study 3: The voice of the land is in our language

In 1965 Joseph Nicholas quit his job as a barber in Bangor, Maine to return to his roots on the Passamaquoddy Indian reservation at Pleasant Point in northern Maine. The Passamaquoddy have lived in that area—"the land where the sun rises first"—for at least three thousand years. Nicholas was haunted by memories of his grandparents and pride in their heritage as "people of the early dawn." Convinced that the voice of the land was in his language, he wanted to pass on the culture of his grandparents to the younger people and do what he could to make sure that one of the last living Indian languages in New England would survive another generation. When Nicholas went back to the reservation, over 80 percent of the Passamaquoddy were unemployed and living in shacks with dirt floors and no plumbing. Average life expectancy was 47 years in a country where the white middle-class population can expect to live nearly three decades longer. The Passamaquoddy were even denied the right to vote in Maine until 1954, despite having fought in every United States war since the American Revolution. English was of course the language of the reservation schools and had already just about totally replaced Passamaquoddy in the home.

The first step in Nicholas's fight to restore Passamaquoddy to its rightful pride of place among the younger generation was to reintroduce traditional dance. Nicholas, now in his 70s, and a former tribal councilman and state representative, worked with linguists at the Massachusetts Institute of Technology to produce a writing system and dictionary for Passamaquoddy. Two tribal elders have ensured that reservation schools are now bilingual. Booklets and videotapes are now available that tell children about Passamaquoddy culture and language. Now the children of the people of the early dawn are able to say in their own language *Nkihcitomitahatomon wetapeksi*, which means "I am proud of my roots."

Other Native American languages in California no longer spoken in communities have benefited from the Master-Apprentice Language Learning program, which has brought together pairs consisting of a fluent elder and a younger learner who use the language in everyday activities.

Settling for less, but getting more?

These examples illustrate that it is possible for indigenous people to find a new niche within dominant cultures and still maintain their language and culture. Each of these languages, however, is at a different stage in the disruption of intergenerational transmission, and the struggle to secure them will have to continue. Many other indigenous people realize that there are some benefits arising from increased interaction with the dominant society, but they want to preserve some autonomy for themselves and to have a say in determining their own fate—in particular, the right to educate their children in their own way. In the cases we examined and many others, people have used schooling as a means of resistance to the encroachment of the dominant culture. The example of the Rough Rock Navajo school in Arizona, for instance, led other native American communities to contract with the US Bureau of Indian Affairs to operate their own schools.

Minority groups who have retained control over their schooling, such as the Old Order Amish in Pennsylvania, have in fact shown greater language maintenance than those who have not. There is no doubt that absence of schooling in one's own language can make maintenance difficult. In Erik Allardt's study of 46 linguistic minorities in 14 European countries, the clearest link to emerge between language and schooling is that a minority language which is not taught tends to decline. Studies of language shift have shown time and time again that schools are a major agent of cultural and linguistic assimilation because formal education is often the first point of contact children have with the world outside their own community.

Immersion in English schools was destructive to Dyirbal-speaking children in Australia for several reasons. Children had to sink or swim in a completely different language and cultural environment. The very fact that Dyirbal had no presence in the school was a signal that it was seen as a useless language. Denied the opportunity of learning in Dyirbal, and expected to assimilate to the norms of white Australia, many children got caught in a vicious circle. Because the school failed to support the home language, skills in it were often poor and deteriorated further. The failure of the school to let children develop in their own language was then used to legitimize further oppression of it. At the same time they often did not progress in the majority language (often for reasons that had nothing to do with language, but which reflected the poorer socio-economic status of the minority in relation to the majority).

While many groups, such as the Hawaiians and Maori, have made enormous gains in securing a place for their languages in the public educational sector, it would be wrong to leave the picture unduly rosy. Provision for schooling in a threatened language will not automatically safeguard its future or lead to a way out of the vicious circle of running continually harder only to end up in more or less the same place generation after generation. Language movements cannot succeed if schools or states are expected to carry the primary burden of maintenance or revival. A frequent decision of language revival groups to start on the educational system can be misguided, particularly if the language in question is spoken primarily by those already past school age.

The lesson to be learned from the experience of some 70 years of state intervention on behalf of Irish is clear. There is an important distinction to be made between learning a language in the artificial environment of the classroom and transmitting it in the natural environment of the home. Schools in Ireland have achieved most of what can be expected from formal language education, namely knowledge of Irish as a second language acquired in late adolescence. They have not led to its spoken use in everyday life, nor its intergenerational transmission. In his assessment of the efforts of the Irish state to revitalize and maintain Irish, Pádraig Ó Riagáin points out that government language policies have almost invariably been out of step with economic policies and social realities. It is difficult to maintain the proficiency achieved by the pupils in Irish-medium schools in an urban environment without adequate community support for the language, and there is a need to create a more supportive social environment for Irish outside school.

Likewise, with no support system in place in the home and community, some of the original cohort of Kōhanga Reo students from 1981–1982 have lost their knowledge of Maori. Usage in society's higher level institutions such as schools and the media does not automatically trickle down to lower levels such as community and home, any more than food aid to famine victims helps prevent drought or other conditions which lead to famine. Schooling comes after intergenerational transmission is secure and reinforces the home-community network, rather than vice versa. By the same token, no amount of television broadcasting aimed at children can compensate for an absence of language use in the family. Experience with television in Irish and Welsh shows that time bought with television is expensively bought indeed because it has no intergenerational transmission payoff.

Because most Maori and Irish people are already using English for most daily activities, it will take an extraordinary amount of ideological commitment for them to undertake the further dislocation of their lives that transferring to another language would entail. Surveys show, for instance, that two-thirds of the Irish people believe the Irish language is crucial for maintaining an Irish identity, but most Irish people do not speak Irish and have not done so for centuries. As one Irish person put it to researcher Reg Hindley, "although we are all *for* Irish as we are for cheaper bus fares, heaven, and the good life, nobody of the masses is willing to make the effort." Most public opinion polls, regardless of topic, show a similar gap between what people claim they support in principle and what they are actually prepared to do. A recent survey on nutrition, for instance, found that 80 percent of people felt it was important to have a healthy diet, but only 50 percent said they did anything about it. No doubt fewer than those 50 percent really did anything at all: it is obviously easier to go to McDonald's, just as it is easier to sing songs, establish schools, and other organizations than to get families to speak a threatened language to their children.

Ideological commitment in sufficient quantity can, however, be generated, as one of the most successful (yet at the same time, widely misunderstood) cases of language revitalization illustrates—that of modern Hebrew in Israel. As we noted in Chapter 4, spoken Hebrew, a language with an ancient heritage, had virtually died from the bottom-up. Although its intergenerational transmission as a written language passed on primarily in religious instruction and practice gave the revitalization movement an excellent foundation, not everyone believed that late nineteenth-century Zionists would be able to secularize Hebrew so that it could be spread as a common spoken language among Jews, and some even actively opposed it. Yet by the 1960s Hebrew was the principal language of 90 percent of the population over the age of 14. This was not achieved by waiting for children to finish Hebrew-medium schools, get married, and raise Hebrew-speaking children. In the days of early Jewish settlement of Palestine there was no Jewish state to champion the language, nor was there a state education system.

A number of factors, however, conspired to make the revival of Hebrew successful—such as its connection with a world religion, nationalist ideology, and widespread emigration to Israel. This made it possible for adults to make a break from their previous language backgrounds and start again in a new country in settlements where they used Hebrew as a second language. It was this conjunction of factors which enabled Hebrew to emerge from its status as an ancient literary language of male elites to become a common language for all Jews in the modern state of Israel. Benjamin Harshav goes so far as to say that it is doubtful whether the State of Israel itself would have come into being without the revival of the Hebrew language and its domination of the whole social network. Land made the language, in other words, and language made the land. Hebrew of course had a historical territorial link to the land of the Jews, and its establishment as the language of the modern nation-state of Israel was viewed as a homecoming to its ancestral land of the

Bible. The very term "Hebrew" became a label for a whole revolutionary package of land, language, and work.

Although the Hebrew example shows it is possible to reestablish spoken intergenerational transmission after it has been lost, the problems faced by Maori, Hawaiian, Welsh, Breton, Passamaquoddy, Dyribal, Basque, and most other languages are quite different because their speakers are of a different ethnic origin than the group in control of the country where they reside. They have suffered from the in-migration of politically more powerful speakers from the majority, and are themselves a minority in the nation-state into which they are incorporated. The languages of the majority, moreover, are in each case ones of considerable international importance.

This is another reason why language maintenance must first begin in the community itself through voluntary efforts and be financed from the bottom-up through community resources in the early stages. The home is a safer space whose boundaries the minority can more easily control when a more powerful group dominates the public spheres. A few well-chosen victories early on will do more than lack of success in larger and often unrealistic goals, which are more likely to be perceived as requiring alteration to existing power structures and potentially resisted as threats to the cohesiveness of the state. For example, as soon as Quebec Francophones took action to increase their political power, particularly in the form of legislation designed to protect French, they lost whatever good will they had among Anglophones. Securing the home front does not rely on the majority's cooperation, nor does it involve major costs.

That is not to absolve the state of responsibility, but financial aid comes at a price. Dependence on state resources undermines the minority's responsibility and right to control its own affairs. Insofar as a minority language represents an alternative point of view and lifestyle that is potentially in conflict with the dominant culture, requests for bilingual education may represent a threat to the powers that be. Such programs may attract adverse criticism if financed from tax funding of the majority's government, particularly in times of economic hardship. The current backlash against bilingual education in California and Arizona are examples. No language or culture can endure if it is dependent on another for its intergenerational transmission.

Every group must decide what can best be done realistically for a particular language at a particular time. As Joshua Fishman stresses, there is no language for which nothing at all can be done. By the same token, judgments of success or failure cannot therefore be absolute, but must take into account the starting point and work from the bottom up.

Because language planning has not restored intergenerational transmission at home, the revitalization of Irish has been widely judged a failure. Yet Irish would certainly be a lot worse off without all the work on its behalf. Many threatened languages will not achieve anything like the relative successes of Irish. Thanks to the efforts of the revivalists, however, Irish people can now live a full and varied cultural existence at all levels of education in Irish if they are willing to make the effort to learn it. Their ancestral traditions are far more easily accessible than are those of their close relatives the Scottish highlanders, for instance, most of whom have little knowledge of Scottish Gaelic and their unique linguistic and cultural heritage.

State support has kept Irish from disappearing completely as a spoken language. That can hardly be considered a failure. The existence of a quarter of a million speakers of Irish should not be totally discounted simply because they are bilingual in English rather than Irish monolinguals. Over the short term, Irish efforts have bought some time until a sound basis for intergenerational transmission can be achieved. That could still happen. Pádraig Ó Riagáin also documents a remarkable recent rise in entirely voluntary (as opposed to earlier state-sponsored and at times compulsory) Irish-medium schooling, primarily in Dublin. Meanwhile, in Northern Ireland, a deliberately created community in Shaw's Road in urban Belfast, where parents who were not native speakers of Irish, have succeeded in raising children who are.

Who's afraid of bilingualism?

Rather than lament the loss of monolingualism, we should embrace the gain of bilingualism. A glass half-full is also half-empty. Similarly, there is another face to the Old Testament story of the Tower of Babel, where multilingualism is a debilitating punishment visited upon humanity for its presumption. The New Testament, by contrast, presents linguistic diversity as a divine boon bestowed upon the apostles, who are empowered by this miraculous gift of tongues. Contrary to the proclamation made by a misinformed Texas senator that if English was good enough for Jesus, it ought to be good enough for the children of Texas, Jesus himself was certainly bilingual, if not trilingual. His native tongue was probably Aramaic, a language widely used in Palestine at the time, and he would have learned Hebrew in his religious training. He may also have known some Latin, the language of the occupying Roman troops and law courts, if not some Greek as well.

It has become fashionable in certain political circles to talk about multilingualism and multiculturalism as if they were recent discoveries instead of what they really are: a condition of life as old as the human species. With the rare exception of small isolated atoll communities (almost none of which are really isolated anymore), human communities were always in contact with other groups and connected to them either economically or socially through exchange of goods, knowledge, and marriage partners. Humans have been managing or mismanaging multi-lingualism for centuries well before terms like "policy" or "planning" came onto the scene.

What is new, however, is the attempt to manage such linguistic and cultural contacts and resulting conflicts within the framework of agencies of the modern nation-state. We have seen how the changing character of multilingualism in the modern world was tied to the rise of nation-states, in which a common national language was generally seen as inseparably bound to the national culture, a sign of loyalty to the nation itself, and essential for modernization and economic progress. Nations may be both multicultural and multilingual from a practical standpoint by virtue of the presence of a number of coexisting groups, while recognizing the validity of only one. In fact, probably most nation-states are multilingual and multicultural in this sense whether they admit it or not. Similarly, most have resisted sharing power with minorities in their midst.

Many minority languages will survive only as second languages in the future, but that is no small victory. Restoration of full monolingualism where it once may have existed is not a realistic goal, because modern life makes it impossible and indeed undesirable to be entirely independent of outside influences. Bilingualism has for a long time suffered from bad press. The overwhelming majority of references to it in the media still stress its alleged disadvantages, both to societies and individuals. Opponents of bilingualism, ignorant of its social functions and human value, offer a number of reasons why they find it divisive, confusing, and a stumbling block to both peace and progress, but none of these claims holds up under careful scrutiny. Bilingualism is not something mysterious, abnormal, or unpatriotic, but has been an unremarkable necessity for most of humanity.

In today's global village, however, increasing bilingualism in a metropolitan language, particularly English, is making the majority of the world's languages in effect minority languages. Even small national languages such as Icelandic with its 100,000 speakers, and larger national languages such as Swedish and Hebrew, substantially protected by political boundaries and institutions, exist in a diglossic relation with English at the highest levels of international communication. This in itself is no cause for alarm. When diglossia is stable, each language has its own set of functions and space without threatening the other. Sweden, for instance, has just introduced the study of English as a second language into the earliest stages of primary education in order to secure high levels of proficiency. Over time, this will mean that the only monolingual Swedes will be preschool children. Yet Swedish and many other small national languages such as Dutch, Icelandic, and Danish are in no danger of not being transmitted intergenerationally. That is because they control their own polities at all levels from home to school to government. The learning of English and other languages of wider communication will continue to take place at school and not at home as long as they retain control of the education system and use their own languages among themselves at home and in communities as markers of in-group identity. The latter point is worth stressing because it can easily be misunderstood by monolinguals—and evidently even by linguists, as the following story indicates.

American linguist Kenneth Pike once asked Danish linguist Louis Hjelmslev why he continued to use Danish even though he was fluent in English. Hjelmslev was so struck by the question that he commented on it at length in a paper he gave in Copenhagen to a Symposium on Heredity, Race, and Culture in 1954. The answer given to Pike was that Danes would never consider abandoning Danish, because it is an essential and indispensable part of being Danish and has been for longer than anyone can remember. Most Americans have no choice but to speak English since it is the only language they know, and they have not learned foreign languages because it has usually sufficed to know English. If we imagine instead, however, that a Dane were to suggest that all Americans should henceforth be taught to speak with a British accent, most would object. Even though British English is not a completely different language, most people would feel that British English was not the right language with which to express their American identity. They would not feel at home in it any more than they would in Danish.

Globalization on an unprecedented scale does not change the fact that most people everywhere still live their lives in local settings and feel the need to develop and express local identities to pass on to their children. Language, along with features such as dress, behavior patterns, religion, or occupation, serves to mark group identity. When one is given up or lost, another may replace it, but inevitably there is a difference. As the ultimate symbolic system, language is well suited to the role of marking a distinctive identity because it conveys cultural content that preserves and transmits meanings and experiences shared by the group who uses it. Because a large part of any language is culture-specific, people feel that an important part of their traditional culture and identity is lost too when that language disappears. As one Native American, Darryl Babe Wilson, put it, quoting his aunt, "We must know the white man language to survive in this world. But we must know our language to survive forever."

People respond to things on the basis of the meanings that they have for them. Some groups feel very strongly about the role of language in the continuation of their identity. René Levesque, former leader of the Parti Québecois and Quebec Prime Minister, has stated "Being ourselves is essentially a matter of keeping and developing a personality that has survived for three and a half centuries. At the core of this personality is

Figure 8.4 Poster from Welsh Language Board: Why choose Welsh education for your children?

[Courtesy of Welsh Joint Education Authority, Cardiff]

the fact that we speak French. . . . To be unable to live as ourselves, as we should live, in our own language and according to our own ways, would be like living without a heart." A Welsh saying expresses the same feeling: *Gwlad neb iaith, gwlad heb galon* ("Land without a language, land without a heart"). Although ethnic identity can survive language shift, a Québecois or Welsh identity expressed through English is not the same as one expressed through French or Welsh. To say they are different does not imply that one is necessarily better than the other. It does mean, however, that to argue for the preservation of French in Quebec or Welsh in Wales is to argue for a people's right to choose the language in which they want to express their identity. We believe that people everywhere should have these rights.

Living without a heart

Some still regard the concept of language rights as regressive because they are seen as encouraging the persistence of ethnic differences leading to antagonisms. A fear of divided loyalties and identities—supposedly the result of unassimilated ethnic groups—underlies the formation of most nation-states. In 1918, then-US president Theodore Roosevelt could say with unshakable certainty, "We have room for but one language in this country and that is the English language, for we intend to see that the crucible turns out our people as Americans, of American nationality and not as dwellers in a polyglot boarding house and we have room for but one loyalty and that is a loyalty to the American people." In the context of American expansionist policy at that time, Roosevelt also found the extermination of native Americans an "unfortunate, but necessary sacrifice to progress."

American unity has never rested primarily on language, but rather on common political and social ideals. Nevertheless, the current movement called US English, a multimillion dollar lobby group with links to the immigration-restriction lobby that is seeking to obtain a constitutional amendment making English the official language of the US, is trying to stir up support for a language-related national identity politics. Although members legitimize the organization's existence as a way of breaking down supposed language barriers and facilitating minority access to the material and other benefits of mainstream America, the irony is that most ethnic minorities do not actually want a self-contained ethnic group where no English would be spoken. Nor, however, do they want to assimilate linguistically or culturally. A majority want to maintain their ethnicity and language while also being American. An unfounded fear of diversity and thinly disguised racism lies behind the backlash against bilingual education in the U.S. and a similar denial of home language instruction to the children of migrant workers in many European countries.

Despite propaganda from US English to the contrary, there were actually 4.5 times as many non-English speakers recorded in the 1890 US census, when immigration reached its highest point, than in the 1990 census. The assimilative forces that absorbed those immigrants and their languages are in fact even more powerful today. Although the number of non-English speakers is increasing, so is the rate of shift to English. Languages other than English are the ones under threat—not English. Spanish is fast approaching a two-generation pattern shift rather than the three-generation model typical of immigrant groups in the past. Without the replenishing effects of continuing immigration, Spanish would scarcely be viable in the US over the long term.

Another irony in the resistance to providing support in the form of bilingual education is that opposition to it in the US and UK has occurred along with increasing concern over the lack of competence in foreign languages at a time when it is seen as critical to defense interests. Thus, while foreign language instruction in the world's major languages in mainstream schools has been seen as valuable both economically and culturally, bilingual education for minority students has been equated with poverty and loyalty to non-mainstream culture, which is deemed to threaten the cohesiveness of the state. The Defense Language Institute in Monterey, California, which teaches more than 40 languages to 6,000 students, spends about $12,000 to provide a 47-week course in Korean. A graduate of such a course can be expected to achieve a lower level of grammatical proficiency than a five-year-old native speaker. In 1986 there were 10,000 Korean students in California's public schools lacking opportunities and encouragement to develop their native language skills. Most of them will lose their knowledge of Korean before reaching adulthood.

The reason there is little enthusiasm for the languages of immigrant minorities, even when the language concerned is a world language such as Spanish (as is the case in the US) or Arabic (as is the case in France and the Netherlands), is that the situation reflects status differences between the majority and minority populations. Distinctive food, dress, or music are often accepted and allowed to be part of the mainstream (witness the popularity of Mexican food in the US, or Indian restaurants in the UK), but language seldom is.

This ostensible concern over language differences masks the fear many middle-class whites have of losing their majority status. Projections indicate that Hispanics may comprise over 30 percent of the US total population soon after the turn of the century; by 2050, 58 percent of schoolchildren will be non-white. Likewise, in Europe estimates suggest that one-third of the urban population under the age of 35 will be composed of ethnic minorities, the result of widespread migration in the 1950s and 1960s when Europe experienced an acute labor shortage. If we calculate the long-range social and economic cost of continuing the present pattern of undereducating these minority children in Europe, the US, and elsewhere, the results are enormous. It is these children who will become the majority and upon whom the economic burden will fall of caring for the next generation of children and the previous generation soon to be retirees. At the same time the highly developed technological economies in Europe and the US will require an increasingly highly educated work force. New member states in the European Union are almost certain to bring with them their own unresolved language problems and tensions between majority and minorities. Conflicts are likely to increase rather than decrease.

The world has seen the disastrous results of enforced cultural homogenization too many times in the past, and much of the world is unfortunately still inimical to pluralism. In both the US and the Soviet Union it was once believed that industrialization, urbanization, modernization, and the spread of education would reduce ethnic consciousness and lead to the demise of narrower loyalties in favor of broader ones. Both countries have awakened to the fallacy of the melting pot. The 1970s saw a wave of resurgent nationalisms, as have the 1990s with the disintegration of the Soviet Union. The perceived solution under Communist ideology involved not simply the replacement of one language with another, but eliminating the whole basis for ethnicity and separate nationhood.

Under Stalin's regime from 1924 to 1953, whole nations and ethnic groups (including, for instance, the Chechens, the Kalmyk, the Crimean Tartars, the Ingush, and others) were deported, resettled, and persecuted. The Russian conquest of the Caucasus, famed for the number and diversity of its languages, was particularly difficult and bloody. By mixing the population in this way and encouraging the expansion of Russians into formerly non-Russian speaking areas, it was hoped that ethnic ties would weaken and territorial boundaries would break down. Mart Rannut estimates that approximately 70 languages perished in the Soviet attempt to create a new generation of Russian-speaking Soviet citizens with a denationalized cultural identity and an allegiance to the Soviet state and working class. The 1926 census recorded a total of 194 ethnic units, but by 1989 there were only 128.

No empire can be held together indefinitely by repressive linguistic policies and flagrant violations of human rights. The transformation process for the newly liberated states of the former Soviet Union has seen a restructuring of societies on the basis of ethnic and linguistic identities over class-based ones. The Chechens, for instance, losing at least one-quarter and perhaps half of their population in transit as they were deported en masse to Kazakhstan and Siberia in 1944, were allowed to return to their ancestral territory in 1957. In the face of continued Chechen rebellion to Russian appropriation of their land, economic resources, and a continued denial of civil rights, Russian media have depicted the Chechens as thugs and bandits responsible for organized crime and street violence in Russia. In late 1992 Russia sent tanks and troops to the north Caucasus, ostensibly as peacekeepers in an ethnic dispute.

The solution is not to try to get everyone to speak the same language, or to impose coercive official identities, or silence voices of dissent, but to try to rectify imbalances in power. Modernization does not have to entail loss of one's language and culture, and local identity. We need to explore other forms of governance as alternatives to the nation-state, which, as we have seen, arose in particular Western historical circumstances and was predicated on the achievement of linguistic unification as part and parcel of political unification.

Many are still trapped in the mistaken idea that all people have only a single identity—that the Irish are only Irish, Nigerians only Nigerians, and so on. Labels such as these are only the beginning and not end points. In today's global village, no one is only one thing. We all have overlapping and intersecting identities. Being Irish, French, or Breton is not incompatible with being a European, just as being Passamaquoddy or Hawaiian need not be in conflict with being American (or a member of the Republican Party, a woman, a Catholic, etc.). We need to divest ourselves of the traditional equation between language, nation, and state

Figure 8.5   Papua New Guinea's education authorities have now recognized the value of introducing vernacular language education in a number of primary schools around the country

[*Photograph by Suzanne Romaine*]

because with a few notable exceptions, it never actually corresponded to reality anyway, in Europe or anywhere else.

We must think locally but act globally: local languages for expressing local identities and global languages for communicating beyond local levels and expressing our identities as citizens of the world. The active cultivation of stable multilingualism can provide a harmonious pathway through the clash of values inherent in today's struggle between the global and local, between uniformity and diversity.

Our continued survival will depend on our seeing the interconnection between ourselves and our local ecosystems. An important lesson for the global ecosystem can be learned from examining the fate of one such local ecosystem, that of Easter Island, a mere 166 square kilometers of land comprising the most remote inhabited island on earth. All that remains of the once vibrant Rapanui culture that flourished there is a wasteland of grass and hundreds of enormous human stone statues, some weighing more than 60 tons, staring silently across a landscape of extinct volcanoes.

The island was first formed about five million years ago and uninhabited by humans until around AD 400, when a small population of Polynesians arrived in canoes from the west. Evolution had provided the island with a collection of original animal and plant species which harmoniously developed along with the island's natural resources. The colonists initially lived frugally, adapting skills from their homeland to the new conditions, planting the taro and bananas they had brought with them. In time, however, all the original vegetation of the island was replaced. The people burned to the ground the forests that had once covered the whole island, to create more farmland to support the growing population. Gradually, the forest pollen declined as new types of pollen produced by the new species they had brought with them increased. Grass spread until crop pollen itself began to decline. Meanwhile, the crops became harder to grow after the forest was cut and the soil laid bare to the drying wind.

A great crash occurred around the middle of the seventeenth century when the island was thrown into war, almost certainly fueled by the fact that the landscape was depleted of natural resources, thus triggering intense competition between the haves and have-nots. In the dark age that followed, protective walls were built around water supplies, and the islanders manufactured weapons to protect themselves from one another. Eventually, they retreated underground as the island's surface became too dangerous a place to live. Having unthinkingly cleared the forests of timber to feed themselves, they were no longer able to build canoes that might have allowed them to escape the devastated island on which they had imprisoned themselves. This small island—our earth in microcosm—built up a population which was no longer sustainable. When the population peaked beyond the carrying capacity of the land's resources, the ecosystem crashed. Just as we are doing now, the islanders ignored a fundamental law: a varied natural system is inherently more stable than a monoculture. When one part fails, another may support both. The islanders ignored the fact that their lives depended on the natural resources around them.

Contact with Europeans further undermined the remaining population of around 3,000 in the middle of the nineteenth century, when a Peruvian ship forcibly removed about half the people to work as slaves in South America. Following pressure from the Bishop of Tahiti, 15 of the islanders were returned, but they carried smallpox, which further reduced the population to about 100 by 1877. Today, there are fewer than 2,000 Rapanui. Hangaroa, the only small town on the island, looks like a shantytown, with mangy dogs and rusting cars along the sidewalks. Women and their daughters sell a sparse selection of vegetables in open markets. Only one supply ship comes a year to restock the small shops selling canned and other Western goods of limited variety, which are sold at a high price.

Planning for survival: languages as natural resources

Before any decision can be taken to save a language, or protect an ecosystem, we must believe that it is worth doing. This decision is basically a subjective one and carries with it certain values about the kind of world we want to live in and pass on to our children. Ron Crocombe explains that cultural and linguistic uniformity would be undesirable because "Nothing would more quickly stultify human creativity or impoverish the richness of cultural diversity than a single world culture. Cultural uniformity is not likely to bring peace: it is much more likely to bring totalitarianism. A unitary system is easier for a privileged few to dominate. Cultural diversity is one of the world's potential sources of both sanity and fulfillment."

While the loss of most of the world's languages and cultures may be survivable, the result will be a seriously reduced quality of life, if not the loss of the very meaning of life itself for some of the peoples whose voices we have quoted in this chapter and throughout this book. As anthropologist Dell Hymes put it, "One way to think about a society is in terms of the voices it has and might have." Allowing languages and cultures to die directly reduces the sum total of our knowledge about the world, for it removes some of the voices articulating its richness and variety, just as the extinction of any species entails sacrificing some unique part of the environment. It is ultimately self-defeating and maladaptive in the long term to exploit the environment because it increases the likelihood of a deprived and diminished existence not just materially (which is the main concern for economists who look primarily at short-term balance sheets and not the long-term bottom line), but in intellectual, cultural, and emotional terms as well. To remove one language from the mix of languages existing today is to remove it from the world forever. With the passing of each voice, we lose a little more of who we were and are, and what we may become. If we strive toward a goal of preserving all the bits and pieces of our environment, we preserve at the same time as we maximize the opportunities for choices in the future. Variety is not just the proverbial spice of life; it is a prerequisite for life.

We have shown how benign neglect or laissez-faire policies can be continued only at the expense of social justice and true cultural democracy. As far as language is concerned, sociolinguist John Edwards has commented that "in many ethnic matters, the best policy [may be] none at all . . . lack of government legislation or action need not always mean ignorance or discrimination; indeed, lack of response may *be* the appropriate action." It is quite naive to delude oneself that a laissez-faire approach represents absence of policy. It is instead a policy *not* to have a policy. Like other policies, it may be politically expedient and opportunistic depending on the context. Continuing to ignore fundamental inequities in the distribution of the world's resources will lead to more conflicts.

Some top-down strategies

In addition to bottom-up strategies for preserving language and diversity, there are also some useful top-down strategies we would like to suggest.

The first one is to make the preservation of languages part of general activism on behalf of the environment. Arguments in favor of supporting linguistic diversity are the same as those used by scientists in favor of protecting biodiversity. The remedies to the present extinction crisis are similar too because risk to both is caused by the same underlying factors: the destruction of habitats. This means that linguists and others will have to become activists and convince other international groups such as Cultural Survival, Greenpeace, Amnesty International, the Sierra Club, and various local civic groups that language preservation is an important task falling within their remit.

The issue of human rights has already received prominent attention, particularly through the efforts of such groups as Amnesty International. Minority rights overlap substantially with linguistic rights insofar as language death is a symptom of loss of self-regulation of a group's affairs. The Universal Declaration of Human Rights accepted by the United Nations specifies the right to a nationality (and also to change one's nationality), the right of parents to choose the kind of education to give their children, and the right to participate in the cultural life of their community. Discussion of a recent Universal Declaration of Linguistic Rights is taking place under the auspices of UNESCO.

Such legislation should guarantee that everyone has the right to identify with his or her mother tongue and have this identification accepted and respected by others, and have the opportunity to learn the mother tongue orally and in writing. In most cases, this requires indigenous and minority children to be educated through the medium of their mother tongue and use the language in official situations such as school, work, and government. And people whose mother tongue is not an official language in the country where they are resident should be fully encouraged to become bilingual (or multilingual, if they have more than one mother tongue), in their mother tongue as well as the official language or languages — according to their choice.

The second strategy is to establish language policies on a local, regional, and international level as part of overall political planning and resource management. Just as every nation should have an energy policy, it should have a language policy as well — one that embodies the principle of linguistic human rights. This means setting up agencies for language maintenance and development where they do not already exist. The Pacific Languages Unit at the University of the South Pacific in Vila, Vanuatu and the Academy of Mayan Languages in Guatemala are two such examples. Another is the Alaska Native Language Center (ANLC), whose aim is to document and help preserve Alaska's twenty native languages. It also seeks to maximize the heritage of those languages for future generations by documenting the languages in dictionaries, grammars, and literary texts in addition to providing training and materials for programs designed to strengthen the languages' position in Alaskan communities.

In New Zealand, Maori activists have seen the efficacy of linking the struggle for language rights with natural resource management and preservation provisions guaranteed to them in the Treaty of Waitangi of 1840, signed by Maori chiefs and the British. In 1975 the Waitangi Tribunal was created to consider Maori grievances over breaches of the treaty. Although the British regard Maori assent to the treaty as the basis for their sovereignty over New Zealand, there are numerous complicating factors surrounding the treaty and its language, which make its interpretation and legal status fraught with difficulties. The terms of the Maori version of the treaty guaranteed to the Maori *te tino rangatiratanga o ratou wenua o ratou kainga me o ratou taonga katoa*, which can be translated as "the full authority of chiefs over their lands, villages, and all their treasures." Maori activists interpret this as a guarantee rather than cession of Maori sovereignty and have pressed land claims as well as support for the Maori language. The Crown acknowledged Maori claims that the treaty obliged it not only to recognize the Maori language as a part of the country's national heritage and a treasured resource on a par with lands, but to actively protect it. Recognition that the Crown had broken its promise required affirmative action rather than passive tolerance.

As examples of larger geographical scope we can take the European Bureau of Lesser Used Languages in Dublin, the MERCATOR network for information and documentation on minority languages (based at the Frisian Academy in Ljouwert, Holland, to support the Frisian language), and the European Charter on Regional or Minority Languages. These are just a few initiatives which have benefited minorities and their languages in the European Union. Language planning on an even more limited regional basis would clearly make better sense for languages such as Saami, Basque, Catalan, and other languages cutting across national boundaries, but this has to be approached with a great deal of caution to avoid charges of interfering with the sovereignty of existing nation-states. Nevertheless, there are encouraging initiatives toward forms of political autonomy and self-government all over the world—for example, home rule in Greenland, the Saami Parliament in Norway, and tradi-

Figure 8.6   Sovereignty demonstration in Honolulu on the overthrow of the Hawaiian monarchy

[*Courtesy of Edward Greevy*]

tional forms of government among Native Americans and First Nations in Canada.

The desire of indigenous peoples all over the world to assert their rights to self-determination has united them in an effort to preserve their languages, cultures, and lands. A resurgence of native activism is taking place at local, regional, and international levels on a scale scarcely imaginable even twenty years ago. Pressure groups continue to pop up, and some of them have successfully challenged the environmentally unsound practices of large multinational corporations. By forging alliances with conservationists and other international activists, the Yonggom people and their neighbors were able to challenge the Ok Tedi mine; in 1996 an out-of-court settlement awarded them approximately US $500 million in compensation for damage done by mining. The Good Road Coalition of the Rosebud Lakota Sioux, for instance, stopped the siting of a 5,000-acre toxic landfill on their lands. In 1992 about 500 native leaders gathered for the First World Conference of Indigenous Peoples at Kari-Oca, Brazil.

Living in some 15,000 distinct groups, most indigenous peoples have until recently remained rooted in their homelands, local cultures, and languages with little access even to their respective centers of national government, let alone the world press and international political forums. Now the global village reaches even the remotest parts of the Amazon, where indigenous people such as the Kayapo have become global activists and have appeared in international media alongside Sting and

other rock stars. Many native peoples and their organizations have websites in English on the internet capable of reaching millions of people
around the globe. Ironically, these same forces of cultural and linguistic
homogenization are now being pressed into service on behalf of indigenous peoples—and so it should be. Although able to speak to one
another about common concerns in English and other international languages, delegates to the 1999 World Indigenous Peoples Conference on
Education in Hilo, Hawai'i were encouraged to address the meeting in
their native languages.

Legislation, treaties, agencies, and websites go only so far, however.
The effectiveness of any initiatives can always be undermined by individual states unless there is some way of guaranteeing the implementation of
language-related measures on a supranational level. There is a great deal
of difference between democratic countries and oppressive regimes with
respect to the degree of compliance with international agreements and
covenants relating to the rights of minorities and indigenous peoples.
Norway, for instance, has taken a number of steps to strengthen and protect the Saami language, such as the Saami Language Act of 1992, and
the US passed the Native American Languages Act in the same year.
Turkey continues a long history of human rights abuses against the
Kurds, however, despite the fact that Turkey is signatory to many international covenants and treaties as well as an aspiring member of the
European Union. Certain groups such as the Kurds, or the Macedonians
in Greece (already an EU member) receive prominent attention only
when it is politically expedient. The United States government found it
convenient to publicize the Iraqi repression of the Kurds since it wanted
to use Kurdish activism to undermine Saddam Hussein's regime. The
result is that many languages are valued only beyond their national borders, at the same time as they are not recognized for educational or other
public purposes within their own areas of concentration. As recently as
1986, then-Japanese Prime Minister Nakasone reasserted that "Japan is
a nation of homogeneous people," continuing a history of violation of
the International Covenants on Human Rights. When in 1991 the government finally admitted the existence of some 100,000 Ainu people as
an ethnic minority as defined by the covenants, it still refused to
acknowledge that the Ainu are indigenous.

It is not politically popular to talk of restricting the scale of human
activities, but with each day the problems to be addressed grow more
serious. We cannot continue behaving like bulls in a china shop, disrupt-
ing ecosystems wherever we go, destroying resources which cannot be
renewed. As primarily post-agricultural people, most of us are no longer
immediately dependent on the local ecosystems in which we live. We
think we do not have to worry about the exhaustion of this or that food-
stuff or resource because there's always more in the supermarket, or, fail-

ing that, a new technology will find substitutes for nonrenewable resources. We all hope for quick fixes, whether in the domain of environmental action or of language preservation, in which someone or something else does the work. Organizations, policies, and legislation at various levels can help, but we must not forget that it is ultimately individuals who do the work.

We must act now to preserve the remaining healthy vestiges of our heritage by viewing them as resources. Unless intact ecosystems are set aside and under the control of those who live there, there is no hope for long-term survival. Unfortunately, it often takes a great deal of time before the results of scientific research begin to reach government planners and the general public. Getting fast international action is difficult even if there is some consensus in the scientific community. As the clock ticks, it is still business as usual for most governments. In the meantime, our cultures and languages are at risk.

It has been said that bilingualism cannot be shoved down people's throats. Neither should monolingualism, either by fiat or benign neglect. As events of the past few years and the present in various parts of the world show, our global village must be truly multicultural and multilingual, or it will not exist at all.

References and Further Reading

Chapter 1

The epigraph to this chapter is from Cuppy (1941, p. 165). The case of Tevfic Esenç is described in an article in *The Economist* magazine (Economist, 1998). The stories of last speakers of other dying languages are to be found in the literature on those particular languages, as outlined below.

Michael Krauss's estimates of global language endangerment are found in his 1992 article. Several edited collections give overviews, statistics, and case studies from across the world. The most important are Dorian (1989), Robins and Uhlenbeck (1991), Brenzinger (1992), Taylor (1992), Grenoble and Whaley (1998), and McCarty and Zepeda (1998).

Surveys of Native American languages, including statistics on numbers of speakers, can be found in Chafe (1962), Kinkade (1991), Zepeda and Hill (1991), and Hinton (1994). The estimate for numbers of speakers of Irish comes from Hindley (1990). R.E. Johannes (1981) has written about indigenous knowledge of fish. The Micmac example comes from an internet posting by Dan Alford (1994). David Bradley (1989) has written about the Ugong language and people of Thailand.

Niles Eldredge (1991, 1998) provides overviews of the biodiversity crisis facing the world today. The statistics on species endangerment are from Juvik and Juvik (1998). C.P. Snow's (1959) book considers the effects of the agrarian and industrial revolutions. McLuhan (1989) outlines some of the major transformations in human history occasioned by the spread of print media and the rise of other communication technologies such as the telegraph, radio, and television. The effects of more recent technology such as the internet have yet to be systematically assessed.

The idea of English being a "killer" language is in Price (1984, p. 170). The spread of English around the world is the subject of many books such as Kachru (1980) and McCrum, Cran, and MacNeil (1986).

The notion of speaking as an act of identity is explained in Le Page and Tabouret-Keller (1985). The quote from Sir James Henare is from Waitangi Tribunal (1986, p. 40). Spolsky and Cooper (1991) discuss how street signs in Jerusalem reflect the changing power relations in the city.

Fishman (1991) addresses the problems faced by minority groups who wish to revitalize their languages. The quote from Marie Smith is from Davidson

(1993, p. 11), which is also the source of the statistics on the death of indigenous people (p. 194).

An edited version of Rupert Murdoch's speech, the 11th annual John Boynthon lecture, appeared in *The Australian* (Murdoch 1994). The story of the American visitor to Finland is in Christophersen (1986). The melting pot theory of ethnicity is discussed in Glazer and Moynihan (1963). Berberglou (1995) provides a good historical overview of many cases of ethnic nationalism around the world.

Chapter 2

The source for the epigraph to this chapter is Carl Sandburg's poem "Languages" (in Sandburg 1916, p. 175). There are a number of compendiums and encyclopedias of language on the market aimed at specialists and nonspecialists. Probably the most comprehensive list of languages is the *Ethnologue*, produced by the Summer Institute of Linguistics (Grimes 1996). SIL also has a searchable website at *http://www.sil.org/ethnologue/* with a vast amount of information on languages, numbers of speakers, and the state of linguistic research. Voegelin and Voegelin (1977) and, at a more accessible level, Crystal (1987) and Comrie, Matthews, and Polinsky (1997), are also useful on the classification and distribution of languages.

Johanna Nichols's study of typological and genetic diversity is published as Nichols (1992). Some linguists, such as Ruhlen (1987), believe that all Nichols's stocks can be reduced to a mere 17 very large families.

We will not discuss the issue of dialect death here, although many varieties of languages are at risk too. On the issue of distinguishing languages from dialects see Chapter 1 of Romaine (1994). For some studies of dialect death see Wolfram and Schilling-Estes (1997), Dorian (1981), Holloway (1997), and Jones (1998).

Krauss (1992) is an attempt to assess the extent of language endangerment. Figure 2.1 is adapted from Nettle (1998a), and Table 2.2 is from Nettle (1999, p. 114). Correlations between linguistic and biological diversity for various areas and for the world as a whole have been shown by Mace and Pagel (1995), Harmon (1996, 1998) and Nettle (1996, 1998, 1999). Larger ramifications of these correlations are explored in Maffi (2001).

For a discussion of how scientists attempt to measure the extent of biodiversity, see May (1992). The map in Figure 2.3 is based on data from Williams, Gaston, and Humphries (1997). Estimates of the rate of species extinction can be found in Wilson (1978) and Eldredge (1998). See also Wilson (1992) on the importance of insects. Eldredge (1991) is the source for the discussion of concepts such as niche-width and Rapoport's Rule. The World Wide Fund For Nature's report based on data from 152 countries was written by Jonathan Loh (released by Agence France Presse, October 1, 1998) and circulated on the Gaia Forest Archives (*http://forests.org*).

A number of sources document the extermination of indigenous peoples through destruction of their habitats in search of resources. See, for example,

Hemming (1978) on the Brazilian Indians, Hong (1987) on Sarawak, Davidson (1993), and the essays in Head and Heinzman (1990), especially the chapter by Jason Clay.

Chapter 3

There are a number of case studies of the last speakers and final stages of native American languages. Lyle Campbell (1975) has documented Cacopera, and, with Una Canger, Chicomuceltec (Campbell and Canger, 1978). Elmendorf (1981) discusses Wappo and Yuki, and Haas (1968) considers Biloxi. The case of Ishi is documented in Kroeber (1964).

Several studies in Dorian (1989) describe the structural changes that accompany gradual shift. See especially the chapters by Campbell and Muntzel and Jane H. Hill. Shield (1984) discusses the revival of Cornish.

The quote about Rossel Island is from Grimshaw (1912, pp. 191–2), and the quote from the French historian about New Caledonia is from Crowley and Lynch (1985, p. 15). The Cherokee example is discussed in Ullmann (1951, p. 49), and Jespersen (1964, pp. 429–30). Hill (1952) discusses the errors in the claims made about the Cherokee and similar examples of supposed primitiveness. Marshack (1965) attempts to measure efficiency in terms of amount of information, while Swadesh (1971) explains why the notion of primitive language is a myth.

The example of evidentiality in Tuyuca is discussed in Palmer (1986, p. 67). Jo Thomas's (1988) review of Leo Dunmore's book appeared in the *New York Times Book Review*. The Dyirbal noun classification system is described by Dixon (1972), and the changes it is undergoing are studied by Schmidt (1985), the source of Figures 3.3 and 3.4. Dixon (1984) has also described some of the interesting linguistic features of Aboriginal languages, along with his field work experiences.

Leanne Hinton (1994) provides many good examples of the rich linguistic diversity to be found in the native American languages of California. The examples of noun classification in Pohnpeian are from Rehg (1981) and the report of its decline from Rehg (1998). Stephen Wurm (1986, 1991) deals with grammatical change in noun classification systems in two articles. See also Laycock (1975). Hale (1992) provides examples of the rich diversity in Australian and other languages. On the issue of what is lost in translation, see the papers by Christopher Jocks and Anthony C. Woodbury, both in Grenoble and Whaley (1998). Linden (1991) documents some of the kinds of indigenous knowledge under threat today.

The discussion of fishing in Palau relies heavily on Johannes (1981). Other useful sources for Tahiti, Hawai'i, and other Pacific islands include Nordhoff (1930), Craighill Handy (1932), Titcomb (1977), Rensch (1988), and Lieber (1994). Pūku'i (1983, p. 5) is the source for the Hawaiian proverb about fishing. Majnep and Bulmer (1977) is a rich catalogue of indigenous knowledge about birds in Papua New Guinea.

Chapter 4

The title and epigraph of this chapter come from Haugen (1972). The cases of Kirtland's warbler, and of the Yanomami gold rush in Brazil, are discussed in Ehrlich and Ehrlich (1991, p. 90), and Clay (1990), respectively.

The idea of a primordial ecosystem comes from Niles Eldredge (1998). An account of the biological richness and fragility of the Pacific is to be found in Mitchell (1990), from which much of the information on species diversity comes.

The linguistic diversity of the Pacific is evident from the sample in Nichols (1992). Statistics on the number of languages and their speakers in Papua New Guinea derive from Nettle (1999). The classification of the languages is discussed by Foley (1986), and Capell (1969) contains typological information.

Foley (1986) gives some information on the sociolinguistic situation, including the quotation about language serving as an indispensable badge of identity (p. 9). More detail is provided by Sankoff (1980), who pays particular attention to traditional multilingualism (pp. 95–132). The quote about language contact and identity comes from there (p. 10). Further discussion is to be found in Laycock (1980). Examples of traditional language shift and diffusion are given by Thurston (1987), where his experience of local multilingualism is described. Ken McElhanon's experiences with the Selepet are described in Kulick (1992, pp. 2–3).

The ecology and subsistence of New Guinean peoples are described by Rappoport (1968, 1971). The study of the Kubo people is Dwyer and Minnegal (1992). Other descriptions of New Guinea society are to be found in Brown (1978) and Rubel and Rosman (1978). The interconnectedness and fluidity of New Guinean societies is argued by Hays (1993), where the quote about people rather than nature creating boundaries comes from (p. 148).

Social capital, pig festivals, and the behavior of big men are discussed in the works by Rappoport and Rubel and Rosman already mentioned, and, for Irian Jaya, in Posposil (1966). The idea of symbolic capital is developed by Pierre Bourdieu in various works, including, in English, Bourdieu (1984) and (1989). The use of language to invoke solidarity is discussed in many sociolinguistics texts such as Romaine (1994) and Chambers (1995). For the perspective of social psychology, see the many works by Howard Giles and his colleagues such as Giles (1977) and Giles and St. Clair (1979).

Parts of the Amazon show similar patterns of high multilingualism to New Guinea, also maintained over long periods of time in small groups, as documented by Grimes (1985) and Sorenson (1971).

The idea of linguistic equilibria is from Dixon (1997), as is the typology of language loss. Discussion of changes in the geography of human language over the very long term is to be found in Dixon's book, and in Nettle (1999).

There is an extensive sociolinguistic literature on the topic of language shift and death. Taylor (1992) and Dorian (1989) are useful anthologies of case studies from around the world. Detailed studies of specific instances of shift can be found in Gal (1979) and Kulick (1992). The Gros Ventres example is from Taylor (1989).

Good discussions of the social, political, and economic transformation of the Hawaiian islands through the introduction of the plantation system are contained in Takaki (1983), from whom the quotation from Hooper's diary is taken (p. 5), and Beechert (1985), from whom the quotation about vagrancy ordinances is taken (pp. 35–6). Dougherty (1992) provides a good account of the post-contact history of Hawai'i through the overthrow of the Hawaiian monarchy and subsequent annexation to the US at the end of the nineteenth century.

Chapter 5

The idea of the Paleolithic equilibrium is inspired by Dixon (1997). On hunter-gatherer societies in general, Sahlins (1972) is still of interest.

Jared Diamond (1997) gives a readable account of the transition to farming, and its importance in giving rise to the different long-term trajectories of the continents. His book is also the source of information on the distribution of grasses and animals in the various continents. A scholarly review of the topic, including the calculation that 99.997 percent of human beings now depend upon food production, is to be found in Ellen (1994). More specialized works on the origins of agriculture include Rindos (1984), which stresses its gradual and nonintentional nature, and Cohen (1978), which stresses the role of population pressure and the deleterious effects, in terms of nutrition and disease, of the transition. Further evidence of these effects on the skeletons of early farmers is given in Cohen and Armelagos (1991).

Discussion of the demography of the prehistoric world and estimates of the impact of the Neolithic on population growth are to be found in Hasan (1981). The idea of waves of farming advance was first put forward by Ammerman and Cavalli-Sforza (1973), and elaborated in Ammerman and Cavalli-Sforza (1984). It has been applied to the spread of Indo-European by Renfrew (1987), and to many other areas as well, as discussed by Renfrew (1991) and by Diamond (1997, especially Chapter 18). The world population estimates used in Figure 5.2 and discussed in the text come from Biraben (1979).

The European expansion as an ecological and demographic transition is the subject of Alfred Crosby's (1986) classic book. Crosby is the source of much information on the spread of plants and animals (including humans), and also the spread of diseases, from Eurasia. Kunitz (1994) gives a summary of the effects of disease on indigenous populations. Economic causes and consequences of the Eurasian population boom are discussed in Jones (1987), as is the vexed question of why it was Europe, rather than China or India, which expanded and later industrialized.

More traditional historical treatments of the European expansions in different areas which we have found useful are as follows. For the Americas, volumes 1 and 2 of *The Cambridge History of Latin America* (Bethell 1984) contain many useful chapters. There are many accounts of North American history; Dee Brown's (1971) is particularly vivid, and is the source of the quote from Red Cloud, which forms the epigraph of this chapter. Also useful is Ward Churchill (1997). Information on the Kaiowa, Nandeva, and Terana tribes of Brazil comes from an article in the *Guardian* newspaper (Rocha and Summa

1992). For the state of Native American languages today, see the chapters on the Americas in Robins and Uhlenbeck (1991), and, for more specific case studies, Hinton (1994) and Kroskrity (1993). On the slave trade, which took perhaps ten million Africans to America, see Curtin (1969).

For Australia and New Zealand, Crosby (1986) contains much useful information, including the quote from Tamati Waaka Nene (p. 251). Day (1996) is one of the most interesting of the "straight" histories, focusing as it does on racial conflict and aboriginal issues. The quotes from the Reverend West, J.D. Lang, and others are from this source (pp. 101, 109). The story of Trucanini is told by Hughes (1988, pp. 422–424). On the plight of Aborigines this century, including the forcible removal of children from their families, see Pilger (1998, pp. 223–248). For information on Australian languages today, see Bob Dixon's chapter in Robins and Uhlenbeck (1991).

The failure of Europeans to penetrate the moist tropics is examined by Crosby (1986), and by Curtin (1989).

Chapter 6

The epigraph for this chapter comes from Landes (1998, p. 305). Language shift in Gapun, Papua New Guinea, is the subject of Kulick (1992), and that in Oberwart, of Gal (1979). Some information on Hórom (Nigeria) is to be found in Nettle (1998b).

The rise of politically unequal societies is considered by Johnson and Earle (1987). Useful overviews of economic takeoff and the industrial revolution are provided by Jones (1987), who discusses the question of causes, and by the papers in Snooks (1994), which provide statistics on economic growth and social development.

The decline of the Celtic languages is well documented. Glanville Price (1984) gives much of the relevant information. Hindley (1990) is useful for Irish. Michael Hechter (1975) is a systematic and interesting approach to the problem from a social science perspective rather than a historical one, though its treatment of language is minimal. Victor Durkacz's (1983) book, despite its general title, is largely restricted to the domains of education and religion. Perhaps the most useful general source of information, though only available in French, is Abalain (1989). One version of the story of Dolly Pentreath is to be found there (Abalain 1989, p. 169). Another is in Price (1984, p. 136).

Sources of quotations about the Celtic languages are as follows: vernaculars as "rustic, stagnant, etc.," Gregor (1980, p. 302); Edinburgh Gaelic School Society, Durkacz (1983, p. 224); school commissioner in Wales, Durkacz (1983, p. 225); penal laws of Henry IV, Hechter (1975, p. 73); Act for the English Order, Habit and Language (Henry VIII), Durkacz (1983, p. 4); Act for the Settling of Parochial Schools (James I/VI), Durkacz (1983, p. 5); Welsh language "disastrous barrier to all moral improvement" and "distorts the truth," Hechter (1975, p. 75); French officials on Breton, Abalain (1989, pp. 209, 210).

The comments made by Lord Salisbury are quoted in Kiernan (1988, p. 28). The source for John of Fordun's description of fourteenth-century Scotland is Dorian (1981, pp. 16–7, 38). See also Fairhurst (1964). Ralph Grillo (1989) traces the establishment of English and French as dominant languages. The description of the British occupation of Ireland in terms of imperialism and genocide is from Greeley (1989, p. 3).

The spread of metropolitan languages in different parts of the developing world is described by many papers in R.H. Robins and E.M. Uhlenbeck (1991), Grenoble and Whaley (1998), and Dorian (1989). Peter Ladefoged (1992) gives the case that conversion to a majority language can be voluntary and progressive, though for a contrasting view, see Nancy Dorian's (1993).

Information about human rights abuses against the Kurds is contained in Tove Skutnabb-Kangas and Sertaç Bucak (1994), from whom our quotations are taken (pp. 347–8).

Telling accounts of how indigenous social organization is suppressed in many developing countries, often directly or indirectly through the influence of the Western powers, are given by Noam Chomsky (1993, 1996), and by Pilger (1998). The quotations about East Timor and the internet come from Ramos-Horta (1999, p. 12), and as José Ramos-Horta says in that article, you can get more information about East Timor from *http://www.easttimor.com* than you can from being in East Timor itself.

Chapter 7

The view that linguistic diversity and national development are opposing objectives is found in Pool (1972, quotation from p. 225). What we have called the *benign neglect* position has not been explicitly stated in the literature, though Ladefoged (1992) seems to come close.

The failure of "development" to help the rural poor is argued by Chambers (1983), and Lipton (1977). The problem of sustainability is discussed by Redclift (1987), the source of many of our statistics on poverty and environmental degradation. *Business Week*'s (1992) article articulates some of the inequalities in consumption of natural resources between developed and developing nations. A special issue of *The Contemporary Pacific* (Barlow and Winduo 1997) provides an overview of the environmental issues surrounding deforestation in Papua New Guinea and the surrounding region. The quote from Yalaum Mosol is from a report about the Papua New Guinea Rainforest Campaign on the Gaia Forest Archives (*http://forests.org*), dated September 12, 1996. Stuart Kirsch (1996) discusses the impact of the Ok Tedi mine on the Yonggom people of Papua New Guinea. Although we have focused here on the impact of resource extinction in developing countries, similar stories can be told for developed countries such as the U.S. The economic benefits of mining, for instance, on native American land, have done little to improve disparities between local communities and mainstream Americans, as Churchill (1993) has shown. Meanwhile, resource development has devastating effects on local environments. Bass (1990) contains many examples of failed "technofixes" funded by international agencies, including the story of the Niger Delta region of Mali. His chapter entitled "The Fourth World" discusses the problems faced by African nomads. Griffiths and Robin (1997) also contains interesting material on the environmental impact of expanding metropolitan societies.

The story of the two Kayapo Indians arrested in Brazil is related in Clay (1990). On projects funded by international agencies such as the World Bank and their consequences: Bass (1990), and Redclift (1987, pp. 56–69, 75–6).

Furnivall (1948, pp. 372, 376, 408) examines some of the mistakes made in colonial education systems. Robinson (1996) deals with some of the problems resulting from development agencies' failure to take into account Cameroon's indigenous languages. See also Ali A. Mazrui's (1997) critique of World Bank education policies, and Mazrui and Mazrui (1998).

Good examples of indigenous knowledge systems, including Gordon Thomasson's study of Kpelle steelmaking, are given in Warren and Brokensha (1995). The Haunóo information is discussed in Chambers (1983, pp. 87–9), and comes from Conklin (1969). The study of Balinese water temples and their role in irrigation is Lansing (1991). The Asian Development Bank quote is from page 124.

Information on the Palauan Congress is to be found in Stolzenberg (1994), and on the Ombessa village development committees in Robinson (1996). The Kuna's initiative in Panama, and the CRIC in Colombia, are described in Clay (1990). The quote from Apolu Nakera, the Turkana pastoralist, is from Bass (1990, p. 185).

Some organizations such as *Survival International* based in London and *Cultural Survival* based in Cambridge, Massachusetts publish valuable newsletters with information about indigenous peoples. Cultural Survival's (1987) publication is a particularly useful survey. Most of these publications, however, generally say little, if anything, about the role of language in cultural survival.

Chapter 8

Ellis and mac a' Ghobhainn (1971) contains some case studies of language revival and is the source of the epigraph to this chapter (p. 144). Fishman (1991) draws on the experience of past and present practitioners of language restoration in the context of current sociolinguistic theory and practice. See also the chapters in Hornberger (1997). Nancy Dorian edits for the *International Journal of the Sociology of Language* a column entitled "Small languages and small language communities," which contains news and information about language maintenance efforts all over the world. Other useful sources include the papers in Reyhner (1997) and Cantoni (1997).

Sources on the revitalization of the Hawaiian language include Kapono (1995) and Wilson (1998). Slaughter and Watson-Gegeo (1988) is the source for the quotations from parents and other participants in Hawaiian immersion programs. Fortune and Fortune (1987) discuss the case of the Karaja Indians. Harshav (1993) provides a good account of the revitalization of Hebrew. On other language revitalization movements, see Allardt (1979), De Vries (1984), and Spolsky (1989).

The story of Joseph Nicholas's efforts on behalf of Passamaquoddy were reported in *Newsweek* (1988). The quote from Darryl Babe Wilson is from Hinton (1994, p. 234). Nora Marks Dauenhauer and Richard Dauenhauer

(1998) explain some of the reasons why language preservation has been difficult in native Alaskan communities. A special issue of the *International Journal of the Sociology of Language* contains a feature article on Canadian language policy by John Edwards (1994), along with commentaries from other scholars. Hinton (1994) contains other examples of Master-Apprentice pairs in California.

Gabrielle Maguire (1991) describes the Shaw's Road community in Belfast, and Ó Riagáin (1997) provides an assessment of the successes and failures of the movement to restore Irish in the Republic of Ireland. See also Hindley (1990), and, for a comparison of the Israeli and Irish experiences, with considerable discussion of Maori and other cases, Wright (1996). The quotation from René Levesque (1977) is from his book documenting Quebec's claims to distinctiveness. Baker and Prys Jones (1998) provides valuable information about the role and status of bilingualism around the world, and is the source of the information on the languages known by Jesus (p. 18). Rannut (1994) discusses Russification policies in the former Soviet Union, as does an article from *The Economist* (1992).

The quote from Dell Hymes is taken from his article (1979, p. 44). The account of what happened on Easter Island is taken from Mitchell (1990). The quote from Ron Crocombe is contained in his book (1983, p. 27). The quotations from Theodore Roosevelt are found in Crawford (1989, pp. 23), and in Roosevelt (1889–96). Crawford is also the source of the information about the costs of language training at the Defense Language Institute. Crawford (1992) has also given an account of the English-only movement. Veltman (1983) and Veltman (1988) provide evidence for the rapid shift to English among immigrants to the US. The story about Kenneth Pike and Louis Hjelmslev is in Christophersen (1986).

The issue of language rights is treated in a special issue of *Language Sciences* (Benson, Grundy and Skutnabb-Kangas 1998), and Skutnabb-Kangas and Phillipson, 1994), which contains a useful appendix of selected extracts from UN documents and other legislation dealing with linguistic human rights. Skutnabb-Kangas (2000) deals more specifically with the educational dimension of linguistic human rights and the consequences for linguistic diversity.

Cultural Survival Quarterly devoted its 1997 Summer and Fall issues to struggles of the indigenous movement in various parts of the world over the last 25 years (see Maybury-Lewis, 1997 and Maybury-Lewis and Macdonald, 1997). Other issues have taken up native education, media, and so on. See especially the Spring 1998 issue on native education and the Summer 2001 issue on endangered languages. The reawakening of Native American activism is documented in Churchill (1993), Deloria (1969), and Cornell (1988). For discussion of the Treaty of Waitangi, see Awatere (1984) and Kawharu (1989). The full text of the Waitangi Tribunal is published by the Department of Justice, Wellington (Waitangi Tribunal, 1986).

There are now a number of organizations devoted to endangered languages. Terralingua, Partnerships for Linguistic and Biological Diversity, is at: *http:// www.terralingua.org*. A number of organizations of professional linguists such as the Linguistic Society of America, Linguistic Society of Japan, and the German Linguistic Society have established standing committees devoted to endangered languages. At a conference held in Paris in November 1993, the UN General Assembly decided to adopt the "Endangered Languages Project" as a UNESCO project. In cooperation with this project, the International Clearing House for Endangered Languages was established as part of the Department of Asian and Pacific Linguistics in the Institute of Cross-Cultural Studies of the University of Tokyo for the purpose of systematically making comprehensive information on endangered languages available. Their database can be accessed on *ftp://tooyoo.L.u-tokyo.ac.jp*. An internet discussion list for endangered languages can be found on *http://carmen.murdoch.edu.au/lists/endangered-languages-l/ell-websites.html*. The Foundation for Endangered Languages puts out a newsletter, *Ogmios*, available by subscription from *http://www.ogmios.org*.

Since the first edition of this book went to press, several important new books on the topic of language endangerment and preservation have appeared. These are Crystal (2000), Skutnabb-Kangas (2000), Fishman (2001), Hale and Hinton (2001), and Maffi (2001).

Bibliography

Abalain, Hervé (1989). *Destin des Langues Celtiques*. Paris: Editions Ophrys.

Alford, Dan (1994). Klangassociation, Whorf & Fetzer Dialogues. *LINGUIST List* Vol-5-606: May 24.

Allardt, Erik (1979). *Implications of the Ethnic Revival in Modern Industrialized Society: A Comparative Study of the Linguistic Minorities in Western Europe*. Helsinki: Societas Scientariarum Fennica.

Ammerman, Albert and Luigi L. Cavalli-Sforza (1973). A population model for the diffusion of early farming in Europe. In Renfrew, Colin (ed.), *The Explanation of Culture Change: Models in Prehistory*, pp. 335–58. London: Duckworth.

Ammerman, Albert and Luigi L. Cavalli-Sforza (1984). *The Neolithic Transition and the Genetics of Populations in Europe*. Princeton: Princeton University Press.

Awatere, Donna (1984). *Maori Sovereignty*. Auckland: Broadsheet Publications.

Baker, Colin and Sylvia Prys Jones (1998). *Encyclopedia of Bilingualism and Bilingual Education*. Clevedon: Multilingual Matters.

Barlow, Kathleen and Steven Winduo (eds.) (1997). Logging the Southwestern Pacific: Perspectives from Papua New Guinea, Solomon Islands, and Vanuatu. *The Contemporary Pacific: A Journal of Island Affairs*, 9.

Bass, Thomas A. (1990). *Camping with the Prince and Other Tales of Science in Africa*. Boston: Houghton Mifflin.

Beechert, Edward D. (1985). *Working in Hawai'i: A Labor History*. Honolulu: University of Hawai'i Press.

Benson, P., P. Grundy, and T. Skutnabb-Kangas (eds.)(1998); Special issue on language rights. *Language Sciences* 20:1.

Berberglou, Berch (1995). *The National Question: Nationalism, Ethnic Conflict and Self Determination in the 20th Century*. Philadelphia: Temple University Press.

Bethell, Leslie (ed.)(1984), *The Cambridge History of Latin America*. Volumes 1 and 2. Cambridge: Cambridge University Press.

Biraben, Jean-Noel (1979). Essai sur l'évolution du nombre des hommes. *Population* 1: 13–24.

Bourdieu, Pierre (1984). *Distinction: A Social Critique of the Judgement of Taste*. Cambridge, MA: Harvard University Press.

Bourdieu, Pierre (1989). *Language and Symbolic Power*. Cambridge: Polity Press.

Bradley, David (1989). The disappearance of the Ugong in Thailand. In Dorian (ed.), pp. 33–40.

Brenzinger, Matthias (ed.) (1992). *Language Death: Factual and Theoretical Explorations with Special Reference to East Africa*. Berlin and New York: de Gruyter.

Brown, Dee (1971). *Bury My Heart at Wounded Knee: An Indian History of the American West*. New York: Holt.

Brown, Paula (1978). *Highland Peoples of New Guinea*. Cambridge: Cambridge University Press.

Business Week (1992). Growth vs. the Environment. *Business Week* 3265 (May 11): 65–75.

Campbell, Lyle (1975). Cacopera. *Anthropological Linguistics* 17: 146–53.

Campbell, Lyle and Una Canger (1978). Chicomucełtec's last throes. *International Journal of American Linguistics* 44: 228–30.

Campbell, Lyle and Martha C. Muntzel (1989). The structural consequences of language death. In Dorian (ed.), pp. 181–96.

Cantoni, Gina (ed.) (1997). *Stabilizing Indigenous Languages*. Flagstaff: Northern Arizona University.

Capell, Arthur (1969). *A Survey of New Guinea Languages*. Sydney: Sydney University Press.

Chafe, Wallace (1962). Estimates regarding the present speakers of North American Indian languages. *International Journal of American Linguistics* 28: 162–71.

Chambers, Jack (1995). *Sociolinguistic Theory*. Oxford: Blackwell.

Chambers, Robert (1983). *Rural Development: Putting the Last First*. Harlow: Longmans.

Chomsky, Noam (1993). *Year 501: The Conquest Continues*. Boston: South End Press.

Chomsky, Noam (1996). *Power and Prospects: Reflections on Human Nature and the Social Order*. Boston: South End Press.

Christophersen, Paul (1986). Pike and Hjelmslev and Attitudes to Language. *Journal of Multilingual and Multicultural Development* 7:519–22.

Churchill, Ward (1993). *Struggle for the Land: Indigenous Resistance to Genocide, Ecocide and Expropriation in Contemporary North America*. Monroe, ME: Common Courage Press.

Churchill, Ward (1997). *A Little Matter of Genocide. Holocaust and Denial in the Americas 1492 to the Present*. San Francisco: City Light Books.

Clay, Jason (1990). Indigenous peoples. The miner's canary for the twentieth century. In Head, Suzanne and Heinzman, Robert (eds.), *Lessons of the Rainforest*, pp. 106–17. San Francisco: Sierra Club Books.

Cohen, Mark N. (1978). *The Food Crisis in Prehistory*. New Haven: Yale University Press.

Cohen, Mark N. and George Armelagos (1991). *Paleopathology and the Origins of Agriculture*. London: Academic Press.

Comrie, Bernard, Stephen Matthews, and Maria Polinsky (eds.) (1997). *The Atlas of Languages: The Origin and Development of Languages Throughout the World*. London: Bloomsbury Publishing.

Conklin, Harold (1969). An ethnoecological approach to shifting agriculture. In Vayda, Andrew P. (ed.), *Environmental and Cultural Behaviour: Ecological Studies in Cultural Anthropology*, pp. 221–33. New York: The Natural History Press.

Cornell, Stephen E. (1988). *The Return of the Native: American Indian Political Resurgence*. New York: Oxford University Press.

Craighill Handy, E.S. (1932). *Houses, Boats, and Fishing in the Society Islands*. Honolulu: Bernice P. Bishop Museum Bulletin, 90.

Crawford, James (1989). *Bilingual Education: History, Politics Theory and Practice*. Trenton, NJ: Crane Publishing Company.

Crawford, James (1992). *Hold Your Tongue: Bilingualism and the Politics of English Only*. Reading, MA: Addison-Wesley.

Crocombe, Ron (1983). *The South Pacific: An Introduction*. Suva: University of the South Pacific.

Crosby, Alfred W. (1986). *Ecological Imperialism: The Biological Expansion of Europe, 900–1900*. Cambridge: Cambridge University Press.

Crowley, Terry, and John Lynch (1985). *Language Development in Melanesia*. Vila, Vanuatu: University of the South Pacific.

Crystal, David (1987). *The Cambridge Encyclopedia of Language*. Cambridge: Cambridge University Press.

Crystal, David (2000). *Language Death*. Cambridge: Cambridge University Press.

Cultural Survival (1987). *Report from the Frontier: The State of the World's Indigenous Peoples*. Boston: Cultural Survival.

Cultural Survival Quarterly (1998). Reclaiming Native Education: Activism, Teaching and Leadership. Spring 1998 Vol. 22.1.

Cuppy, William J. (1941). *How to Become Extinct*. New York: Ferris Printing Company.

Curtin, Phillip (1969). *The Atlantic Slave Trade: A Census*. Madison: University of Wisconsin Press.

Curtin, Phillip (1989). *Death by Migration: Europe's Encounter with the Tropical World in the Nineteenth Century*. Cambridge: Cambridge University Press.

Dauenhauer, Nora Marks and Richard Dauenhauer (1998). Technical, emotional, and ideological issues in reversing language shift: examples from Southeast Alaska. In Grenoble and Whaley (eds.), pp. 57–99.

Davidson, Art (1993). *Endangered Peoples*. San Francisco: Sierra Club Books.

Day, David (1996). *Claiming a Continent: A History of Australia*. Sydney: HarperCollins.

Deloria Jr., Vine (1969). *Custer Died for Your Sins: An Indian Manifesto*. New York: Macmillan.

De Vries, John (1984). Factors affecting the survival of linguistic minorities: A preliminary comparative analysis of data for western Europe. *Journal of Multilingual and Multicultural Development* 5: 207–16.

Diamond, Jared (1997). *Guns, Germs and Steel: The Fates of Human Societies*. New York: Norton.

Dixon, Robert M.W. (1972). *The Dyirbal Language of Queensland, North Australia*. Cambridge: Cambridge University Press.

Dixon, Robert M.W. (1984). *Working with Aboriginal Languages. Memoirs of a Field Worker*. Chicago: University of Chicago Press.

Dixon, Robert M.W. (1997). *The Rise and Fall of Languages*. Cambridge: Cambridge University Press.

Dorian, Nancy C. (1981). *Language Death. The Life Cycle of a Scottish Gaelic Dialect*. Philadelphia: University of Pennsylvania Press.

Dorian, Nancy C. (ed.) (1989). *Investigating Obsolescence: Studies in Language Contraction and Death*. Cambridge: Cambridge University Press.

Dorian, Nancy C. (1993). A response to Ladefoged's other view of endangered languages. *Language* 69: 575–79.

Dougherty, Michael (1992). *To Steal a Kingdom: Probing Hawaiian History*. Waimānalo, HI: Island Press.

Durkacz, Victor (1983). *The Decline of the Celtic Languages*. Edinburgh: John Donald.

Dwyer, P.D. and M. Minnegal (1992). Ecology and community dynamics of Kubo people in the tropical lowlands of Papua New Guinea. *Human Ecology* 20: 21–55.

Economist (1992). Ethnic cleansing comes to Russia. *The Economist* November 28.

Economist (1998). English kills: Dying languages. *The Economist* June 6.

Edwards, John (1994). Ethnolinguistic pluralism and its discontents: a Canadian study, and some general observations. *International Journal of the Sociology of Language* 110: 5–85.

Ehrlich, Paul R. and Anne H. Ehrlich (1991). *Healing the Planet: Strategies for Resolving the Environmental Crisis*. Reading, MA: Addison-Wesley.

Eldredge, Niles (1991). *The Miner's Canary: Unraveling the Mysteries of Extinction*. New York: Prentice Hall.

Eldredge, Niles (1998). *Life in the Balance: Humanity and the Biodiversity Crisis*. Princeton: Princeton University Press.

Ellen, Roy (1994). Modes of subsistence: From hunting and gathering to agriculture and pastoralism. In Ingold (ed.), pp. 197–225.

Ellis, Peter B. and Seumas mac a' Ghobhainn (1971). *The Problem of Language Revival*. Inverness: Club Leabhar.

Elmendorf, William (1981). Last speakers and language change: Two Californian cases. *Anthropological Linguistics* 23: 36–49.

Fairhurst, H. (1964). The surveys for the Sutherland Clearances, 1813–1820. *Scottish Studies* 8:1–18.

Fishman, Joshua A. (1991). *Reversing Language Shift: Theoretical and Empirical Foundations of Assistance to Threatened Languages*. Clevedon: Multilingual Matters.

Fishman, Joshua (2001). *Can Threatened Languages Be Saved? Reversing Language Shift, Revisited: A 21st Century Perspective*. Clevedon: Multilingual Matters.

Foley, William (1986). *The Papuan Languages of New Guinea*. Cambridge: Cambridge University Press.

Fortune, David and Gretchen Fortune (1987). Karaja literary acquisition and sociocultural effects on a rapidly changing culture. *Journal of Multilingual and Multicultural Development* 8: 469–91.

Furnivall, J.S. (1948). *Colonial Policy and Practice.* Cambridge: Cambridge University Press.

Gal, Susan (1979). *Language Shift: Social Determinants of Linguistic Change in Bilingual Austria.* New York: Academic Press.

Giles, Howard (ed.)(1977). *Language, Ethnicity and Intergroup Relations.* London: Academic Press.

Giles, Howard and Robert St. Clair (eds.) (1979). *Language and Social Psychology.* Oxford: Blackwell.

Glazer, N. and Daniel P. Moynihan (1963). *Beyond the Melting Pot.* Cambridge: MIT Press and Harvard University Press.

Greeley, A.M. (1989). Review of R.F. Foster, *Modern Ireland 1600–1972* (New York: Allen Lane/The Penguin Press). *The New York Times Book Review* June 4, p. 3.

Gregor, D.B. (1980). *Celtic: A Comparative Study of the Six Celtic Languages, Their History, Literature and Destiny.* Cambridge: Oleander.

Grenoble, Lenore and Lindsay Whaley, (eds.) (1998). *Endangered Languages: Current Issues and Future Prospects.* Cambridge: Cambridge University Press.

Griffiths, Tom and Libby Robin (eds.) (1997). *Ecology and Empire: Environmental History of Settler Societies.* Edinburgh: Keele University Press.

Grillo, Ralph (1989). *Dominant Languages: Language and Hierarchy in Britain and France.* Cambridge: Cambridge University Press.

Grimes, Barbara F. (1985). Language Attitudes: identity, distinctiveness, survival in the Vaupes. *Journal of Multilingual and Multicultural Development* 6:389–403

Grimes, Barbara F. (1996). *Ethnologue: Languages of the World.* 13th edition. Dallas: Summer Institute of Linguistics.

Grimshaw, B. (1912). *Guinea Gold.* London: Mills and Boon.

Haas, Mary R. (1968). The last words of Biloxi. *International Journal of American Linguistics* 34:77–84.

Hale, Ken (1992). The human value of local languages. *Language* 68: 4–10.

Hale, Ken and Hinton, Leanne (eds.) (2001). *The Green Book. Language Revitalization in Practice.* San Diego: Academic Press.

Harmon, David (1996). Losing species, losing languages: Connections between biological and linguistic Diversity. *Southwest Journal of Linguistics* 15: 89-108.

Harmon, David (1998). Sameness and silence: Language extinctions and the dawning of a biocultural approach to diversity. *Global Biodiversity* 8: 2-10

Harshav, Benjamin (1993). *Language in the Time of Revolution.* Berkeley: University of California Press.

Hassan, Fekri (1981). *Demographic Archaeology.* New York: Academic Press.

Haugen, Einar (1972). *The Ecology of Language.* Stanford: Stanford University Press.

Hays, Terence (1993). "The New Guinea Highlands": Region, culture area, or fuzzy set? *Current Anthropology* 34: 141–64.

Head, Suzanne and Robert Heinzman (eds.) (1990). *Lessons of the Rainforest.* San Francisco: Sierra Club Books.

Hechter, Michael (1975). *Internal Colonialism: The Celtic Fringe in British National Development.* Berkeley: University of California Press.

Hemming, John (1978). *Red Gold: The Conquest of the Brazilian Indians*. London: Macmillan.

Hill, Archibald (1952). A note on primitive languages. *International Journal of American Linguistics* 18: 172–79.

Hill, Jane H. (1989). The social functions of relativization in obsolescent and non-obsolescent languages. In Dorian (ed.), pp. 149–64.

Hindley, Reg (1990). *The Death of the Irish Language: A Qualified Obituary*. London: Routledge.

Hinton, Leanne (1994). *Flutes of Fire: Essays on Californian Indian Languages*. Berkeley: Heyday Books.

Holloway, Charles E. (1997). *Dialect Death: The Case of Brule Spanish*. Amsterdam: John Benjamins.

Hong, Evelyn (1987). *Natives of Sarawak: Survival in Borneo's Vanishing Forests*. Penang: Institut Masyarakat Malaysia.

Hornberger, Nancy H. (ed.) (1997). *Language Planning from the Bottom Up: Indigenous Literacies in the Americas*. Berlin: Mouton de Gruyter.

Hughes, Robert (1988). *The Fatal Shore*. London: Collins Harvill.

Hymes, Dell (1979). Sapir, competence and voices. In Fillmore, C.J., D. Kempler, and W. S.-Y. Wang, (eds.), *Individual Differences in Language Ability and Behavior*, pp. 33–46. New York: Academic Press.

Ingold, Tim (ed.) (1984). *Companion Encyclopedia of Anthropology: Humanity, Culture and Social Life*. London: Routledge.

Jespersen, Otto (1964). *Language: Its Nature, Development and Origin*. New York: W.W. Norton & Co.

Jocks, Christopher (1998). Living words and cartoon translations: Longhouse "texts" and the limitations of English. In Grenoble and Whaley (eds.), pp. 217–34.

Johannes, R.E. (1981). *Words of the Lagoon: Fishing and Marine Lore in the Palau District of Micronesia*. Berkeley: University of California Press.

Johnson, Allan and Timothy Earle (1987). *The Evolution of Human Societies: From Foraging Group to Agrarian State*. Stanford: Stanford University Press.

Jones, E.L. (1987). *The European Miracle: Environments, Economies and Geopolitics in the History of Europe and Asia*. 2d. edition. Cambridge: Cambridge University Press.

Jones, Mari (1998). *Language Obsolescence and Revitalization. Linguistic Change in Two Sociolinguistically Contrasting Welsh Communities*. Oxford: Oxford University Press.

Juvik, Sonia P. and James O. Juvik (eds.) (1998). *Atlas of Hawai'i*. 3rd edition. Honolulu: University of Hawai'i Press.

Kachru, Braj (ed.) (1980). *The Other Tongue*. Oxford: Pergamon.

Kapono, Eric (1995). Hawaiian language revitalization & immersion education. *International Journal of the Sociology of Language* 112: 121.

Kawharu, Ian Hugh (1989) (ed.). *Waitangi: Maori and Pakeha Perspectives of the Treaty of Waitangi*. Auckland: Oxford University Press.

Kiernan, Victor G. (1988). *The Lords of Human Kind*. London: The Cresset Library.

Kinkade, M. Dale (1991). The decline of native languages in Canada. In Robins and Uhlenbeck (eds.), pp. 157–76.

Kirsch, Stuart (1996). Return to Ok Tedi. *Meanjin* 55(4): 657–66.

Krauss, Michael (1992). The world's languages in crisis. *Language* 68: 4–10.

Kroeber, Theodora (1964). *Ishi, Last of His Tribe*. Berkeley: Parnassus Press.

Kroskrity, Paul V. (1993). *Language, History, and Identity: Ethnolinguistic Studies of the Arizona Tewa*. Tucson: University of Arizona Press.

Kulick, D. (1992). *Language Shift and Cultural Reproduction: Socialization, Self and Syncretism in a Papua New Guinean Village*. Cambridge: Cambridge University Press.

Kunitz, Stephen J. (1984). Disease and the destruction of indigenous populations. In Ingold (ed.), pp. 297–326.

Ladefoged, Peter (1992). Another view of endangered languages. *Language* 68: 809–11.

Lansing, J. Stephen (1991). *Priests and Programmers: Technologies of Power in the Engineered Landscape of Bali*. Princeton, NJ: Princeton University Press.

Laycock, Don (1975). Observations on number systems and semantics. In Wurm, Stephen (ed.), *New Guinea Area Languages and Language Study. Vol I. Papuan Languages and the New Guinea Linguistic Scene*, pp. 219–23. Canberra: Pacific Linguistics Series C., No. 38.

Laycock, Don (1980). Multilingualism: Linguistic boundaries and unsolved problems in Papua New Guinea. In Wurm, Stephen (ed.), *New Guinea and Neighbouring Areas: A Sociolinguistic Laboratory*, pp. 81–100. The Hague: Mouton.

Le Page, R.B. and Andrée Tabouret-Keller (1985). *Acts of Identity: Creole-based Approaches to Language and Ethnicity*. Cambridge: Cambridge University Press.

Levesque, René (1977). *An Option for Quebec*. 2d. edition. Toronto: McClelland and Stewart.

Lieber, Michael D. (1994). *More Than a Living: Fishing and the Social Order on a Polynesian Atoll*. Boulder: Westview Press.

Linden, Eugene (1991). Lost Tribes, Lost Knowledge. *Time*, September 23.

Lipton, Michael (1977). *Why Poor People Stay Poor: Urban Bias in World Development*. London: Temple Smith.

Mace, Ruth and Pagel, Mark (1995). A latitudinal gradient in the density of languages in North America. *Proceedings of the Royal Society of London, B* 261: 117-21.

Maffi, Luisa (ed.) (2001). *On Biocultural Diversity: Linking Language, Knowledge, and the Environment*. Washington, D.C.: Smithsonian Institution Press.

Maguire, Gabrielle (1991). *Our Own Language: An Irish Initiative*. Clevedon: Multilingual Matters.

Majnep, Ian Sam and Ralph Bulmer (1977). *Birds of My Kalam Country*. Auckland: Auckland University Press.

Marschak, J. (1965). Economics of language. *Behavioral Science* 10: 135–40.

May, Robert M. (1992). How many species inhabit the earth? *Scientific American* October: 42–48.

Maybury-Lewis, David (ed.) (1997). 25 Years of the Indigenous Movement: Asia and Africa. *Cultural Survival Quarterly* Vol. 21.3 (Fall).

Maybury-Lewis, David and Theodore Macdonald, Jr (eds.)(1997). 25 Years of the Indigenous Movement: The Americas and Australia. *Cultural Survival Quarterly* Volume 21.2 (Summer).

Mazrui, Ali A. (1997). The World Bank, the language question and the future of African education. *Race and Class* 38: 35–48.

Mazrui, Ali A. and Alamin A. Mazrui (1998). *The Power of Babel: Language and Governance in the African Experience*. Chicago: University of Chicago Press.

McCarty, Teresa L. and Ofelia Zepeda (eds.) (1998). Indigenous Language Use and Change in the Americas. *International Journal of the Sociology of Language*, Volume 132.

McLuhan, Marshall (1989). *The Global Village: Transformations in World Life and Media in the 21st Century*. Oxford: Oxford University Press.

McCrum, Robert, William Cran, and Robert MacNeil (1986). *The Story of English*. New York: Viking Penguin Inc.

Mitchell, Andrew (1990). *A Fragile Paradise: Nature and Man in the Pacific*. London: Fontana/Collins.

Murdoch, Rupert (1994). Power of technology to liberate. *The Australian* October 21, p. 11.

Nettle, Daniel (1996). Language diversity in West Africa: An ecological approach. *Journal of Anthropological Archaeology* 15: 403-38

Nettle, Daniel (1998a). Explaining global patterns of language diversity. *Journal of Anthropological Archaeology* 17: 354–74.

Nettle, Daniel (1998b). Materials from the South-Eastern Plateau languages of Nigeria (Fyem, Hórom and Mabo-Barukul). *Afrika und Übersee* 81: 253–79.

Nettle, Daniel (1999). *Linguistic Diversity*. Oxford: Oxford University Press.

Newsweek (1988). Amway salutes Joseph Nicholas. *Newsweek* July 18.

Nichols, Johanna (1992). *Linguistic Diversity in Space and Time*. Chicago: University of Chicago Press.

Nordhoff, Charles B. (1930). Notes on the offshore fishing of the Society Islands. *Journal of the Polynesian Society* 39: 137–73, 221–62.

Ó Riagáin, Pádraig (1997). *Language Policy and Social Reproduction*. Oxford: Oxford University Press.

Palmer, Frank (1986). *Mood and Modality*. Cambridge: Cambridge University Press.

Pilger, John (1998). *Hidden Agendas*. London: Vintage.

Pool, Jonathan (1972). National development and language diversity. In Fishman, Joshua (ed.), *Advances in the Sociology of Language*, Volume 2, pp. 213–30. The Hague: Mouton.

Posposil, L. (1966). *The Kapauku Papuans of West New Guinea*. New York: Holt.

Price, Glanville (1984). *The Languages of Britain*. London: Edward Arnold.

Pūku'i, Mary Kawena (1983). *'Ōlelo No'eau: Hawaiian Proverbs and Poetical Sayings*. Bernice P. Bishop Museum Special Publication No. 71. Honolulu: Bishop Museum Press.

Ramos-Horta, J. (1999). Site seeing. *The Guardian*, January 11, p. 12.

Rannut, Mart (1994). Beyond linguistic policy: the Soviet Union versus Estonia. In Skutnabb-Kangas, Tove, and Robert Phillipson, in collaboration with Mart Rannut (eds.), *Linguistic Human Rights: Overcoming Linguistic Discrimination*, pp. 179–209. Berlin/New York: Mouton de Gruyter.

Rappaport, Roy (1968). *Pigs for the Ancestors*. New Haven: Yale University Press.

Rappaport, Roy (1971). The flow of energy in an agricultural society. *Scientific American* 225: 116–32.

Redclift, Michael (1987). *Sustainable Development: Exploring the Contradictions*. London: Methuen.

Rehg, Kenneth L. (1981). *Ponapean Reference Grammar*. Honolulu: University of Hawai'i Press.

Rehg, Kenneth L. (1998). Taking the pulse of Pohnpeian. *Oceanic Linguistics* 37:323–345.

Renfrew, Colin (1987). *Archaeology and Language: The Puzzle of Indo-European Origins*. London: Jonathan Cape.

Renfrew, Colin (1991). Before Babel: Speculations on the origin of linguistic diversity. *Cambridge Archeological Journal* 1: 3–23.

Rensch, Karl H. (1988). *Fish Names of Eastern Polynesia*. Canberra: Pacific Linguistics, Series C., No. 106.

Reyhner, Jon (ed.) (1997). *Teaching Indigenous Languages*. Flagstaff: Northern Arizona University.

Rindos, David (1984). *The Origins of Agriculture: An Evolutionary Perspective*. San Diego: Academic Press.

Robins, Robert H. and Eugenius M. Uhlenbeck (eds.) (1991). *Endangered Languages*. Oxford: Berg.

Robinson, C.D.W. (1996). *Language Use in Rural Development: An African Perspective*. Berlin: Mouton de Gruyter.

Rocha, Jan and Giancarlo Summa (1992). The tribe that lost its will to live. *The Guardian* February 21, 1992, p. 28.

Romaine, Suzanne (1994). *Language in Society: An Introduction to Sociolinguistics*. Oxford: Oxford University Press.

Roosevelt, Theodore (1889–1896). *Winning the West*. New York: G. Putnam's Sons.

Rubel, Paula and Abraham Rosman (1978). *Your Own Pigs You May Not Eat*. Chicago: University of Chicago Press.

Ruhlen, M. (1987). *A Guide to the World's Languages: Vol. l: Classification*. Stanford: Stanford University Press.

Sandburg, Carl (1916). *Chicago Poems*. New York: Henry Holt and Company.

Sankoff, Gillian (1980). *The Social Life of Language*. Philadelphia: University of Pennsylvania Press.

Sahlins, Marshall (1972). *Stone Age Economics*. Chicago: Aldine.

Schmidt, Annette (1985). *Young People's Dyirbal: A Case of Language Death from Australia*. Cambridge: Cambridge University Press.

Shield, Lesley E. (1984). Unified Cornish—Fiction or fact? An examination of the death and resurrection of the Cornish language. *Journal of Multilingual and Multicultural Development* 5: 329–37.

Skutnabb-Kangas, Tove and Sertaç Bucak (1994). Killing a mother tongue—how the Kurds are deprived of linguistic human rights. In Skutnabb-Kangas, Phillipson, in collaboration with Mart Rannut (eds.), pp. 347–71

Skutnabb-Kangas, Tove and Robert Phillipson, in collaboration with Mart Rannut (eds.) (1994). *Linguistic Human Rights: Overcoming Linguistic Discrimination*. Berlin / New York: Mouton de Gruyter.

Skutnabb-Kangas, Tove (2000) *Linguistic Genocide in Education- or World-wide Diversity and Human Rights?* London: Lawrence Erlbaum Associates.

Slaughter, Helen B. and Karen Ann Watson-Gegeo (1988). *Evaluation report for the First Year of the Hawaiian Language Immersion Program.* A Report to the Planning and Evaluation Branch, Department of Education, State of Hawai'i.

Snooks, Graeme D. (ed.) (1994). *Was the Industrial Revolution Necessary?* London: Routledge.

Snow, C.P. (1959). *The Two Cultures: and a Second Look.* New York: Mentor.

Sorenson, Arthur P. (1971). Multilingualism in the Northwest Amazon. *American Anthropologist* 69: 670–84.

Spolsky, Bernard (1989). Maori bilingual education and language revitalisation. *Journal of Multilingual and Multicultural Development* 10: 89–106.

Spolsky, Bernard and R.L. Cooper (1991). *The Languages of Jerusalem.* Oxford: Oxford University Press.

Stolzenberg, William (1994). The old men and the sea. *Nature Conservancy* November/December, pp. 16–23.

Swadesh, Morris (1971). *The Origin and Diversification of Language.* Chicago and New York: Aldine Atherton.

Takaki, Ronald (1983). *Pau Hana: Plantation Life and Labor in Hawai'i 1835–1920.* Honolulu: University of Hawai'i Press.

Taylor, Allan R. (1989). Problems in obsolescence research: The Gros Ventre of Montana. In Dorian, (ed.), pp. 167–79.

Taylor, Allan, R. (ed.) (1992). Language Obsolescence, Shift, and Death in Several Native American Communities. *International Journal of the Sociology of Language* 93.

Thomas, Jo (1988). Review of Leo Dunmore, *Senatorial Privilege. The Chappaquiddick Cover-up. New York Times Book Review* October 23: 1820.

Thurston, William (1987). *Processes of Change in the Languages of North-Western New Britain.* Canberra: Pacific Linguistics Series B, No. 99.

Titcomb, Margaret (1977). *Native Use of Fish in Hawai'i.* 2nd ed. Honolulu: University of Hawai'i Press.

Ullmann, Stephen (1951). *Words and Their Use.* New York: Philosophical Library.

Veltman, Calvin J. (1983). *Language Shift in the United States.* Berlin: Mouton.

Veltman, Calvin J. (1988). *The Future of the Spanish Language in the United States.* Washington, DC: Hispanic Policy Development Project.

Voegelin, C.F. and F.M Voegelin (1977). *Classification and Index of the World's Languages.* New York: Elsevier.

Waitangi Tribunal (1986). *Findings of the Waitangi Tribunal Relating to Te Reo Maori and a Claim Lodged by Huirangi Waikarapuru and Nga Kaiwhakapumau i te Reo Incorporated Society.* Wellington, New Zealand: The Wellington Board of Maori Language.

Warren, D. Michael, L. Jan Slikkerveer, and David W. Brokensha (eds.) (1995). *The Cultural Dimension of Development.* London: Intermediate Technology Publications.

Williams, P.H., K.J. Gaston, and C.J. Humphries (1997). *Proceedings of the Royal Society, Biological Sciences* 264: 141–48.

Wilson, E.O. (1978). *Life on Earth.* Sunderland, MA: Sinauer Associates.

Wilson, E.O. (1992). *The Diversity of Life.* Cambridge: Harvard University Press.

Wilson, William H. (1998). I ka ʻōelo Hawaiʻi ke ola: "Life is found in the Hawaiian language." *International Journal of the Sociology of Language* 132:123–37.

Wolfram, Walt and Natalie Schilling-Estes (1997). *Hoi Toide on the Outer Banks: The Story of the Ocracoke Brogue.* Chapel Hill: University of North Carolina Press.

Woodbury, Anthony C. (1998). Documenting rhetorical, aesthetic, and expressive loss in language shift. In Grenoble and Whaley (eds.), pp. 234–58.

Wright, Sue (ed.) (1996). *Language and the State: Revitalization and Revival in Israel and Eire.* Clevedon: Multilingual Matters.

Wurm, Stephen (1986). Grammatical decay in Papuan languages. In *Papers in New Guinea Linguistics* No. 24: 207–11. Canberra: Pacific Linguistics Series A., No. 70.

Wurm, Stephen (1991). Language decay and revivalism: The Äyiwo language of the Reef Islands, Santa Cruz Archipelago, Solomon Islands. In Blust, Robert (ed.), *Currents in Pacific Linguistics. Papers in Honour of George Grace,* pp. 207–11. Canberra: Pacific Linguistics Series C., No. 117.

Zepeda, Ofelia and Jane Hill (1991). The condition of Native American Languages in the United States. In Robins and Uhlenbeck (eds.), pp. 135–56.

Index

DATE DUE